RESURRECTION

RESURRECTION

The Miracle

Season That Saved

Notre Dame

Jim Dent

THOMAS DUNNE BOOKS ☙ St. Martin's Press, New York

THOMAS DUNNE BOOKS.
An imprint of St. Martin's Press.

RESURRECTION. Copyright © 2009 by Jim Dent. All rights reserved. Printed in the United States of America. For information, address St. Martin's Press, 175 Fifth Avenue, New York, N.Y. 10010.

www.thomasdunnebooks.com
www.stmartins.com

Library of Congress Cataloging-in-Publication Data

Dent, Jim.
    Resurrection : the miracle season that saved Notre Dame / Jim Dent.
        p. cm.
    Includes bibliographical references and index.
    ISBN 978-0-312-56721-7
    1. Notre Dame Fighting Irish (Football team)—History.   2. University of Notre
Dame—Football—History.   3. Parseghian, Ara, 1923–4.   4. Football coaches—United
States.   I. Title.
    GV958.N6D47 2009
    796.332'630977289—dc22

                                                                                    2009016738

First Edition: September 2009

10   9   8   7   6   5   4   3   2   1

This book is dedicated to former Notre Dame coach Ara Parseghian, one of the best to ever grace the sport of college football, and to his outstanding work for the Ara Parseghian Medical Research Foundation since 1994. The foundation is a non-profit organization dedicated to finding a treatment for Niemann-Pick Type C disease as quickly as possible.

"Ara Parseghian is an excellent coach, citizen and father who cares about people most of all," said his great friend Lou Holtz, another Notre Dame former coach. "Nowhere is there a greater challenge than to save the lives of young people. This is a time in his life when Ara should be sitting back, playing golf, doing the things that retired people do. But he accepted this challenge because he not only wanted to help his grandchildren, but other children as well."

Michael Parseghian lost his battle with NP-C in 1997 at the age of nine, and Christa passed away at age ten in October, 2001. Marcia was the third of the Parseghian family to succumb to the disease at the age of sixteen in 2005.

Thanks to the tireless efforts of the Parseghian family, along with the staff and countless volunteers, the foundation has raised more than $32 million that has gone directly into research. Cindy Parseghian, Ara's daughter-in-law, is the president of the group and is assisted by executive director Glen Shepherd and assistant director Peg Romano.

We sincerely encourage you to make a donation to the cause, and there are many ways you can do it: First, you may go to Parseghian.org and click onto "Donate Now." You may also contact the foundation at victory@parseghian.org, or by calling 520-577-5106. Here is the mailing address: 3530 E. Campo Abierto, Suite 105, Tucson, AZ 85718.

—JIM DENT, September 2009

CONTENTS

RESURRECTION

Chapter 1

TOUGH IRISH KID

Snow was blowing sideways on a Chicago morning in December of 1963 when Tony Carey aimed the '53 Chevy into the parking lot at Marshall Field's department store. His fingers drummed the steering wheel to the beat of "Louie Louie." His mind drifted back to Notre Dame and the trouble that had gone down.

Carey's mood reflected the low, gray clouds rolling off Lake Michigan. Life should have turned out better. No one ever expected him to get kicked out of Notre Dame, even for one semester, and as a result, his football career almost crashed. In three years in South Bend he had yet to suit up for one game. How could this happen to a tough Irish kid from the south side of Chicago?

Not long ago, Carey had greatness written all over him. In 1960, he quarterbacked Mount Carmel High to a 28–7 victory over archrival St. George in the Chicago Catholic League championship game, and the Caravan proceeded to win the overall city title by defeating Taft High as Carey won Most Valuable Player honors. He could still feel his cleats digging into the thick grass at Soldier Field; his ears remained filled with the cheering of 80,000 fans. You could fill a dozen scrapbooks with the stories they had written about Tony Carey.

Once upon a time, Notre Dame had been the passion of his life. The Fighting Irish existed in his genes. His father, Robert, had competed on the Notre Dame track team and graduated with a law degree from the university in 1926. His brother, Tom, had played quarterback for legendary coach Frank Leahy in the early fifties. So how was it possible that this grand old football program had gone straight into the toilet? How in the name of Knute Rockne had an American brand name bigger than General Motors become yesterday's news? It seemed that no one cared anymore. The nine national championships, the five Heisman Trophies, and the Four Horsemen were memories and nothing more. It could be said that the Notre Dame program was suffering through a period of Famine, Pestilence, Destruction, and Death.

Word from the Chicago newspapers was that Notre Dame would soon depart from the ranks of big-time college football to join Stanford, Northwestern, Army, Navy, Vanderbilt, Rice, and others of a lesser football heritage in a conference certain to inspire mediocrity. Collegiate powers like Michigan State, Iowa, Wisconsin, Purdue, and USC would be crossed off the schedule. It would be a quasi-Ivy League existence instead of an annual chase for number one. Good-bye Frank Leahy. See you later, Johnny Lujack. Forget about those rollicking Saturdays at Yankee Stadium in the twenties, thirties, and forties, when Notre Dame versus Army captured the imagination of an entire nation. Ignore the fact that Rockne and Notre Dame had once salvaged college football's reputation as a scandal-ridden blood sport. Quash the notion that Notre Dame in the twenties had single-handedly transformed college football from a lowly outsider into an American institution.

That frosty morning in '63, Tony Carey, his life going nowhere, shifted the Chevy into neutral and gazed at the gathering storm. Not once had he felt so alone. Never could he remember being on the outside looking in. Giving up was getting closer than hanging on. Oh, he probably would return for spring practice in March, hoping to jump-start his career, but his focus at this time was pursuing his diploma and preparing himself for law school.

Then it hit him. Why had the music stopped? Carey looked down at the radio now silent in his dashboard. He heard static and then a voice: "We interrupt our regular programming to bring you this news bulletin."

Carey would say for decades that he did not remember climbing onto the hood of the '63 Chevy that day, but in a matter of seconds, he was dancing and yelling. Snow was sticking to his flattop. His high-top, rough-suede hush puppies, a.k.a. Polish gym shoes, were getting soaked. People were watching him. Still, nothing was about to calm that piston inside his heart.

"*We are back! We are back!*" he yelled.

A new coach was coming to Notre Dame. The football program would have a fighting chance. It would be a huge gamble against great odds. But the man they were talking about on the radio had that look in his eye.

Chapter 2

BLUEPRINT FOR DEFEAT

G iven the glorious past of Notre Dame football, it seemed preposterous that a powerful force would set out to tear it all down. Actually, it was the work of two people, and both were insiders.

The fall of Notre Dame football was set in motion in 1953. The reason was simple: President Rev. Theodore M. Hesburgh hated the term
"football factory." Fair or not, this was how Notre Dame was perceived
across America. Father Hesburgh was driven to change the entire scheme
and to clean up the image. To him, the sins of the institution had begun
under Knute Rockne back in the 1920s. The Roaring Twenties was the
decade of excess, and Notre Dame football was the epitome of that over-
indulgence.

For years, Father Hesburgh had studied the football program and wondered how it could have gotten so out of control. How could a brutish
game come to overshadow an entire university? So at the end of the 1953
season, about a year after he ascended to the office of the presidency, the
priest set out to dismantle the factory. Academia would be number one.

Father Hesburgh, starting in the early 1950s, fought the odds to
transform the university into the "Harvard of the Midwest." If football
had to suffer, so be it. His closest friend and leading supporter in this
quest was Father Edmund P. Joyce, who recently had been elevated to
the title of executive vice president and chairman of the faculty board in
charge of athletics. Together, the two men began their crusade. They
slashed athletic scholarships and started to rein in the program. First,
they had to do something about coach Frank Leahy, a rogue who had

built his own fiefdom while bending many rules. Fathers Hesburgh and Joyce could have cared less that Leahy had been college football's most successful coach over the past two decades.

When Fathers Hesburgh and Joyce set out to fix the university's reputation, they dumped the old Notre Dame thinking that was the foundation for this relentless pursuit of championships. Regardless of the amount of glory it shined upon the university, football was about to take a fall.

Father Joyce was quick to support this philosophy. "Naturally, we would like to have a winning football team," he said, "but it is not so important as all that. I can understand the attention that the football team has received, because of the past, but you must remember that Notre Dame is a great academic institution and it has been for many years."

Had they forgotten that Notre Dame was nothing more than a remote outpost out on the cold Indiana plains when Rockne took over as coach in 1918? If not for football, Notre Dame would have remained a forgotten sectarian college. When Notre Dame and Army met in the legendary 1913 game at West Point, the Cadets admitted they had never heard of Notre Dame—could not even pronounce it. Army players simply referred to the team as the "Catholics."

It was Rockne who spread the Notre Dame fame far and wide in the twenties. Who could forget the visage of Pat O'Brien playing the Rock in the movie *Knute Rockne: All American*. "Pass that Ball! Run that Ball! Fight! Fight! Fight!"

Since the beginning of time, it seemed, Notre Dame had been all about the old pigskin. Why else would a campus statue of Father William Corby with his right hand held up be called "Fair Catch Corby?" Why would everyone shout "We're No. 1!" when they set eyes on the statue of Moses with his forefinger pointing to the sky? Why else would the Sacred Heart Church be the place where students and alumni alike went to seek forgiveness for beating Iowa by only two touchdowns?

Needless to say, this overhyped notion did not sit well with Father Hesburgh. He was still disturbed over the troubling issues from the 1920s when players were not required to attend classes. Halfback George Gipp might have been the greatest player of this era, but he was a heavy drinker and a gambler who bet on his own team. During a tongue-lashing from Rockne at halftime of the 1919 Army game, Gipp supposedly said, "Ah, don't worry, Rock. We'll win in the second half. I've got five hundred bucks bet on this game."

Gipp had played professionally on Sundays under an assumed name, just as Rockne and others had done during their playing days at Notre Dame.

In the 1930s, after Rockne perished in a plane crash in Bazaar, Kansas, Notre Dame football leveled off for a few years, then sprang back into the national consciousness when Frank Leahy took over in 1941. Six undefeated seasons, three national championships, a thirty-nine-game unbeaten streak, and four Heisman Trophy winners matched the standards that Rockne once set. No one could deny Leahy his place among the greatest coaches of all time.

For all of his upside, though, Leahy could be an embarrassment. His petulant behavior was well chronicled as he coached his players to fake injuries in order to save time-outs. That little trick not only incensed opponents but the Notre Dame alumni as well.

Father Hesburgh's dim view of Notre Dame football began to take shape when he was promoted to executive vice president and athletics chairman in 1949. That is when the priest and the coach started to tangle. Father Hesburgh got his first tour of the factory and quickly came to know Leahy and his greedy deeds. He did not like what he saw. Notre Dame might have enjoyed the greatest run in the history of college football, but things had to change.

Father Hesburgh's appointment to head of athletics was made by Notre Dame president Father John J. Cavanaugh, who had originally hired Leahy in 1941. Cavanaugh was not aware at the time of his hiring that Leahy, a former player under Rockne, possessed a blueprint that would create endless tension between the university president and the coach. Leahy with his capricious personality wanted to run the football program the way he saw fit, and who could blame him? In 1941, his first team finished unbeaten, and in 1943 he won his first national championship.

Leahy's streak of independence irritated Father Cavanaugh to no end. Cavanaugh was further frustrated that Leahy's name became synomous with Notre Dame, while the rest of the university played second fiddle to football. When General Dwight D. Eisenhower brought his presidential campaign to Notre Dame in the early fifties, he stopped first at the office of Frank Leahy. It was Leahy, not Father Hesbugh, who at the 1952 Republican National Convention seconded Eisenhower's nomination.

At the height of Leahy's successful run in 1947, Father Cavanaugh slashed football scholarships from thirty-two to eighteen a year. Two years later, when Father Cavanaugh moved Father Hesburgh to athletics, the president ordered him to get control of Leahy. Father Hesburgh would write in his 1990 biography, *God, Country, Notre Dame,* that this was no easy task. "The problem, as Cavanaugh explained it to me, was that while the administration theoretically controlled athletics and had its own representative as an overseer, the reality was that Frank Leahy was doing whatever he pleased. Not that he was doing anything wrong, only that he was operating independently of the university administration. In other words, he was running what amounted to be an autonomous fiefdom."

In 1949, when Father Hesburgh moved to athletics, Leahy refused to talk to his new boss. When Father Hesburgh summoned Leahy to his office, the coach usually sent an assistant coach. It was no way to start a relationship.

Leahy's behavior was rarely predictable. After losses, he was known to walk into the corner of the dressing room and cry. At halftime of the 1951 Michigan State game, he accused the players of throwing the game for the purpose of winning their bets. His practices were often as brutal as those being conducted by Paul "Bear" Bryant at Kentucky and later at Texas A&M. In 1954, more than seventy players quit Bryant's A&M team during a brutal ten-day preseason camp in Junction. Leahy might have outdone Bryant. He ordered players to attend illegal summer practices at a farm near Cleveland and worked them until their tongues hung out.

Leahy was both revered and reviled, but no one could argue with his success. When Father Cavanaugh started chopping scholarships in 1947, Leahy was in the midst of a four-season run without a loss. For all that, health issues in 1953 gave Notre Dame an excuse to part with its infamous and pain-in-the-ass coach. Halfway through the '53 season, Leahy fainted at halftime of the Georgia Tech game. This case of acute pancreatitis quickly cleared up, and he was back on the sideline in two weeks. By the end of the season, however, Fathers Hesburgh and Joyce were telling everyone that Leahy's fragile health was casting doubts on his ability to coach.

"Leahy spoke with friends who told him to retire before he killed himself," Father Joyce said, but Leahy denied ever saying that to anyone. He believed his health was fine and that he could continue to coach for years.

When Leahy was eased out the door at the end of the 1953 season, he claimed it was the conspiratorial work of Fathers Joyce and Hesburgh. Practically everyone with knowledge of the situation supported Leahy's contention that he was fired. They believed that the health issues were trumped up by Fathers Hesburgh and Joyce, and, in reality, Leahy would live for another twenty years.

"No way that Frank Leahy quit Notre Dame," said Paul Hornung, the 1956 Heisman Trophy winner who was recruited by Leahy. "I know that for a fact. The reason I came to Notre Dame in the first place was to play for Frank Leahy. When they got rid of him, I knew the program was in deep shit."

Leahy's record of 87-11-9 came close to topping Rockne's final mark of 105-12-5. He would finish with one more undefeated season than Rockne.

The firing of Leahy opened the door for Fathers Hesburgh and Joyce to trash the old blueprint and to begin the process of de-emphasis. Football would be reined in by reducing scholarships, but there was more. Notre Dame was about to hire a coach with some serious white space on his resume. Leahy was soon replaced by twenty-five-year-old Terry Brennan, a productive halfback in the glory years of the late forties, but a coach who might have been better suited for a place like Wabash. He had been the head coach at Mount Carmel High for three years and spent one year on Leahy's staff tutoring the freshmen.

Within days after Leahy left, Brennan was rewarded with the biggest job in the history of college football. It was like elevating an assembly line worker to the top of the Ford Motor Company. One witness to this remarkable moment in Notre Dame history was Tom Carey, brother of Tony Carey, who had played quarterback at Mount Carmel under Brennan before being recruited and signed by Notre Dame. When Brennan made the leap from South Chicago to South Bend, Carey knew something was going down—literally.

"At the time, my father knew some of the Notre Dame trustees," Carey told author Steve Delsohn in his book *Talking Irish*. "And when Notre Dame started recruiting me, my father told me what would happen. He said they would de-emphasize Notre Dame football and that Terry would go down there and replace Leahy. That's exactly what happened. Hesburgh and the others knew they couldn't de-emphasize football at Notre Dame until Frank Leahy was gone."

Father Hesburgh was now operating under a radically different philosophy than his predecessors. The win-at-all-costs mandate was about to change. Hello, Rhodes scholars. So long, football factory. Fathers Hesburgh and Joyce were on the brink of setting a national institution back by fifty years.

IN 1954, WITH Leahy out of the picture and the novice Brennan running the show, the Fighting Irish were still blessed with remarkable talent. Leading the way was a blue-eyed sophomore quarterback/running back/defensive back with blond, curly hair, the one they called "Golden Boy." Paul Hornung had been the top high school recruit in the country two years earlier. Brennan could also thank Leahy for players like Ralph Guglielmi, end Dan Shannon, and tackle Frank Varrichione.

What Brennan accomplished during his first two seasons at Notre Dame should have earned him a contract extension. His first two teams compiled an overall record of 17-3 with losses to the highly respected programs of Purdue, Michigan State, and USC. His 1954 team finished fourth in the country. There were no embarrassing moments. The team was fundamentally sound, the fans were buying tickets in record numbers, and the sporting press held firm to the belief that Notre Dame remained one of the preeminent programs in the country.

As more football scholarships were slashed, however, and fewer big names were coming to South Bend, the writing was on the wall. Clearly, Brennan was able to succeed in his first two seasons because of the players recruited by Leahy during an era when football was still king.

Nevertheless, the Notre Dame winning machine began to belch smoke during the 1956 season, when the Irish finished 2-8. Fans could see the numbers dwindling along the bench. Moreover, the quality of the athletes had greatly diminished since Leahy.

One afternoon in 1956, Heartley "Hunk" Anderson strolled onto the practice field at Cartier Field and shook his head. Possibly no one outside of Leahy knew the history of Notre Dame football better than Hunk. He was an All-American tackle for Rockne in the early twenties when famed sportswriter Grantland Rice called him "the roughest human being pound for pound that I have ever known." Growing up in the upper peninsula of Michigan, Anderson was a close friend of George Gipp's and followed the famous running back to Notre Dame.

Anderson became the line coach for Rockne in the midtwenties. His second job was playing tackle on Sundays with the George Halas–coached Chicago Bears. His third job was at Edwards Iron Works in South Bend. After a grueling twelve-hour workday, Anderson would hustle over to Cartier Field just in time for the start of practice. He was normally in a foul mood and was known to take it out on the linemen.

About twenty minutes into practice, Rockne would say, "Ah, Heartley, would you be good enough to bring the behemoths over here?"

"Hell, Rock," Anderson would reply. "They ain't even bleeding yet."

Anderson had replaced Rockne as head coach when he died in 1931. In spite of his physical intensity and fanatical loyalty, Anderson would last only three years as head coach.

More than two decades later, when Anderson saw the talent Brennan had to work with, he knew the great Notre Dame football tradition was no more. What he witnessed that day were thin bodies and thinner ranks. He looked around and said, "Where is the freshmen team?" Somebody pointed to a small group of players.

"Come on," Anderson said. "Don't shit your old friend Hunk. Where're you hiding them?"

When it was explained that the ranks were fading because scholarships were dwindling, Anderson shook his head again.

"You guys are gonna get slaughtered," he said to the coaches. "You can't run this program with these numbers, and I'll tell you what else. When the shit comes down, you guys will be the fall guys."

After the disastrous 1956 season, Anderson organized a group of monogram winners (Notre Dame lettermen) to speak to Fathers Hesburgh and Joyce about restoring some of the scholarships.

"Father Hesburgh, I respect what you are doing with our fine university," Anderson began. "I do feel it is the prerogative of the university to determine what is good for the school. But I also feel that we should give the Notre Dame football team and coach Terry Brennan a fighting chance."

The plea meant little to Father Hesburgh. No more scholarships were coming. They would go 7-3 in 1957, and 6-4 in 1958. The high points in that stretch were Hornung winning the Heisman Trophy in 1956, and the Irish pulling off one of the biggest upsets in the history of college football against an Oklahoma Sooners team riding a 47-game winning streak in 1957. On November 16, Oklahoma was celebrating its fiftieth birthday as a state. As the game began, the sky turned coal black and the wind howled out of the south. The game was still scoreless with 3:50 to play. The Fighting Irish faced a fourth and goal from the 3-yard line. In the huddle, quarterback Bob Williams looked halfback Dick Lynch in the eye and said, "I want you to haul ass around end. Keep your eye on the ball." Williams flipped an overhand toss to Lynch, who scooted into the end zone untouched. Final score: Notre Dame 7, Oklahoma 0.

Conspicuous by his absence that day was Father Hesburgh. He had decided not to make the trip to Norman, believing the Irish had no chance to win.

Beating Oklahoma actually saved Brennan's career, but everyone knew he was hanging by a thread.

"To me, Terry Brennan was a great coach," Hornung said later, "and I think I know what a great coach looks like. I played for the greatest coach of all time, a guy named Vince Lombardi."

At the end of the 1958 season, Hunk Anderson's prediction about Terry Brennan being the next fall guy came true. In spite of a decent 32-18 overall record, he was fired on December 21. Arthur Daley wrote in the *New York Times*, "No college in the country, in all probability, has as many unrestrainedly devoted followers as Notre Dame. Here is the 'People's Choice' in a most sentimental form, all of it packed inside the roseate glow of pure idealism. Yet this is the school that gave the sack to a thirty-year-old father of four children for Christmas."

All Notre Dame could do now was pray for a happier New Year.

Chapter 3

"JOE MUST GO"

Football in the early sixties at Notre Dame was like playing behind the Iron Curtain.

—TACKLE ED BURKE

The Old Fieldhouse was constructed in 1898 at the behest of university president Andrew Morrissey during an era when football was just a passing thought at Notre Dame. Knute Rockne was ten years old at the time. The place burned down a year after it was finished, and Father Morrissey was quick to rebuild one of the country's largest gymnasiums with concrete and steel. This is not to suggest Father Morrisey was committed to big-time athletics. He did, however, support the athletic notion *mens sana in corpore sano* ("a healthy mind in a healthy body"). He had no idea that this gray, castellated edifice would someday become the spiritual center of Notre Dame athletics.

Beginning with Rockne in the twenties, Notre Dame staged pep rallies so boisterous that the sound carried for miles beyond the farms that ringed campus. Students from the all-male university packed the place for the purpose of outyelling each other. These spirit-builders propelled the Fighting Irish players toward victory week after week. Rockne, the originator of the fiery halftime speech, frequently practiced amateur psychology on his team, so, naturally, he cherished those Friday nights at the Old Fieldhouse, where the bedlam sent an electrical charge racing up the spine.

"To me, the greatest thing about Notre Dame was the Old Fieldhouse," Paul Hornung remembered. "My old roommate Sherrill Sipes and I went to the Old Fieldhouse in 1953 for the first time as freshmen and, man, it was rocking."

That day in '53, the students gathered to provide some solace to an

Irish team that had suffered a setback. As a heavy favorite, No. 1 Notre Dame had tied Iowa 14–14. It would be the only blemish in a 9-0-1 season.

The students were raising the roof when tight end Don Penza, the team captain, took the microphone. No words came out of his mouth. He started to cry. The crowd responded by cheering even louder.

"Penza had dropped a pass in the end zone that would have won the game for Notre Dame," Hornung said. "They gave Penza a thirty-eight-minute standing ovation. I know. I timed it. That was absolutely amazing and it made me love Notre Dame even more."

Dr. Charlie Kenny, a history major from the class of 1963, came to love the pep rallies at the old, decrepit building almost as much as he loved the university. "It was kind of like going to the circus without the elephants," he said.

Growing up in New York, Kenny could have cared less about playing tackle football. All he wanted to do was to fill his eyes and ears with the game. Because he was Catholic, and because Notre Dame was America's torchbearer for Catholicism and football, Kenny hurried to South Bend as fast as he could. One of his first stops as a freshman was the Old Fieldhouse on a day in 1959 when a pep rally had been scheduled to christen Joe Kuharich as the new Notre Dame football coach. Kuharich would be replacing Terry Brennan.

Inside the old rectangular building with a dirt floor and the color scheme of a dungeon, the students stood shoulder to shoulder, 5,000 strong, shouting their lungs out. They climbed up on each other's shoulders and created human pyramids. This was the kind of moment Kenny had been living for, and he was not disappointed. The first thing he did was check his watch and make a mental note of the time.

Kuharich was positioned on the balcony at the west end of the antique building, which, after sixty-four years of existence, was starting to fall down around itself. Kuharich's eyes were filled with dismay. A massive jug-eared man, Kuharich held up his right hand in an attempt to quiet the masses. After several minutes of the ear-splitting cacophony, Kuharich held up both hands. That did not work, either.

"It was so loud that you couldn't hear the person next to you if they were trying to talk to you," Kenny said later. "That day, the Old Fieldhouse was kind of like the Romans going to the Colosseum." The students somehow believed that the firing of Brennan and the hiring of Kuharich would instantly turn the program around.

Kenny checked his watch again. Almost ten minutes had passed and Kuharich had yet to speak, or yell, a single word above this human freight train of sound. He looked baffled. The steel balcony shuddered beneath his feet as Kuharich stepped back from the microphone again and held up both hands.

"I actually think that Kuharich was in a state of shock," Kenny remembered. "But you had to remember that there were a bunch of pent-up needs inside these students. We were hungry for a winner."

That fall of 1959, Notre Dame had forgotten what the top 20 looked like. Elite teams like Oklahoma, LSU, and Ohio State seemed on the verge of lapping them. Not once since 1954 had the Fighting Irish finished in the top five teams, and no one could forget the 2-8 fiasco in 1956, the worst season in the school's history.

What the university needed was a man with a quick fix. Was this Joe Kuharich the savior? At age forty-three, here stood a man with pluses and minuses. He had played tackle three seasons for the Fighting Irish back in the midthirties and his roots ran deep. As a kid growing up in South Bend in the twenties, Kuharich had sneaked into Cartier Field to watch his beloved team practice. Knute Rockne admonished the youngster, then let him stick around and watch. Kuharich felt an emotional connection that day to Notre Dame that would never die.

In the opinion of Theodore Hesburgh and Edmund Joyce, Kuharich was the man who would bring Notre Dame back from the darkness. He was a "brother of Notre Dame," and that was the most important criterion of all. All the coaches dating back to Rockne had played football for Notre Dame and were part of the sacred bond.

The second thing going for Joe Kuharich was that he really wanted the job. In fact, he practically begged for it. He informed Father Hesburgh that he would take a 50 percent pay cut from his job as the head coach of the Washington Redskins. Kuharich was ready to make a clean break from eccentric Redskins owner George Preston Marshall, and the feeling was mutual.

Upon Kuharich's departure, Marshall told the *Washington Post*, "Good riddance that bastard is gone."

In five seasons with the Redskins, Kuharich had only one winning season and finished 26-32 overall—hardly the numbers you would expect from the new messiah. Prior to that, he had coached the Chicago Cardinals in 1952 to a 4-8 record, getting canned after one season.

Based on his pro record, Kuharich looked like a washed-up, second-rate coach who was more qualified for Iowa State, but there was one remarkable season on his resume that no one could deny—or explain, really. In the fall of 1951, Kuharich coached the University of San Francisco Dons to a 9-0 record. That season, the roster read like a Who's Who of football heroes. Nine players would make it to the pros, five were selected to the Pro Bowl, and three superstars—Gino Marchetti, Ollie Matson, and Bob St. Clair—were elected to the Pro Football Hall of Fame. It could be argued that San Francisco that season was the best team in America, even better than No. 1 Tennessee, coached by the legendary General Robert Leyland.

At the end of the 1951 season, when it was time to hand out bowl bids, San Francisco was left out in the cold. Neither the Orange nor Cotton Bowl would bend the rules in order to accept USF's two black players. In the final Associated Press poll, the Dons finished fourteenth—a slap in the face for an undefeated team. They would soon be forgotten. Football was dropped the next season at USF for financial reasons.

One more notable name from the Dons' football program was Pete Rozelle, who graduated from the university in 1950 and was the athletics publicist in '51. That season was the beginning of a long friendship between Kuharich and the future NFL commissioner.

That first day at Notre Dame, Kuharich continued to stand on the balcony of the Old Fieldhouse, peering down at the crazies, wondering what the hell he had gotten himself into. Stress was etched on his face. He knew these wild-eyed, disorderly students were not giving up. The noise finally began to subside and Kuharich took two quick steps toward the microphone. Kenny checked his watch. The standing ovation—if you could call it that—had lasted eighteen minutes.

Kuharich threw a fist into the air and shouted, "Notre Dame will come back! I promise you that we *will* come back!" Those words should have provoked a thunderous ovation. Those words should have sent 5,000 rowdies running up the stairway to lift this massive man onto their shoulders. Instead, the students stopped cheering. They could barely believe their ears. Some looked at each other in disbelief. The voice emanating from this barrel of a man was more like the squeaking of a mouse. It was so high-pitched that it sounded womanly.

NOTRE DAME, IN spite of the scholarship losses, boasted a small group of talented, experienced players in 1959. The sporting press has always been a sucker for a new coach, and this was especially the case when Kuharich hit town. Both the *Chicago Tribune* and the *Sun-Times* picked Notre Dame to finish in the top 10. Some of the writers believed that stars like Myron Pottios, sophomore Nick Buoniconti, George Izo, and Monty Stickles could bring the Irish back in one season.

But Kuharich did not agree. He told the Chicago newspapers that he was appalled by the absence of good players left behind by Terry Brennan.

"What do they expect me to do this first season?" Kuharich said. "I'm supposed to match up against Purdue, Michigan State, Georgia Tech, and Pitt with this kind of talent? Not this year."

Either Kuharich owned a crystal ball, or he knew his stuff. The Irish lost to Purdue, Michigan State, Georgia Tech, and Pitt. They were also defeated 30–24 by Northwestern, a team coached by an up-and-comer named Ara Parseghian.

Notre Dame finished with a 5-5 record, and, for those keeping score, that was one more loss than Brennan had suffered during his final season of 1958. The Fighting Irish were going nowhere fast. The pro-oriented coach with the high-pitched voice was no messiah.

In 1960, after the eighth game of the season, Charlie Kenny walked into the Old Fieldhouse for a pep rally and could not believe his eyes. Or ears. The place was so empty that you could hear pigeons rattling around in the rafters. The band was not playing. No one was cheering. Kenny, instead of checking his watch, began counting heads.

"There were only eighteen kids in the crowd," Kenny said. "When the football team walked onto the balcony I felt embarrassed. There were more players on the balcony than students in the cheering section."

Fourteen months had passed since they had cheered their hearts out for the new coach. By that time, Notre Dame was in the midst of an eight-game losing streak. In the second game of the season, Purdue had scored 6 touchdowns in the second quarter alone en route to a 51–19 defeat of Notre Dame. Even more embarrassing was that Kuharich during the off-season had welcomed Purdue coach Jack Mollenkopf into his office on the Notre Dame campus for four days to learn his offensive and defensive systems. Mollenkopf then turned the tables on the teacher to the tune of a 32-point defeat.

In the fifth week of the season, Ara Parseghian and Northwestern had defeated Notre Dame for the second straight year, this time 7–6. Navy, a team that Notre Dame once handled with ease, beat the Irish 14–7 in Philadelphia.

As the football team slid further down the tubes, the students grew more restless—and bored. Notre Dame in the fall of 1960 was a cold, womanless world with a ten o'clock lights-out curfew and five mandatory masses per week. The closest females were over at St. Mary's and they were practically locked down around the clock. You held better odds of breaking into Fort Knox than working your way into one of those dorm rooms. Just ask the Fighting Irish team that pulled off the biggest upset in the history of college football back in 1957. Upon returning to campus after breaking the Oklahoma Sooners' monumental forty-seven game winning streak, the players decided to celebrate in the most logical manner. They took off en masse for St. Mary's—*panty raid*! The players naturally felt they deserved the intimacy of a few good women. What they found instead on the edge of campus was a phalanx of priests toting flashlights and wearing hard expressions. Not even the conquering heroes were going to penetrate that line.

With its strict rules and an absence of women, Notre Dame in the early 1960s felt like a boarding school and a military institute rolled into one. Not until 1973 would females be allowed to attend the university. Students in 1962 lived in spartan rooms with no carpeting, and the primary entertainment on the weekend beyond football was the TV show *Bonanza*, which was so popular among the Domers that the priests were willing to schedule Sunday Night Benediction around it.

The conservative fifties were dead and gone, but not at Notre Dame. At most colleges in America, it was time to party, party, party. A Friday afternoon kegger with a fifty-fifty male-female split was far more important than Keats or calculus.

America was changing, and changing fast. President John F. Kennedy was a visionary with a different agenda. In 1962, John Glenn became the first American to orbit the earth in Friendship 7. Soon, Kennedy set a goal of landing a man on the moon before the end of the decade. Political unrest could be felt around the world as the Cold War intensified. The Soviet Union placed ballistic missiles on Cuban land just ninety miles from the Florida coast. For a short time, the world stood on the brink of nuclear war and possible self-destruction. Kennedy called the Russians' bluff by threatening war if the missiles were not removed, and they were. About the same time, America started training South Vietnamese pilots for a possible war in Asia.

More than any event, pop music signaled radical changes to come in that era. The Beatles produced their first hit single, "Love Me Do," in 1962, and Beatlemania would soon make its way from England to America in 1964. Folk music was just beginning to evolve into protest music thanks to a young artist named Bob Dylan. Years later, protests would sweep across most of America's major universities. At Notre Dame, however, discipline was spelled with a capital D and the priests continued to rule with a heavy fist. They were the first and last line of authority.

Notre Dame remained a quiet, pastoral university blessed with the architectural magic of the Golden Dome and the Basilica. It seemed that every structure pointed toward the heavens. The Dome looked like a gold skullcap glistening in the bright Indiana sunlight. The rust and amber of the trees brought to mind the great tradition of the university. A walk around the lakes, or down to the Grotto to light a candle and say a prayer, brought peace to many lives.

In spite of this beauty, Notre Dame was not exactly the wealthiest university in America, ranking just inside the top 150 for alumni donations. (Today, Notre Dame ranks fifteenth in the country). One of the reasons for its dwindling bank account was the performance of the football team. Domers with big bucks were more accustomed to national championships than losing to Northwestern.

Students of that era remember the high winds blowing out the glass of the windows of Washington Hall, one of the main structures on campus. Weeks passed before the windows were repaired.

This losing trend was especially unfortunate when you consider that football was about the only entertainment on campus. "We didn't have a lot to do in those days," Charlie Kenny remembered. "We all looked forward to the games and the pep rallies. Football and the Old Fieldhouse was really about the only entertainment we had. So when the football team got so bad, we really had nowhere to turn. There were guys on campus who were absolutely penniless. Even the guys with money had trouble sneaking out to the beer joints. My first date at Notre Dame was four couples at the campus bowling alley."

One afternoon, the students were sitting around the dorm when another student, Chet Ronidella, started picking on Kenny about being out of shape. Kenny was not an athlete and never would have considered going out for the football team.

"I bet you can't do ten push-ups," Ronidella said.

"I bet I can do thirty," Kenny shot back.

Kenny won the bet by doing thirty-five, and then offered another wager.

"Set a time for the 440-yard dash and I bet I can beat it."

Another student, Bob McGowan, set the over/under at a minute and thirty seconds.

Ten students marched over to the Old Fieldhouse to see if Kenny could back up his boast. They were amazed when he came chugging around the final turn at a fairly brisk pace. Kenny was breathing hard, and he was seeing stars when he crossed the finish line. Still, he won yet another wager and a nickname that would last for the rest of his days at Notre Dame—the "Iron Duke," from an old John R. Tunis novel. It was appropriate that English major Carl Wiedemann, one of Charlie's best friends, gave him the nickname.

At a time when football was the center of Charlie Kenny's universe, he did the unthinkable. Step 1: Stop going to watch football practice.

"I will admit that I learned how to curse at a Catholic university," Kenny said. "But Kuharich was so vile in his language to the players that I couldn't take it anymore. On top of that, the practices were absolutely brutal, and I could tell it was killing the players. They were scrimmaging on Thursday for hours when other teams were tapering off and letting their legs rest."

Step 2: Stop pulling for his beloved Irish after they lost six straight games in 1960.

"A lot of kids thought the best thing that could happen would be more losses," he said. "That way Kuharich would be fired. I remember pulling against Notre Dame in the Miami game. I watched that game on TV and just could not believe the utter incompetence. Bill Clark twice tried to fall on the ball and missed it."

The 28–21 loss to Miami was the seventh straight of the season, and Iowa the following week (28–0) was number eight. By now, the entire campus was split over Kuharich. The greatest institution in the history of college football was now the laughingstock of America.

"Students were arguing and fighting in the dorms," Kenny said. "There were even some fights breaking out in the stands over what should be done."

Knute Rockne had lost twelve games in thirteen seasons. By the end of the 1960 season, Kuharich had lost thirteen games in *two* seasons.

"Kuharich was the most disorganized coach I've ever seen," said Joe Doyle, the former sports editor of the *South Bend Tribune*, who started covering Notre Dame football in 1949. "He didn't even have the sense to have quarterback meetings. He was trying to coach the way you do in the pros and he had no idea how to handle the college game. The other coaches were beating his brains out."

In spite of the 2-8 record in 1960, the sporting press predicted Kuharich would make his move in '61. Notre Dame returned an experienced team, with a strong-armed quarterback named Daryle Lamonica.

That season's preview in *Sports Illustrated* contained everything but pictures of blue and gold pom-poms: "For the first time in three years at Notre Dame, the only thing green about this team will be the uniforms it wears. Properly hardened by several seasons of adversity, the Irish are ready to march through a traditionally tough schedule to national ranking."

When the Irish opened the season with a 19–6 victory over Oklahoma, *Sports Illustrated* was talking national championship. This in spite of the fact that Oklahoma, the preeminent team of the fifties with three national championships, was coming off a 3-6-1 season. Roy Terrell wrote in the magazine, "On Saturday, the Notre Dame Golden Dome, freshly gilded, flashed back to the rays of autumn sun until Our Lady danced in the air like some celestial vision. On the cover of the game program, wearing his old magical, twisted grin, was Knute Rockne, back to haunt Notre Dame opponents once again. The only thing missing was George Gipp. . . . It was a victory that set Notre Dame fans from Puget Sound to Omsk talking about the days of Rockne and Frank Leahy."

When Notre Dame defeated Purdue 22–20, then went to 3-0 with a 30–0 victory over USC, the Irish rose all the way to No. 4 in the national rankings. But by the first of November, all the cheering would stop. The Irish lost three straight to Michigan State, Northwestern (for the third straight year), and Navy. Kuharich finished the season on a 5-5 thud as the students once more stayed away from the Old Fieldhouse on Friday nights.

The players had lost all respect for Kuharich and, behind his back, were now calling him "The Kook."

The opening game of the 1962 season was scheduled at Oklahoma, and as the Irish were preparing for the trip, Kuharich gathered his players around him at Cartier Field. These Kuharich pep talks could be pretty interesting. He was known to utter some inane phrases. Like:

"That is a fine kennel of fish."
"Now the shoes is on the other side of the table."
"That is a horse of a different fire department."

This day, Kuharich cleared his throat and studied the ground. He looked nervous. Given that the Irish had defeated Oklahoma the previous season, Kuharich should have been brimming with confidence.

"Boys," Kuharich began. "I want you to listen to me. After we go down to Norman to play that great Oklahoma team, I don't want to feel any repercussions from our administration after we get back."

Tony Carey remembers how the players shook their heads in disbelief. "We couldn't believe what he was saying," Carey said. "We were astounded. He didn't say that we were going to go down there and beat them. He didn't say we were going down there to show them our stuff. He said we were going to lose and that he didn't want to feel any repercussions when we got back."

In Norman, the Irish defeated Oklahoma for the third time in six seasons. Again, Notre Dame fans across America rejoiced at the prospects of their team finally returning to the glory years, but in a matter of days, the Irish stumbled into a four-game losing streak that included yet another loss to Paraseghian and Northwestern. This 35–6 shellacking was especially hard to swallow.

"Let's face it," Carey said. "According to our tradition, we should have been beating Northwestern every year. They had the fewest players in the Big Ten and traditionally they had been the worst, but the fact of the matter was that their coach was a helluva lot better than our coach. We knew that Northwestern's coach really had it together and ours really didn't."

The football program was upside down halfway through the 1962 season. The Notre Dame offense had become so predictable that the Irish failed to score 10 points in four consecutive losses. Pro scouts knew that Lamonica was the best quarterback prospect in the land, but Kuharich rarely let him throw.

As the story goes, a Notre Dame priest noticed Lamonica walking across campus one fall afternoon toting his golf clubs. The priest began, "May I ask you, Daryle, are you not going to football practice today?"

"Nah, Father," Lamonica said. "We've only got two plays and I know 'em both."

The next afternoon, the priest saw Lamonica headed toward Cartier Field. "So you're going to practice today, are you, Daryle?" the priest said.

"Yes, father," Lamonica said. "Joe is going to tell us today which of the two plays we're going to run in Saturday's game."

Here is the most telling part of Kuharich's naiveté concerning offensive strategy. In the pros, Lamonica would pass for more than 20,000 yards with 164 touchdowns, earning the nickname the "Mad Bomber." In three seasons at Notre Dame, he finished with a grand total of 1,363 passing yards and 8 touchdowns.

Lamonica would be named the Most Valuable Player in the AFL for the 1967 and 1969 seasons. Oakland Raiders coach John Madden said he would never trade Lamonica for O. J. Simpson, the most coveted player in either the NFL or AFL in the late sixties and early seventies.

At Notre Dame, playing in the stodgy Kuharich system, Lamonica and the other players thought they would die of boredom. Practices were so disorganized in 1962 that Kuharich failed to notice that many of the players were not showing up. A few had quit without even telling the coach.

"Back then, if you got a football scholarship, they wouldn't take it away if you quit the team," Carey said. "If you kept going to class, you could keep your scholarship. Back then, things were really terrible at Notre Dame. You just wouldn't believe how bad it really was."

For several weeks that season, Kuharich failed to assign someone to coach the freshman team. So they started choosing up sides and holding their own scrimmages on the east end of Cartier Field. They were also having a lot of fun and making lots of noise. One day, Kuharich marched down the field and yelled, "If you guys don't shut up, I'm going to throw you out of here."

The next day, most of the freshmen did not show up for practice, and Kuharich did not notice.

In the final weeks of the 1962 season, it was obvious that Kuharich had totally lost the team. Moreover, the fans had given up. Notre Dame Stadium, which held 59,075, was normally overflowing on game days, but not against North Carolina in the eighth week of the season. The 3-4 Irish managed to draw just 35,553 fans. The crowd began chanting, "*Joe must go.*"

Covering the game for the *South Bend Tribune,* Joe Doyle recognized that Lamonica was changing the plays at the line of scrimmage. When Kuharich sent in a substitute with the next play, Doyle made a note that Lamonica tried to stop him from entering the huddle. Asked about this odd maneuver, Lamonica told Doyle, after the game, "Ah, we never lis-

ten to that guy [Kuharich] anymore, and I didn't want a substitute telling me which play to call."

In December of 1962, after completing yet another 5-5 season, Hesbugh and Joyce let Kuharich know that he could stick around for at least
one more season. Instead, he stayed until the middle of March, when
it was too late to hire another coach from the outside. Out of the blue,
Kuharich's old friend, NFL commissioner Pete Rozelle, had created a
brand-new position called "supervisor of officials." Kuharich was out of
South Bend before you could say *"Joe must go."*

This left everyone to wonder why Kuharich was hired in the first
place. Joyce tried to explain: "I knew Joe for many years. I was one year
behind him at Notre Dame. He was a good student, fine football player,
and an intelligent guy."

Kuharich rarely displayed his intelligence at Notre Dame—or at his
next stop with the Philadelphia Eagles. Kuhrich was the NFL supervisor of officials for one year before joining the Eagles. His first act as head
coach was to trade All-Pro quarterback Sunny Jurgensen to the Redskins. Prior to the 1966 season he traded defensive back Irv Cross and
linebacker Maxie Baughan to the Rams. He got virtually nothing in
return. He coached the Eagles to one winning season. Even when
Kuharich was winning, the Eagles were losing. Philadelphia lost the first
eleven games of the 1968 season, but won the season finale, costing the
team the drafting rights to O. J. Simpson.

Eagles running back Timmy Brown (not the Notre Dame Heisman
Trophy winner) later said, "Kuharich was the worst coach I ever played
for. I hate him with a passion."

So did the fans. An airplane once flew over Franklin Field with a banner that read JOE MUST GO. Buttons with that exact message were worn by
fans to the games. Snowballs were fired at Kuharich from the stands just
before Christmas of 1968. Weeks later, he was fired and never coached
another season.

It was clear that Hesburgh and Joyce did not know what they were
doing when Kuharich was hired back in 1959. Or they wanted the Notre
Dame program to fail.

Chapter 4

WALK-ON

Nick Rassas knew at age five that he was going to play football at Notre Dame. Nothing would ever stand in his way.

That dream began on a cool November morning in 1947 when the Rassas family boarded the South Shore Line of the Illinois Central Railroad at Union Station in South Chicago. As the train headed east toward Indiana, Nick's mother, Frances, sat to his left and his father, George, to his right. Also on the trip was George Rassas Jr., one year older than Nick and also a diehard Notre Dame fan.

Big George Rassas once was a tough, scrapping, talented tight end for the Notre Dame Fighting Irish from 1938–1940 under coach Elmer Layden, one of the famed Four Horsemen from the twenties who played for Knute Rockne.

As the train clattered past the hectic streets of Chicago, then into the cornfields on the western edge of Indiana, young Nick felt his heart accelerate. All of the stories about Notre Dame had conjured up images of Oz—lions and tigers and wizards—in a mysterious place with a Golden Dome and a band that never stopped playing. It was even larger than a little boy's imagination. He could already sing every word of the "Victory March," and could not wait to sing it for the first time inside Notre Dame Stadium.

"Mom, I'm going to play football at Notre Dame when I get big," he said. "You can count on it."

"Little Nick," she said. "You're going to have to grow up really big like the other football players. If not, maybe you can play in the band."

Nick looked out the window at the passing countryside and the farms turning the color of winter hay.

"No way, Mom," he said. "No way."

Two hours later, the train filled with boisterous Notre Dame fans pulled into the rail platform next to St. Mary's College, the private all-girls school that existed in a parallel universe with Notre Dame. St. Mary's, on St. Joseph's Avenue, bordering the St. Joseph's River, was seventy-five acres of rolling hills, green, manicured lawns, and buildings of Gothic architecture resembling Notre Dame. It was constructed in 1844 by the Sisters of the Holy Cross for the purpose of educating female collegians, who were not allowed to walk across the street and attend all-male Notre Dame.

The rail stop at St. Mary's was a mile walk from Notre Dame Stadium, but Nick could feel the electricity in the air when he stepped onto the platform. In the distance, he could hear the band playing. The game was still two hours away, but people still walked fast, as if they had a train to catch. Men wore herringbone suits with fedoras, and the women were decked out in chiffon dresses and silk stockings.

These were the Camelot days at Notre Dame, when World War II had been won and the Fighting Irish were in the midst of four straight unbeaten seasons. A year earlier, the Irish had suffered a frustrating tie with Army, but still won the national championship. At the moment, they were 5-0 with a rematch against Army that afternoon. As the Rassas family walked briskly toward the stadium they saw fans cooking brisket and others drinking champagne.

What amazed little Nick was the number of people who recognized his father. Several approached him, slapped him on the back, and shook his hand. Indeed, George Rassas had been a fan favorite less than a decade earlier, when he had led the Irish in receiving for two seasons, but he was a humble man who rarely talked about his collegiate career. At 6'1" and 220 pounds, Rassas, known as the "Big Greek," was quite large for the time in college football. He was tabbed a preseason All American in 1940, and likely would have made the first team if he had not shattered a cheekbone in the opening game of the season against the College of the Pacific. In an era of leather helmets and no facemasks, George Rassas had taken a brutal hit. If it hadn't been for the injury, though, he likely would have never met Frances McGuire, and the Rassas family would not be standing in the bright sunshine outside of Gate 14.

In the fall of 1940, Rassas had been examined by the Notre Dame doctors, who determined he would need more extensive care than could be afforded in South Bend. He was put on a train to Chicago. Hours later, he was sitting on an examining table at Mercy Hospital in South Chicago, when Dr. Walter McGuire walked in. He prescribed surgery and an anesthesiologist was called in. After performing the procedure, Dr. McGuire left the hospital and returned home.

The McGuires had six daughters, and each one was sitting in the living room when their father walked in.

"Girls," McGuire began. "There is a big, strong, handsome football player from Notre Dame at Mercy and I think he might enjoy some company. I just fixed his broken cheekbone and he's in room—"

Before he could recite the room number, Frances checked the Notre Dame program for a picture of George. She liked what she saw. She was out the door, and her other five sisters could not catch her. She arrived first at the hospital and wasted little time making her introduction. Even through the bandages, Frances liked what she saw. The couple was married on August 30, 1941, and little Nick arrived two years later.

Much of the credit for the McGuire-Rassas marriage went to Dr. Walter McGuire, who had something of an ulterior motive when he arranged for the introduction of Frances to George. McGuire, a native of County Sligo in Ireland, emigrated to New York in the early 1900s and was among the first of Notre Dame's "subway alums" in the twenties. You could count on McGuire being one of the first on the subway en route to Yankee Stadium to see Knute Rockne's famous teams. It was said that McGuire's blood was actually Notre Dame green. By the thirties, the McGuire clan was loading up the train from South Chicago over to Notre Dame on football weekends. Just like the Rassas family, they never missed a Notre Dame game.

Dr. McGuire once made the suggestion, which came in the form of an order, that no marriages or funerals would be scheduled on a "Notre Dame Saturday."

Standing outside of Gate 14, holding hands with his mother and father, Nick's eyes brightened when his dad handed him and little George a bag of salted peanuts. Then, Frances put Notre Dame pennants in the hands of both boys.

At that moment, Little Nick knew what heaven looked like, or, at least, felt like. But the best was yet to come.

Walking up the portal that led from Gate 14 to their seats, Nick's eyes became fixated on the emerald green grass. The entire field shimmered. He saw the green jerseys and the gold leather helmets. Johnny Lujack was warming up and whipping the brown pigskin to Leon Hart. George Connor, with his wide, ferocious face, was tossing his teammates around like rag dolls. After the war, Connor had transferred to Notre Dame from Holy Cross College in Worcester, Massachusetts. This change of scenery to Notre Dame was preordained. Connor was stationed at Pearl Harbor in 1945 when he was called into the office of a commanding officer with a name that sounded familiar—Frank Leahy. It was the same Leahy who had taken a two-year leave from Notre Dame to join the war effort in the South Pacific, the same Leahy who had tried to recruit Connor out of De La Salle Institute in Chicago. Leahy seized the moment and convinced Connor to make the move to South Bend. Recruiting rules were lax in the postwar years, and players frequently changed schools.

His first year at Notre Dame in 1947, Connor would win the Outland Trophy as the best lineman in America while leading his team to yet another undefeated season and a national championship.

Now Leahy walked slowly from the long tunnel at the south end of the field. He was dressed in a dark, double-breasted suit with a wide fedora. In an era when many college coaches preferred T-shirts and parkas, Leahy was a dashing figure with movie star looks.

Leahy stopped next to the goalpost, removed his hat, and turned his eyes into the bright sunlight. He pulled a Camel from his pocket and lit it. He took a deep drag, his eyes surveying a field of players that included two future Heisman Trophy winners—Lujack and Hart—along with future All Americans Ziggy Czarobski, Bill Fischer, Emil Sitko, Marty Wendell, Jim Martin, and Connor, a consensus choice from the previous season. This was a Notre Dame team unmatched at practically every

position. It had taken Leahy less than two years after the war to assemble
a collection of stars that any coach would die for. Not since the days of
Rockne had the Notre Dame swagger been more pronounced.

Sitting on the 45-yard line, eating peanuts, and dropping the shells,
little Nick Rassas drank it all in like a twelve-ounce glass of cold lemon-
ade. Watching the players get ready for Army was so much better than
watching *Howdy Doody*. Now the little boy's eyes widened as he heard
the Notre Dame band strike up behind him. He turned to see more
than a hundred members of the band marching down the aisle just to
his left. They were playing the "Victory March" and soon he was singing along:

> *Cheer, cheer for Old Notre Dame*
> *Wake up the echoes cheering her name*
> *Send the volley cheer on high,*
> *Shake down the thunder from the sky*

Little Nick could have reached out and touched the musicians. Just
then his mother turned and said, "See, Nick, how great the band is?"

Nick shook his head.

"No, Mom," he said. "I'm going to play football at Notre Dame."

Minutes later, the ball flew off the tee and into the arms of Irish
return man, number 25—Terry Brennan. He took off toward the
right sideline like a rocket and Nick swore number 25 was running
right at him. Brennan glided behind the picket line of blockers and
sprinted down the sideline before the Army defenders had time to
blink—95 yards to the end zone without being touched. This was accomplished against an Army team that had won back-to-back national
championships in 1944–1945, and was ranked No. 4 coming into
this game.

Five minutes later, Brennan scored again on a 14-yard sweep. In the
second half, Bob Livingstone added a 6-yard touchdown run and fullback Larry Coutre lumbered in from the eleven. That day, Notre Dame
would rush for a remarkable 361 yards, leaving a fine Army team down
on its knees. Even more amazing, the 27–7 pounding ended one of the

greatest continuous rivalries in the history of college football. After thirty-four years, dating to 1913, the schools were calling it quits.

IN THE SEVENTH grade, Nick wrote his autobiography and dedicated it to his mother and father. To his mother, he inscribed "The Chauffeur of the Year Award." The book was four pages, handwritten, and contained four chapters. Like all great works of literature, it got off to a rollicking start:

It was a cold and snowy day in Baltimore, Maryland, when I was born. My aunts and uncles called me the terror of Baltimore. When I was one and a half, my aunt had lots of dollar pieces in her room and when she got back they were all over the house. Then we moved to Chicago, Illinois. Then in 1946, we moved to Winnetka and in that year there were some painters doing over the rooms in our house. When they left, they left a bucket of pink paint. My brother, George, and my sister, Margot, and I painted my mother's station wagon pink. We also painted the wheelbarrow pink. Then, when I was three, there wasn't a day when my brother, George, and I didn't fight. When I was four and it was Christmas, we didn't have enough bulbs for our tree, so we went to a house nearby and took their bulbs! But we had to give them back. Then, when I was five, my mother was going to Florida but each time she would be ready to go, we always got the chicken pox or something like that.

Nick ended the book with his life's goals:

My future hope is to go to Loyola High School and Notre Dame College. Then I might get married or play pro football with the Chicago Bears. Whatever I do, I hope that I am successful.

He signed off with, "Written by Nick Rassas Himself!"

To his horror, Nick Rassas weighed only 96 pounds when he reached the ninth grade. His mother's premonition back in 1947 had come true.

"Nick, you will not be going out for the football team," his father said. "You're too small, but we will see what we can do."

Rassas looked at his mother and said, "Mom, I can't play in the band. I don't even know how to play an instrument."

"Maybe you can be the drum major," she said.

The boy turned, walked into his bedroom, and closed the door.

In the ninth grade, Rassas endured a painful season as the manager of the football team, but the Rassas family developed a strategy that soon would put Nick on the field. George Rassas located a Hungarian weight-lifter who had once competed in the Olympics. He owned a store in the family's North Chicago suburb of Winnetka. He kept racks of weights in the back of the store, and soon Nick was there every day, pumping iron. Frances Rassas started feeding her son six meals a day, and each one included a bountiful helping of pasta.

By the time Nick reached the twelfth grade, he was all the way up to 150 pounds. At Loyola Academy, he finished the season as the No. 1 rusher in the Catholic League on the North Side of Chicago. After the final game, his coach, Lenny Jardine, accepted a job at Purdue University and hoped to take his star halfback with him.

"Coach, I love you like a brother," Nick told Jardine, "but I am not going to Purdue. I am going to Notre Dame."

Rassas received thirteen scholarship offers, including one from coach Ara Parseghian, just seven miles away at Northwestern.

"I am going to Notre Dame," Rassas told Parseghian. "Period. End of story."

There was only one problem. Notre Dame never called. Notre Dame never wrote. Rassas mailed a letter to coach Joe Kuharich and never got a response. What frustrated Nick was that Don Hogan, the leading rusher from the South Side of Chicago, had received a Notre Dame scholarship, while the leading ground gainer from the North Side never got a five-cent postcard.

"Don and I were pretty equal in talent," Rassas remembered. "Our fathers even played at Notre Dame during the same years. But he got a scholarship and I didn't."

Players from the South Side were regarded as tougher competitors than the North Siders in those days. That is why the North Siders were called "cake eaters." South Side teams were better coached and played a more rugged brand of football. They also won more city championships. Players like Nick Rassas often fell through the cracks, but that was not going to slow him down. Forget the scholarship. He was going to walk on at Notre Dame.

"Nick," his father said, "Coach Kuharich likes big guys. He's got running backs that weigh 240 pounds. I'm not so sure you're going to fit in with his plan."

Nick smiled. "I am going to Notre Dame, Dad," he said. "Period. End of story."

Maybe it was his Irish-Greek ancestry, but Nick Rassas was more stubborn than a mule pulling a four-bladed plow. It was a trait that would help him survive. For two seasons and eight games, the walk-on worked as hard as anyone on the team. He gained weight, maintained a cheery disposition, sang the "Victory March" at every pep rally, and kept his grade-point average above a three. But he was never promoted past the fifth string.

The scrubs at Notre Dame were officially known as the "Red's Raiders" because coach Red Stephens was in charge of the bottom-feeders. What everyone really called this group was the "Shit Squad." Rassas was stuck on the Shit Squad for almost three full seasons.

Nick often wondered if it was all his fault. Or should he blame the coaches? Joe Kuharich had been a disastrous choice. Joe didn't know an All American from an intramural player. That might be a stretch because Kuharich knew how to recruit; he was just a miserable failure as a coach. Columnist Joe McGinnis once wrote, "A lot of people don't like Joe Kuharich. He is a stupid coach, they say." It was further suggested that Kuharich could not coach ducks to fly.

Like a good soldier, Rassas kept his mouth shut and did not complain. Most players after more than two seasons on the bench would start asking questions, or simply quit the team. But not Rassas. He sat in the stands and watched the home games. He did most of his ventilating to his dad in long letters written from his dorm room. This one was dated September 21, 1962, and mailed to Mr. George Rassas at his office, 609 North Wells Street, Chicago, Illinois, with two four-cent stamps.

Dear Dad:

I have been quite depressed and p.o.ed the last couple of days. If I had known this was going to happen to me, I would have gone elsewhere and played ball. I bet I could be on the first string of any other Catholic univer- sity in the country. I bet I could start on any Big Ten team. But at Notre Dame, they've got me still on the last string. I am basically holding dum- mies for the other players. My prediction for the opening game is Okla- homa 20, Notre Dame 6. I am being quite general. But I truly think we are going to get killed. These coaches don't know what they are doing.

I keep thinking of Kook [Kuharich] and maybe someday I will just walk up to him and tell him to eat. . . . In the meantime, I will continue to march to the "Victory March" and hang in there. Maybe I'm not play- ing because they don't want me to make the other team look bad.

So long from the kid that someday might tell Kuharich to eat. . . .

Love, Nick

Rassas knew that things were not going to get any better for the 1963 season in spite of Kuharich's departure. Hughie Devore, promoted from the Freshman team as the interim coach to replace Kuharich, was liked even less. Devore was so impressed with Rassas that he mailed a letter to him in the summer of 1963 and ordered him *not* to report to preseason camp. Nick was certain that his football career at Notre Dame was over.

This was the form letter that Hughie Devore sent to Rassas and dated August 22, 1963:

Dear Nick:

The coaching staff has determined that only 55 Varsity players will be invited back for early practice this year. We feel that each coach can work effectively only if the number of candidates is small enough to give each player extensive personal attention.

After reviewing game films and films of spring scrimmages, the coaches have determined that it will not be possible to include you in this group. If you are on scholarship, this will in no way affect your financial aid.

If you are interested in rejoining the team, please drop by the football office when you return to school.

Sincerely yours, Hugh Devore, Head Football Coach

Rassas broke into tears when he read the letter. Not being invited to fall practice meant the coaches were not interested in him anymore.

Little did he know, though, that he had a guardian angel—or more accurately, a safety net. When word reached Monsignor Daniel F. Cunningham, head of the St. Augustine Parish in South Chicago, the priest went ballistic. Father Cunningham was a close friend of Notre Dame president emeritus John J. Cavanaugh, and a longtime associate of Dr. Walter McGuire. He fired off a letter to Devore that read, in part, "if you do not allow Nick Rassas to come to the preseason camp, he will be the last football player you ever get out of Chicago."

Upon hearing that Monsignor Cunningham had gone to bat for him, Rassas waited, hoped, and prayed. He needed a reprieve in the worst way.

"I was crushed," he remembered. "Here I was, a Notre Dame diehard fan since I was a kid, and I was getting kicked off the team. I had turned down thirteen other scholarships so I could walk on at Notre Dame. I could have played football just about at any other college in America. And now they were telling me to *stay home.* I knew that Monsignor Cunningham was writing a letter, and I might still have a chance, but waiting for that answer was the hardest thing I ever went through."

On August 30, eight days after the letter from Devore had been mailed, a telegram arrived at the Rassas home in Winnetka. It had been wired by Devore at 5:15 EST. Rassas read it with shaking hands.

Nicholas Rassas, 58 Woodly Rd., Winnetka, Il.
Coaching staff has determined you should return Tuesday September 3rd. If unable to be here, contact us by phone at 284-6265.

"Thank God," Rassas yelled after he finished reading it. "Thank God and thank God for Notre Dame!"

In spite of this joyous news, Rassas dreaded walking through the gate at Cartier Field for the first day of practice. As expected, no one looked at him, and for the entire day, nobody spoke to him. The coaches acted as if he did not exist.

"I went straight back to the Shit Squad," he said. "I could tell that Hughie Devore and the rest of the other coaches didn't want me. My teammates were walking up to me and saying, 'What the hell are you doing here?' In truth, I was an outcast."

Days and days passed without anyone acknowledging he was there. He felt lucky that the equipment manager had issued him a uniform. Finally, Tom Harding, an All-State linebacker from Chicago Marion Central, started conversing with him. Before long, all of the Chicago players were treating him like a teammate again.

"If not for Tom Harding, I don't know what I would have done," Rassas said. "He was the only guy on the team that treated me like a human. Because he started talking to me, the Chicago guys felt that they should, too. Chicago guys always stuck together back then."

Sadly, ten other players who were told to stay home during preseason camp were never invited back to the team. If not for the twelfth-hour Hail Mary from Monsignor Cunningham, Rassas's Notre Dame dream would have died, too. Now, more than ever, he was determined to hang on.

Each day, Rassas walked onto the practice at Notre Dame, and each day the weight on his shoulders seemed heavier. Devore and the other coaches would not give him the time of day. He spent all of his time with the Shit Squad. Now in his third year on the team, he felt that he was regressing. Week after week, Rassas sat in the stands on game days at Notre Dame Stadium and watched his beloved team play. When the Irish played on the road, he was always left behind. He felt quite alone, but he continued to practice with the Shit Squad and did his best.

He went home to Winnetka one weekend and bared his soul to his mother and father. He was hopelessly buried on what amounted to be the junior varsity team. To make matters worse, the varsity was losing week after week, and team morale was lower than a groundworm.

"Look, Mom and Dad, I can go to Purdue in a heartbeat and I'm thinking about it," he said. "I need to play football. Lenny Jardine will take me at Purdue in a heartbeat. He's told me that a million times. They have a scholarship waiting for me. They'll put me in the starting lineup next season. It's almost too good to be true."

Frances and George Rassas tried to convince him to stick with his dream. The next day, Nick grabbed a ride on South Shore Line back to South Bend. A few days later he received this letter from his mother, Frances,

My dearest Nick:

You know that it is always easier for me to express myself in a letter. You know how sentimental I am. I hope you won't be embarrassed about having a very sentimental mother.

Believe me when I tell you that you must keep going and give it all you've got. Promise me that you won't give up. You are being tested whether you believe it or not. Some afternoon, take a walk around the "factory" as you like to call it. Go down to the Grotto and say a prayer. Walk past the Rockne Memorial, past the café [south dining hall], past Dillon Hall, the Alumni Hall and turn toward Sacred Heart. Stand under the Golden Dome, and as you look up at Our Lady so splendid in gold, think of these words: "Though the deed be great or small, Old Notre Dame will win over all."

Young man, you are not a quitter. I know you've had to come the hard way at Notre Dame. What I want you to do is listen to me. You are surrounded by some people who do nothing but complain. Granted, you haven't gotten a fair shake. But don't listen to the guys who are taking the lumps. All they want to do is complain. Just be honest to one person—yourself.

A long time ago, a very young boy once told me this when I said it was better to sit in the stands with a pretty girl on a beautiful Saturday and watch a game: "Mom, I got news for you. I'm going to get on that football field even if I have to lead the band."

My dearest Nick, next year you are going to play for Notre Dame.

Remember that you are not Irish-Greek-American for nothing. Don't for a minute let it get you down. Remember that I love you and I know you've got guts.

Love, Mom

The next day, he took his mother's advice and walked down to the Grotto. Nestled in the trees in the shadow of the Golden Dome, the Grotto is also known as the "Cave of Candles." Morning, noon, and night, visitors come to the Grotto to say a prayer, light a candle, and seek peace. The Grotto was the dream of Father Edward Sorin and it was constructed three years after his death by Father William Corby in 1896. It was Father Sorin's wish that Notre Dame Grotto would replicate that of the Grotto of Our Lady of Lourdes, situated in the small French town of Lourdes, site of the largest Catholic pilgrimage in the country. Domers like to say that reaching God from the Grotto is always a local call.

Rassas, now down on the kneeling board, lit a candle and looked skyward.

"I need to talk to the number-one lady," he said. "I need some help here. I feel like I've been patient and I want to thank you for that. I also thank you for everything that I have. But I need a break here. Is there any way you can help me here? I don't know how much longer I can hang on. I pray to you, Our Lady, and I hope you can make it fast."

A week later, the Notre Dame varsity took off for Palo Alto, California, to play Stanford. Naturally, Rassas was left behind. While the team was gone, the Shit Squad scrimmaged at Cartier Field. Assistant coach Brad Lynn decided to film the practice. That day, Rassas ran wild. He looked like a player who deserved to be on the varsity. Unfortunately, Lynn forgot to tell Devore about Rassas's great performance when the team returned from California, but he did remember to put the film canister on the edge of Devore's desk. That is where it sat for several weeks.

Saturday after Saturday, the Fighting Irish continued to lose. Notre Dame began the 1963 season with losses to Wisconsin and Purdue, then somehow managed to defeat USC and UCLA, before reeling off four straight losses during a stretch that saw Navy Heisman Trophy winner Roger Staubach rip them apart to the tune of 35-14.

Everyone knew that the game had passed Devore by. Hesburgh and Joyce had chosen Devore as the head coach because he was part of the Notre Dame brotherhood. He had been on the freshmen team during Rockne's final season in 1930, and he had spelled Leahy as interim head coach in 1945 when he was serving in the Navy. He was serving as freshman team coach in 1963 when Kuharich quit, and was credited with recruiting many of the players on the 1963–1964 team. But he was about as qualified to be the head coach at Notre Dame as Dean Martin or Frank Sinatra were to be pope. Moreover, the players enjoyed many laughs at his expense. At age fifty-three, he was known more around campus for his drinking than his coaching. It seemed that everything Devore did was wrong.

Later in the season, Devore became so incensed with the officials during the Pitt game that he ran all the way to the center of the field to confront the referee, who, naturally, threw his flag.

"Our captain, Bob Lehman, had to go out there and drag Hughie off the field," Carey remembered. "It was the most embarrassing thing that I've ever seen a coach do. The whole team was embarrassed for him."

They were even more embarrassed with the 27–7 loss that dropped the record to 2-5. The Fighting Irish were going nowhere with Sandy Bonvechio at quarterback, so in the week leading to the Michigan State game, Devore promoted John Huarte to first string. It seemed that everyone but Devore knew that Huarte had far more talent. Huarte was an accurate passer with a sidearm delivery that seemed a bit funky. Still, he always managed to get the job done during practice, moving the offense far better than Bonvechio.

When game day arrived against Michigan State, Devore stumbled into the locker room about five minutes before kickoff, looking disheveled as usual, his face still red. In the corner of the locker room, Bonvechio sat on his helmet, peeling an orange, knowing his playing days that season were likely over. Huarte's chinstrap was buckled and he was ready to go.

"Okay, boys," Devore said. "At quarterback, it'll be . . . Sandy Bonvechio." Bonvechio dropped the orange and blurted, "Who?" Huarte felt as if his heart had been ripped out. He had to stand on the sideline and watch the offense score one touchdown in a 12–7 loss.

In the ninth week of the season, Devore sat down to watch the game film of the Michigan State loss. He spooled the film into the reel, turned off the lights, and sat back to take notes. What he saw caused him to stand up behind his desk and yell one of his favorite phrases: "What the *hell* is going on with this team?"

Devore had put the wrong film in the projector. What he saw instead of Notre Dame–Michigan State was the Shit Squad scrimmage from a few weeks earlier. Right before his eyes was little Nick Rassas, running all over the field. He broke several long runs from the halfback position, and returned two punts for touchdowns. He also intercepted two passes and returned one for a touchdown. Devore had never seen anything like it.

Devore flipped off the projector and took off for Cartier Field.

That day, as the Irish were prepared for practice, Rassas was still on the Shit Squad. He walked into Cartier Field knowing it would be another two hours of pure drudgery—holding dummies and trying to stay out of the way. All of a sudden he heard Devore yelling his name. The head coach was running toward Rassas, waving his arms.

When the two were face-to-face, Devore yelled, "Why didn't you fucking tell me? Why didn't you fucking tell me, Nick?"

Rassas turned his palms up. "Why didn't I tell you what?"

Devore grabbed him by the jersey. "Why didn't you tell me about the film. Why didn't you tell me what you did in that scrimmage?"

Devore's eyes were growing wider by the second. Rassas wondered if the coach had been drinking again.

"I don't know what film you are talking about," Rassas said.

"The film of the scrimmage," Devore said. "The film that Brad shot when I was gone to Stanford. The film of the scrimmage when you went off like a roman candle."

"Oh, that film. I guess I didn't think you cared. Besides, coach Lynn should've been the one who told you."

Devore pulled off his cap and slammed it to the ground. "Lynn didn't tell me shit," he hollered.

Devore then turned and started yelling, "Manager! Manager! Somebody get this man a gold jersey. Get Nick Rassas a gold jersey! Now! He's going to first string."

"Coach," Rassas stammered. "I-I am going from fifth string to first string?"

"That's right. You'll be starting against Iowa in five days. You'll be going both ways. You'll be returning kickoffs and punts. You'll be on the field the whole *damn* day."

"Coach, I don't even have a game jersey," he said.

"Don't worry. We'll find you one that fits."

Rassas slipped on a gold practice jersey and trotted out to join the defensive huddle. This did not make sense, but it certainly was what he had wanted his whole life.

ON THE FRIDAY before the Iowa game, the team was basically goofing off in the final pregame practice while Devore and the other coaches smoked cigarettes and paid little attention.

Remembering that very low point in the history of Notre Dame football, Ken Maglicic said, "Getting to the end of that season, nobody cared. The administration didn't care. The fans didn't care. The players had lost hope. We felt like the Notre Dame spirit was dead and gone."

It had been a season of backbiting and bickering among the coaches. A common scene was an assistant coach walking up to a group of players and saying, "You know they should have hired me as the head coach instead of Hughie. Hughie doesn't know what the hell he's doing."

The Irish were trying to finish off a season that everyone wanted to forget. Two games were left, and it was almost time to fly to Iowa City. After finishing his cigarette, Devore walked to the middle of the field and blew his whistle, signaling the end of practice. Just then one of the team managers shot through the side gate of Cartier Field. He was blabbering words that made little sense.

"Coach, Coach, there has been a shooting in Dallas."

"Hold, on, son," Devore said. "A shooting in Dallas doesn't really affect us much."

"No sir, but somebody in Dallas shot the president."

A silence fell over the field. Devore reached for another cigarette and lit it. "Is the president going to die, son?"

"Nobody knows yet," the boy said.

One by one, the players dropped to their knees on the muddy practice field and prayed. They crossed themselves. Several said Hail Marys.

When they were back on their feet, Devore said, "Everybody hit the showers. Pack your shit. We've got a bus to catch. The plane takes off for Iowa City in about an hour."

Devore apparently never stopped to think that President John F. Kennedy was the first Roman Catholic to hold the highest office in America. He never stopped to think that Notre Dame was the most prestigious Catholic university in the country. He never thought about contacting Father Hesburgh. He never considered that the Saturday college games might be cancelled due to the death of a president.

An hour later, the Notre Dame chartered flight took off from St. Joseph's County Airport for Iowa City. Father Hesburgh would be incensed when he got the word.

AS THE MOTORCADE of President John F. Kennedy passed through downtown Dallas on November 22, 1963, there was wild cheering in the streets, some of it so loud that it drowned out the sounds of gunfire coming from the Texas School Book Depository.

As the midnight blue 1961 Lincoln limousine made the slow, wide turn from Houston Street onto Elm Street, the first shot rang out at precisely 12:30 Central Time. At that moment, Kennedy put his hands over his head and turned toward his wife, Jacqueline. His expression changed from a smile to one of astonishment. Secret Service agent Roy Kellerman yelled to limousine driver William Greer, "Let's get out of here," but the driver's reaction was slow, and it was reported that he actually tapped the brake. Now, Kennedy was squarely in the sniper's sights. The first bullet exited through the neck. Doctors would speculate that he might have survived that wound, but the next bullet slammed into the side of his head, sending two chunks of skull and part of the president's brain rolling along the back of the limousine. Jacqueline Kennedy jumped from her seat and crawled along the top of the trunk, trying to recover the matter.

The limousine sped away at eighty miles an hour en route to Parkland Hospital, just four miles away. Upon arrival at approximately 12:37 P.M., Kennedy still had a faint heartbeat, which quickly stopped. His wife tried to hide his lifeless body with her own. One of the agents placed a suit coat over his head. Kennedy was pronounced dead at one o'clock.

The thirty-fifth president of the United States had stood for many widely accepted virtues and beliefs and had been a strong and popular leader during a time of crisis in America. A country suffering through the Cold War with the Soviet Union, along with the looming threat of a nuclear holocaust, had come to lean on John F. Kennedy and the hope he exuded.

One of Kennedy's passions was football. All four Kennedy brothers had played the game at Harvard, and young Ted once scored a touchdown in the famous rivalry game against Yale. Football was an integral part of patriarch Joseph Kennedy's "grand plan" because it was a demonstration of American principle and ruggedness that would help reduce the prejudices his children would face for being wealthy, Irish, and Catholic.

The president often played upon the football theme during his public speaking. He compared the almost unthinkable dream of putting an American on the moon to "Rice beating Texas." He once said, "Politics is like football. If you see daylight, go through the hole."

The morning after the assassination, Hesburgh made sure the Notre Dame football charter was back on the ground in South Bend bright and early. There was no way on God's green earth that the Fighting Irish would play a football game one day after the death of the first Catholic president of the United States. The only games contested that day were Arkansas–Texas Tech, Miami–Florida, Brigham Young–Colorado State, and Nebraska–Oklahoma. For the rest of his life, Oklahoma coach Bud Wilkinson, an adviser to Kennedy and a great admirer of the president, would express his regret for his team's participation that day.

After the plane landed at the St. Joseph County Airport, and the team bus weaved its way toward campus, the players were amazed at the lack of activity. There were no trucks, combines, or plows in the cornfields. Not a single automobile besides the Notre Dame bus moved along the highway. When they turned onto Notre Dame Avenue, normally a bustling place on an autumn Saturday, not a single student could be seen.

"It was like a shadow came over Notre Dame," Ken Maglicic said. "Kennedy was Catholic. When he was elected president, it was like we had our own leader, and when he got shot down, I remember thinking, *What is it about Catholics? What did we do wrong to deserve this?*"

At Notre Dame, the death of a president engendered a more intimate sadness. The students felt as if they had known him personally.

"He was a very, very likable and respected president," said freshman Larry Conjar, "but let's face it. He meant even more to the Catholics. We felt it more than the rest of the people."

Father Hesburgh had been a close friend and counselor to the president. He personally pledged to the Kennedy family more than a hundred masses in his honor. In his official statement, he said, "May this sad day not be one of darkness, nor triumph for the powers of evil, but the birth of a great new life that for years to come will inspire great deeds, come what may."

It seemed that everything was upside down at Notre Dame. Nick Rassas wondered when it would all turn around. Just as his life was about to turn around, the year grew even sadder.

Chapter 5

DEATH IN THE BRONX

Yankee Stadium on the afternoon of November 28, 1963, possessed all of the charm and ambience of a wet sponge. The day was damp and exceedingly dark for one o'clock. A gun-metal gray sky reflected the gathering gloom. Even the playing field was a disaster. For six months, the bright green grass had been ripped to shreds by the cleats worn by Yogi Berra and Mickey Mantle. Then the New York Football Giants had trampled the playing surface into a batch of kitty litter. To rectify the problem, the grounds crew had mixed a substantial amount of animal manure into the mushy sod, hoping to improve the texture. The House that Ruth Built now smelled like a stockyard.

The only decent news was that Nick Rassas would start the first game of his college career against Syracuse that day. Everyone was anxious to see him play.

Notre Dame football on any other Thanksgiving would have been a day-long orgy of Irish stew and wild whiskey laughter, but not on this cloudy, windy, listless afternoon. Just three days had passed since President John F. Kennedy's funeral procession had wound through the streets of the nation's capital past 800,000 mourners as millions more watched on television. Still fresh on everyone's mind was the dramatic vision of Kennedy's three-year-old son, John Kennedy Jr., saluting his father's flag-draped coffin as it lay on a caisson drawn by six white horses.

Now the general attitude around the country this Thanksgiving morning was that life should return to normal. The games would be played. A little Thanksgiving football might just lift the spirits. Few could imagine

Notre Dame not playing its annual game in New York. For more than four decades, the Irish had been a huge part of that city's sports parade. Notre Dame fans were known to turn the city into a drunken bash on the weekend of the Big Game. New York is where legendary coach Knute Rockne built a national reputation for the program, where the Notre Dame "subway alumni" had been born.

Subway alums were comprised mostly of the Irish-Catholic fans who had never set foot on campus, but loved Notre Dame football as much as and possibly more than the actual alumni. They were the biggest reason that every seat was occupied when the Irish made the annual thousand-mile trek to New York to play at Yankee Stadium.

Notre Dame's games in New York during the Roaring Twenties were Mardi Gras and Saint Patrick's Day rolled into one. *New York Times* columnist Paul Gallico wrote in 1934, "Tomorrow is the annual gathering of that amazing clan of self-appointed Notre Dame alumni which will whoop and rage and rant and roar through the town from sunup until long after sundown in honor of a school to which they never went."

They were dubbed the subway alums because they packed the cars of the Lexington Avenue Line of the Interborough Transit Company that emerged from beneath 149th Street and stopped at the Bronx Concourse Station, right outside the front gates of Yankee Stadium. The subway alums arrived in huge columns with victory on their minds. The tethering of poor Irish Catholics to Notre Dame football was as natural as the evolution of bathtub gin during Prohibition. Other than religious faith, Catholics of the urban ghetto had little to cling to. A century after IRISH NEED NOT APPPLY signs were first seen in large cities, they were still the target of widespread bigotry. Many Americans believed after World War I that the Catholics pledged their allegiance to the pope in Rome rather than the president in Washington.

Be that as it may, faith, religion, and political allegiance were thrown out the window that Saturday afternoon at Yankee Stadium. That day, Notre Dame football was measured by the boisterous masses and their ethnic diversity. They came in all shapes, sizes, religions, and nationalities—Poles, Germans, Italians, Armenians, Anglos, Catholics, and Protestants. Football, more than anything, accelerated the Americanization of the Irish Catholics. Notre Dame graduate Scott Eden, in his book titled *Touchdown Jesus,* explained it thusly, "In their immigrant enclaves, these Catholics had for almost a century faced a hard choice: assimilate and ditch their Old World ethnicity, or maintain their culture and lose out on the American Dream. For the most part, they chose to assimilate and ditch. But in some sense, rooting for Notre Dame perhaps let them have it both ways. It was assimilation through victory."

Rockne had capitalized on this outpouring of passion and turned it into emotional ammo for his team. Even as a young coach, Rockne possessed both the vision and the burning desire to make things happen quickly. In 1920, he grabbed the nation's attention when Notre Dame pulled off a huge upset over No. 1–ranked Army at West Point. That day, fabled running back George Gipp tore through college football's most respected defense for 150 yards on 20 carries. Gipp also passed for 123 yards on five completions, and gained another 112 yards on kick returns, bringing his total for the day to 385—an astounding statistic for an era when offensive football was the equivalent of the horse and buggy. Gipp's heroics helped the Irish overcome a 17–14 halftime deficit to win 27–17.

Before the game, famed sportswriter Ring Lardner had asked Army coach John J. McEwan what he thought of Gipp's talents.

"Who the hell is Gipp?" McEwan snarled.

After the game, Grantland Rice asked McEwan the same question.

"Gipp is no football player," McEwan said. "He is a runaway *sonofabitch.*"

The *Chicago Herald-Examiner* wrote, "George Gipp of Notre Dame is heralded as the wonder man of football in New York today. Every New York newspaper declares that Gipp is All-American timber."

After the 27–17 victory over Army, Notre Dame football stood on the brink of greatness. The Irish had risen from an ill-equipped and obscure team to national prominence. That season, Gipp was regarded as one of the two greatest college players in the country, along with Ohio State's two-time All-American halfback Pete Stinchcomb.

Gipp died two months after the historic game. He caught a cold while teaching a group of high school kids his drop-kick technique. The cold gave way to pneumonia and finally to a massive throat infection known as streptococcus. Penicillin could have saved him, but its accidental discovery by Scottish scientist Alexander Fleming did not occur until 1928. Gipp died in the early morning hours of December 14 at St. Joseph's Hospital in South Bend, and when the lights flickered off and then back on at the downtown Oliver Hotel about 3:30 A.M., Gipp's gambling buddies knew it was a signal from the hotel host that Gipp was gone.

The Gipp spirit never died, and Rockne was not about to stop now. Rockne recognized that New York was the place to build a brand name during the "Golden Age of Sports" of the 1920s. New York was a town of big dreams—and, more important, seven daily newspapers. It was a city that loved to be dazzled. The twenties was the decade of the Big Party when the bootleg gin flowed, gangsters flourished, and flappers were the new eye candy.

Men like Theodore Hesburgh however, regarded this era with disdain. It was a time when the Notre Dame football factory started cranking. Meanwhile, academic goals were either ditched or placed on the shelf. In the 1920s, football was No. 1. Academics be damned.

Rockne was forever seeking a bigger stage, and he was running Notre Dame by the early twenties. In 1921, he scheduled a game against Rutgers at the legendary Polo Grounds in New York City. Of course, to the elitist powers of eastern football, Rockne's bold move was considered an invasion of enemy turf.

With his crooked nose, stout build, and Gatling-gun speech, Rockne seemed like an alien to the tweed suits of the East. Little did they know that he had designs on their precious playground. No longer would Notre Dame football be constrained to the cornfields of northern Indiana, and why not? Rockne was already a big hit with the sporting press. Here was the greatest salesman that college football had ever seen. Moreover, Notre Dame was the perfect fit for this sports-hungry town. Rockne was keenly aware of its huge contingency of Irish Catholics searching for hope. Rockne already had two undefeated seasons under his belt (1919 and 1920) and he was out to prove that Notre Dame was not some poor little Catholic college way out yonder.

In November of 1921, the Polo Grounds was the center of the sports universe. Just three weeks earlier, it had hosted the most celebrated

World Series ever—the New York Yankees versus the New York Giants. For the first time in the history of the Series, every game was played in one venue. This occurred because the Yankees had been subleasing from the Giants since 1913, forcing Babe Ruth and the gang to share space with their hated National League rivals.

Ruth had rocked the baseball world again that season by smashing 59 home runs. In comparison, the Giants' George "High Pockets" Kelly was second in the Major Leagues with only 23. Ruth's home run numbers from 1919 through '21 (29, 54, and 59) had already changed the game for all time.

The Yankees, playing in their first World Series, built a 3-1 lead, but Ruth injured his knee in Game 5. He saw limited action the rest of the way as the Giants came from behind to seize the World Series 5 games to 3. (This would be the last of the experimental nine-game World Series.) As Ruth made a temporary exit in late September of that year, Rockne rolled onto his stage. This had been his dream for years.

Rockne would later write that "the nationwide discussion of Notre Dame by football followers after the first Army game had tremendous effect on our varsity spirit. Everybody in the school, save the older professors, wanted to be football players."

That October of 1921, Notre Dame dispatched Rutgers 48–0, and the sporting press was loving every minute of it. Two years later, Army agreed to move the annual game from West Point to Ebbetts Field, home of the Brooklyn Dodgers. Rockne had Army right where he wanted them. He also had one foot inside the Big Apple.

The 13–0 defeat of Army in 1923 was merely a warm-up act for the 1924 contest at the Polo Grounds attended by 80,000 fans. Witnessing Notre Dame's 13–7 victory over Army from the press box, Grantland Rice stormed into the most dramatic newspaper lead in the history of sportswriting, one that would make him forever famous, "Outlined against a blue-gray October sky, the Four Horsemen rode again. In dramatic lore, they are known as Famine, Pestilence, Destruction, and Death. These are only aliases. Their real names are Stuhldreher, Miller, Crowley, and Layden. They formed the crest of the South Bend Cyclone before which another fighting Army team was swept over the precipice."

In truth, it had been a fairly dull game with no dramatic comeback. Imagine what Rice might have written about Red Grange's performance that same day against Michigan. Grange scored 4 touchdowns in the first twelve minutes, accounting for 6 overall, as Illinois defeated Michigan 39–14. Based on that performance, Rice would dub Grange the "Galloping Ghost." But while the ghost was galloping in the Midwest, Rice enjoyed a comfortable seat in the press box at the Polo Grounds, stoking the Notre Dame fires.

Like most of the leading sportswriters of the time, Rice rarely missed a Notre Dame game in New York during the 1920s. With Rockne and Notre Dame on the rise, the eastern press could not be sated. Before "Rock" swaggered into the national consciousness, college football was a two-bit sport that had been beset by scandal, injuries, and death.

The Golden Age of Sports was already gaining momentum, and Rockne had taken his seat in the front row. In the twenties, a rising middle class was responding more to the exploits of Ruth, Jack Dempsey, and Bobby Jones than to the crime-ridden, mob-infested front page. Irish immigrants across New York were plunking down pennies for the pleasure of reading Rice, along with the likes of Damon Runyon and Ring Lardner. Sports editors quickly learned that hitching their pages to the rising stars like Notre Dame was the best way to shepherd the masses. College football before Rockne had been a one-column headline. Now the "Show" was spread across the top of page one. The boys up in the press box were enamored of the manner in which Notre Dame fought back and won in the most dramatic of ways.

Rice's story on the 1924 Notre Dame–Army game was elevated from the sports section of the *New York Herald Tribune* to the front pages. So many forces were hyping the Fighting Irish that Notre Dame versus Army was moved in 1925 to the largest venue in America—Yankee Stadium.

More than 80,000 fans, a mind-boggling number for the era, packed the House that Ruth Built for the October 17th contest between the two greatest powers in college football. Temporary bleachers were erected along the left- and right-field lines. It was a crowd larger than any to ever see Babe Ruth and Lou Gehrig play.

For New Yorkers, Notre Dame–Army was larger than the stock market, more fashionable than the Cotton Club. Among the celebrity A list in 1925 were New York City mayor Jimmy Walker, a legendary playboy and sports lover, and Babe Ruth, Lou Gehrig, and former heavyweight champ Gene Tunney, who sat in the same row. Tim Mara, the owner of the New York Football Giants and one of the biggest bookmakers in town, occupied one of the suites, as did Arnold Rothstein, the gambler who had fixed the 1919 World Series. Also in the house was Joseph Kennedy, a renowned bootlegger and a fiercely ambitious Irish Catholic who would rise to membership in the Notre Dame Board of Lay Trustees. His son, John F. Kennedy, would receive an honorary degree from Notre Dame not long after he ascended to the White House in 1961.

More than 750,000 tickets were requested from both schools. A general-admission ticket cost an outrageous $50 (the equivalent of more than $500 today). Tickets were scalped for as much as $300 apiece (more than $3,000 today). Officials from Notre Dame and Army agreed to allow NBC and CBS radio to broadcast the games free as a way of building a larger magnet.

The elite rich could have cared less if Notre Dame 13, Army 7 lacked exciting scoring or a fourth-quarter comeback. Just being a part of the Big Game exhilarated the subway alums, and when it ended, they were already making plans for next season's game.

ROCKNE'S IMPROBABLE RISE to the kingdom of college football could have never happened without New York. Rockne grew up as a player and a man in the 1913 game against Army at West Point. Back then, Rockne was a clumsy, short, and pudgy end who struggled to learn the fundamentals of the game. The oldest player on the team, he became so frustrated at times with his inadequacies that he repeatedly threatened to quit. When quarterback Gus Dorais threw the ball Rockne's way that first time, he tried to pin the ball to his chest with his elbows. Rockne was lucky to have a coach like Jesse Harper.

Harper was a quiet and humble gentleman with a solid football mind developed during his years at little-known colleges like Alma and Wabash. Upon his arrival at Notre Dame, the name "Harper" did not register with Notre Dame fans, but this hardly mattered since Notre Dame was barely known beyond the Indiana state borders in 1913. These were the dark ages of college football when the forward pass, legalized only seven years earlier, was about as effective as snake oil. But Harper held much larger plans for football's newest gimmick.

On October 28, 1913, nineteen Notre Dame players boarded the train from South Bend for the thousand-mile journey to West Point. Only fourteen had football cleats.

The Cadets were unaware that Harper was transporting a secret weapon all the way from the Midwest to New York called the forward pass—the real forward pass. Several teams had experimented with the forward pass since its legalization in 1906, but there were not many risk-takers in this era. Receivers rarely caught the ball on the run and were mostly stationary targets. The soft underhand toss was the most popular form of delivery.

Harper, however, was about to change the game. That previous summer, he had taught Dorais the overhand throwing motion. Harper, a former college baseball player at the University of Chicago, believed the quarterback should deliver the ball like a pitcher, and the result was a spiral that could travel 20, 30, even 40 yards.

Rockne would become Dorais's favorite target simply because he and the quarterback were best friends. The duo had been thrown together as freshmen roommates. During the summer before the 1913 season, the two seniors-to-be worked as restaurant clerks at a resort on the Ohio shores known as Cedar Point. During free time, they brought along a football to the beach to practice this dandy little maneuver they were about to spring upon the most powerful college football team in the land.

"People at the beach didn't know that we were two college seniors making painstaking preparations for our final season," Rockne remembered. "They probably thought we were crazy. Once a bearded old gentlemen took off his shoes to get in the fun, seizing the ball and kicking it merrily with bare feet, until a friendly keeper came along to take him back where he belonged."

Receivers at Notre Dame were taught to run medium-to-deep routes and to catch the ball over the shoulder. They were also instructed to keep their hands open and relaxed. Harper referred to this as "soft hands." Dorais and Rockne spent many hours perfecting their pass routes and techniques at Cedar Point.

In the first quarter at West Point, Dorais shocked the Cadets when he uncorked a 40-yard spiral that Rockne hauled in at the 2-yard line and trotted into the end zone. On the next possession, Rockne faked an injury and began limping about the field. When the Cadets' defense began to ignore him, Dorais floated another 40-yard touchdown pass his way. That touchdown provided the Irish with a 14–6 lead.

For the day, Notre Dame would score 2 touchdowns via the pass; 3 more were set up by it. Not long after the 35–14 victory, every college team in the country was copying the Harper formula. Long, spiraling passes became the trend that would overhaul the game. What Harper and Notre Dame accomplished was the equivalent of a junior college team toppling the NCAA's top-ranked Division I team.

The headline in the *New York Times* the next day blared, "NOTRE DAME OPEN PLAY AMAZES ARMY." *Times* columnist John Kieran wrote, "The Dorais to Rockne forward passing combination wakened the East to the possibilities of the new open game on the gridiron. Others had used the play before and had used it well, but it so happened that this Dorais to Rockne tandem was the inspiration and example for a new system and new spirit in football over a wide territory."

In spite of the praise from the national press, Harper downplayed the notion that Notre Dame–Army was the birthplace of the passing game, but without a doubt it was the launching pad for a man named Rockne. The awkward end who had threatened to quit the team was named to Walter Camp's All-American team at the end of the season—albeit as a third-teamer.

After graduating from Notre Dame, Rockne worked as an assistant under Harper. In 1918, when Rockne officially took over as head coach, Harper handed him the keys to the program and said, "Rock, keep the Army game on your schedule. One day it might be big enough to play in New York City."

Rockne wasted no time capitalizing. He did so with a fervor that inspired memories of the late P. T. Barnum, the hard-driving showman who invented the circus in the 1800s and brought to life "The Greatest

Show on Earth." Before long, Rockne was beginning to resemble a carnival barker. Sportswriters could not get enough of this colorful quote machine. One of Rockne's best: "To hell with the guy who will die for Notre Dame. I want the man who will fight to keep it alive."

The most notable game in New York City, at least in the minds of the Notre Dame romanticists, occurred in 1928 when Rockne delivered the famous "Win one for the Gipper" speech. Gipp had supposedly told Rockne from his deathbed to deliver an inspirational talk to the team in his memory. Rockne found just the right moment. At halftime against Army, Notre Dame trailed 6–0. Rockne dramatically recalled for the players what Gipp said in the early morning hours of December 14, 1920, just hours before his death: "I've got to go, Rock. It's all right. I'm not afraid. Sometimes when things are going bad, when the breaks are beating the boys, tell them to go out and win one for the Gipper. I don't know where I will be then, Rock, but I'll know about it and I'll be happy."

So inspired were the Irish players that they practically took the hinges off the locker room as they roared back onto the playing field for the second half. The Irish would rally for 2 touchdowns to beat Army 12–6 in one of the most historic games in college football.

Not even the crash of the stock market a year later could kill the Notre Dame–Army rivalry. It merely redistributed the tickets at Yankee Stadium. Now the working stiffs, mostly the Irish Catholics, got a chance to buy tickets. For years, their appetites had been appeased by cheap newspapers and the free airwaves. Now the gates on Lexington Avenue were swinging open and the Average Joe Magills were strolling in. They packed the subway cars to the ceiling, drank whiskey from flasks, and sang the "Victory March" at the top of their lungs.

Nothing was more entertaining than Notre Dame–Army. Many of the games were down-to-the-wire finishes. Rockne's final five games against Army were decided by 7 or fewer points. The margin of victory greatly widened over Army in 1941, when Frank Leahy took over as coach. Then the pendulum swung mightily toward Army when Leahy, along with many of his key players, went off to war for the 1944 and '45 seasons. The Cadets were psyched for revenge during those war years, when Colonel Earl "Red" Blaik put two of his strongest teams on the field. While most college teams were losing players to combat, Blaik was actually rounding them up in Europe and the South Pacific and bringing them home.

In 1944 and 1945, Notre Dame lost 59–0 and 48–0 to Army. Revenge was squarely on the minds of the Notre Dame players when the 1946 game at Yankee Stadium arrived. Not in the history of the rivalry was the setup more dramatic. No. 1–ranked Army was coming off two straight national championships and working on a twenty-five game winning streak. Doc Blanchard had picked up the Heisman Trophy in 1945, and Glenn Davis was about to do the same in 1946. No. 2 Notre Dame, with its famous coach having returned from World War II, was hell-bent on reestablishing itself as the premier football program in the country.

The *Los Angeles Times* called it "The College Gridiron Battle of the Century" and Notre Dame's "Holy Crusade." There was enough hate on both sides of the ball to start another war. Both teams were averaging more than 30 points per game, but defense would become the central issue in this contest. Notre Dame smothered Blanchard and Davis, and the Army defense was equally rough on quarterback Johnny Lujack. The closest thing to a touchdown for Army came when Blanchard was caught from behind out of nowhere by Lujack at the 16-yard line. Never before had the Irish fans seen Lujack run that fast. He was merely atoning for the interception he had thrown just minutes earlier.

In the second half, Notre Dame faced a fourth and one at the Army 4-yard line. A field goal would win the game, but Leahy's stubbornness spoiled the victory. Forsaking the short kick, Billy Gompers ran off tackle and failed to make the first down. Notre Dame 0, Army 0.

Angry tight end Jim Mello said after the game, "We would have won that game if Frank Leahy had stayed in South Bend. We should have kicked the damn field goal."

In spite of the scoreless tie, the national sporting press called it the "Game of the Century." Red Smith wrote in the *New York Times*, "Notre Dame's Pyrrhic bid for vengeance over real and fancied grievances of the immediate past died of its own frustration in a bloodless 0–0 tie with the Army today as a carnival crowd of seventy-four thousand rocked and tottered."

That would be the last game ever played between Army and Notre Dame at Yankee Stadium. Fights in the stands between opposing fans were the biggest reason. Notre Dame blamed West Point fans for blatant Catholic bigotry. Both universities cited widespread gambling in the stands as a reason to leave New York. Bookies worked the stadium from one end to the other. Red Smith wrote, "It was estimated that $15 to $25 million was wagered on the result—which of course was unfortunate. There wasn't any."

The game was moved to South Bend in 1947, a contest won by the Irish 27–7, giving Notre Dame a 23-9-3 advantage in the series. After 1947, Notre Dame–Army was scheduled on an occasional basis, and the rivalry fizzled.

ON THE NIGHT before Notre Dame–Syracuse in 1963, Charlie Kenny attended a party with friends at the Plaza Hotel in honor of Matthew H. McCloskey, the United States ambassador to Ireland. McCloskey had been appointed by Kennedy just a year earlier. A Philadelphia contractor and one of America's richest and most powerful men, McCloskey had served as treasurer of the Democratic National Party in the midfifties and was hyped as a Superman-like fund-raiser. Widely known as a member of Kennedy's "Irish Mafia," McCloskey was approached by the president in early November about returning to the endowment game.

"Matt, the party is running into debt and we need you back here," Kennedy said.

McCloskey shook his head. "No, no, Mr. President. Leave me alone. I'm happy where I am."

That would be their final conversation.

Kenny's invitation to the Plaza Hotel had come via Matt McCloskey III, his close friend and classmate at Notre Dame. Matt was the grandson of the U.S. ambassador. A humble young man, Matt had never mentioned to anyone at Notre Dame that his famous grandfather was a high-ranking politico, but upon returning from Easter vacation his senior year, Matt had a story to tell. "Boy, did I have fun," he told Charlie. "I got to play golf with the president and one of the golf bags was stuffed full of submachine guns."

An ironic remark, indeed, considering the controversial lack of protection afforded the president that tragic day in Dallas.

The McCloskey affair turned out to be an extension of the Kennedy wake. Six days after the assassination, Matt McCloskey's mother was still dressed in black. She could barely carry on a conversation without crying. Her best friend was Jacqueline Kennedy.

"We had two drinks and left," Kenny said. "It was sad."

That somber mood carried over into the next morning as fans prepared for the trip to the stadium. Any other Notre Dame game on Thanksgiving would have been a boisterous and festive event in the Bronx. Kenny experienced a mixture of feelings as he passed through the front gate and strolled down the aisle toward his seat. He had graduated the previous May, and this was his first autumn away from campus since 1959. He could barely fathom how he had managed to miss most of the season. He would be seeing the Irish play in person for the first time in 1963. The college kid who had never missed a game was finding the real world a bit square. He was about to discover that his seat, planted behind a wide concrete pillar, would partially obscure his view of the field. Maybe the football gods were telling him something.

As he took his seat, Kenny realized that the stadium was slightly more than half full. He was practically overcome with sadness. How could the Notre Dame football program he loved so dearly have fallen this far? The band started playing, but Charlie was in no mood to sing.

"The words of the Victory March had become hollow," remembered Kenny. "They had lost their meaning."

Ten minutes until kickoff, down in the Notre Dame locker room, the players awaited the pregame pep talk to be delivered by coach Hughie Devore, who sauntered into the cramped space wearing the "Spencer Tracy Hat," so named by the players because it resembled the one worn by Spencer Tracy in the movie, *It's a Mad, Mad, Mad, Mad World.* It was actually a worn-out, grease-stained fedora smashed down on the top. Devore loved to throw his hat when he got mad.

With kickoff approaching, the players could only imagine the nonsensical words about to fly from his mouth. Here was a man who had played for Knute Rockne back in the twenties. Too bad he could not recall those famous brimstones delivered by Rock—the hand-clapping, the "Fight! Fight! Fight! Fight!" Otherwise, Notre Dame might have played some inspired football in 1963—perhaps inspired enough to win more than two games.

Devore's clothes looked as though they had been slept in. His face was red from a long night of drinking. The sagging jowls and the bloodshot eyes spoke to his fatigue, but who wouldn't be exhausted? Pressures from a 2-6 season at Notre Dame were enough to send a sane man to the nuthouse. Throw in Hughie's other bad habits—like drinking and chasing officials around the field—and you had a recipe for disaster.

Devore removed his hat to reveal his disheveled hair. The players formed a circle around him. Devore began, "This has been the toughest year of my entire life. I honestly cannot believe that we have lost all of these games. I do *not* want to lose another game. Listen to me. I do not want to lose another game! I would rather take little Joey out to midfield and stab him to death than to lose another game."

Players were shocked into silence. Puzzled looks crossed several faces. Center Norm Ricola leaned toward Ken Maglicic and whispered, "What the hell did he just say?"

Maglicic cleared his throat. "I think he just said that he'd rather kill his twelve-year-old kid than to lose another game."

Just then, Devore spun around and flailed his arms. Words rolled from his tongue that no one could understand. That is when his dentures came flying out of his mouth.

"It was amazing," Ken Maglicic would remember. "With his right hand, Hughie grabs the dentures out of midair and sticks them back into his mouth. He didn't miss a beat. We all ran outside laughing."

This pregame buffoonery provided some comic relief. At least the Fighting Irish could laugh in the face of defeat. Call it the resiliency of youth, but the Notre Dame players seemed to be gliding on air as they sprinted down the tunnel toward the playing field.

Nick Rassas was smiling like a kid waking up on the morning of his twelfth birthday party. He had waited almost three full seasons to wear a Notre Dame game uniform, and that day against Syracuse he was actually going to start and go both ways. He was going to return punts and kickoffs. He might actually be on the field for the full sixty minutes. His eyes were getting moist as he approached the dugout steps and the sounds of the stadium erupted.

That is when Rassas heard the voice in his head. It belonged to his father, George Rassas:

Son, someday you will suit up for Notre Dame at Yankee Stadium. It will be the greatest day of your life. The subway alums will fill the place, and when they see the team run out onto the field in those green jerseys, they will yell so loud, and stomp their feet so hard, that the whole stadium will rock back and forth. It will be a day you will never forget.

In that moment, Rassas felt his life changing. Blood rushed through his arteries like the subways delivering the last-minute arrivals to the Bronx. For the first time, he was going to play a real game for Notre Dame. The rumble he heard as he reached the dugout steps sounded like a locomotive. Everything was just as his father had predicted. He looked up into a hazy light; the dust was forming brownish clouds all the way up to his waist. Notre Dame fans were stomping the steel floor behind the dugout with such force that dust was going everywhere. Rassas brushed it off his pants as he tore up the steps and onto the playing surface. The Notre Dame band belted out the "Victory March," and, as he sang the words, tears flowed down his cheeks.

Not far behind Rassas, Ken Maglicic bounced along like a child on a pogo stick. At last, Maglicic was living his dream, romping into legendary Yankee Stadium. A native Clevelander, he had for years followed one of the greatest rivalries in the major leagues. Maglicic loved the Indians with the same passion he had for Notre Dame.

Maglicic was one of the last Irish players out of the dugout. He was planning something far different than the usual jog across the field. As his teammates sprinted across the infield grass, Maglicic took off for home plate. He stomped on it with both feet, then looked down the right-field line at the foul pole only 296 feet from the batter's box and thought about all the home runs slapped into that short porch by

Roger Maris and Mickey Mantle. That historic sixty-first home run by Maris on the final day of the 1961 season had landed in the right-field seats.

After he was finished with home plate, Maglicic ran toward the pitching mound. This was a spot made famous by the feet of the Yankees' Whitey Ford and the Indians' Bob "Rapid Robert" Feller. Maglicic jumped on the mound, his heart in full sprint. He raised both arms over his head. He turned and ran toward the Notre Dame bench located down the right-field line. He was revved to play football, and, for the most part, so were the Fighting Irish.

Rassas's moment had finally arrived. He was lining up to return the opening kickoff with the swirl of Yankee Stadium around him. His back was to the third-base dugout and his eyes were focused on the Syracuse kicking team lining up in right field. Tommy McDonald, the other kick returner, was standing beside Rassas. Together, they waited for the football to come spinning out of a gray sky. Then came the voice of the public address announcer:

"Welcome, ladies and gentlemen, to Yankee Stadium for the final game of the 1963 season between Notre Dame and Syracuse. Set to return the kickoff for Notre Dame is Tommy MacDonald, number 25, of Los Angeles, California. The other returner is number 27 . . . " Rassas heard a hand scrape across top of the microphone. He heard the announcer say softly to someone to beside him, "Who the hell is this other kid?" Rassas smiled. He knew his name was not even in the game program. The Notre Dame roster that day, printed on page twenty-nine of the game program, skipped from the name Dave Pivec to Herb Seymour.

After a long pause, the announcer finally said, "The other return man for Notre Dame is Nick Rassas out of Winnetka, Illinois."

His heart sang with joy.

Rassas prayed the ball would be kicked to him. Instead, it tumbled out of the ever-darkening clouds and straight into the arms of MacDonald, who fell on the ball at the Notre Dame 15-yard line.

Rassas stepped into the huddle. It was now official. He was in the starting lineup for the first time at Notre Dame. Even better, quarterback

Sandy Bonvechio called his number on the first play. Rassas took the pitch around the right end and carried the ball four yards up the sideline. Then he heard over the booming speakers, *"That was number 27 Nick Rassas of Notre Dame."*

He saw a flash, but could not imagine what it was. A photographer from the *New York Times* had captured the moment on film, and the picture of him carrying around right end would appear on the front of the sports section the next day.

In spite of his impressive beginning, the Notre Dame offense was the same old sputtering, out-of-synch, smoke-belching engine. Everyone knew that John Huarte, not Bonvechio, should have been the starting quarterback. Every time the Irish needed a big play, Bonvechio misfired.

Devore was soon up to his old tricks as he felt a sudden urge to talk to one of his coaches in the press box. He picked up the sideline phone and yanked the receiver off the cradle, failing to notice he was holding it upside down. Instead of yelling into the mouthpiece, his words were bouncing off the earpiece. As the players watched, he slammed the phone to the ground and yelled, "I can't believe those bastards up there won't answer me."

In the second quarter, Syracuse scored first on a 6-yard pass from quarterback Walley Mahle to Billy Hunter. Notre Dame tackle Dick Arrington blocked the extra point and the Orangemen led 6–0.

Late in the second quarter, Devore had seen enough of Bonvechio's wobbling passes, so he inserted quarterback Frank Budka at right halfback. The Syracuse defense was not tipped to the fact that Budka had come into the game for a bit of trickery. Devore's hunch worked out as Bonvechio pitched the ball around right end to Budka, who stopped and lofted a pass that found MacDonald open in the middle of the end zone for a 20-yard touchdown. Ken Ivan's extra point gave Notre Dame a 7–6 lead with a minute to go before halftime.

Time and again in the third quarter, Syracuse threatened to score and was stopped. The Orangemen reached the Notre Dame 1-yard line and fumbled as Maglicic recovered. Other drives were stopped at the 5, 16, 22, 25, and 28-yard lines. Syracuse would double the Fighting Irish in total yards while establishing an 18-9 advantage in first downs, but the Notre Dame defense, led by linebackers Bob Lehmann and Maglicic, made the biggest stops when it really counted.

Trailing Notre Dame 7-6 with the clock winding down in the fourth quarter, Syracuse worked the ball to midfield. Maglicic was fighting off two blockers when running back Mike Koski broke off left tackle. Maglicic was in a desperate situation when he reached out with his left hand and grabbed Koski's facemask. Flags flew everywhere. The ball was moved 15 yards to the Notre Dame 35.

On the next play, with slightly less than three minutes to play, Koski broke through the line and into the Notre Dame secondary as the safeties moved in for the tackle, but Koski did not have the ball. He had fooled them all. He was actually the primary receiver on this play and was quickly behind the Notre Dame secondary, hauling in the pass from quarterback Rich King at the 21. He sprinted straight to the end zone for the winning touchdown. Syracuse executed the 2-point conversion as King passed to Dick Bowman in the end zone.

Three minutes later, at the sound of the final gun, Maglicic remembered lying on the ground as the last seconds ticked away. Syracuse had won 14-7. All Maglicic could hear was the celebration of the Syracuse fans. All he could see were backsides of the Notre Dame fans trudging up the aisles toward the exits.

"If I hadn't gotten the facemask penalty, I really think we would have won the game," he remembered. "That was the break they needed to get the offense going."

This was an odd confession coming from a linebacker who had led the team in tackles that day with 18. He also recovered a fumble. If there had been an award for the defensive player of the game, it would have gone to Maglicic.

Still, it was easy to see why all seemed lost. As the sun set behind the monuments at Yankee Stadium, Notre Dame football was facedown in the Bronx mud. The 2-7 record was not the worst in school history, but likely would have tied the record of 2-8 if the Iowa game had not been cancelled.

In the Notre Dame locker room, Devore greeted reporters with his normal sad look.

"I would like to come back as coach next year, but that is up to the school," he said in his gravelly voice. "We are a good football team, but we never seem to get enough points. Nick Rassas gave us more speed than we've had in a long time, but he was kind of slow coming along this season."

Rassas carried 8 times for 33 yards and received a good grade that day for his defensive play, but it was not enough. In truth, Notre Dame in 1963 was one of the worst teams in all of college football. The numbers from that season were abysmal. Notre Dame's offense gained only 1,980 yards with just 54 completions for just 654 passing yards. (A college team today working from the spread offense might approach those passing numbers in one game.) Notre Dame scored only 15 touchdowns all season—4 by the defense.

Frank Budka had led the Irish in passing that season with 239 yards. *Preposterous.* Forty years earlier, when the forward pass was still in its infancy, 145-pound quarterback Gus Dorais had passed for 243 yards in one game against Army. That was in 1913.

On that cold November evening in New York, there seemed to be no relief in sight. Given Father Hesburgh's stubborn position, Notre Dame could expect the same kind of torture for the 1964 season. The football factory was in a million pieces.

In the last nine years, Notre Dame had lost forty-four games. Compare that to the previous sixty-seven years when the Irish lost eighty-one games. That's an average of nearly five losses per year versus an average of 1.2. The Fighting Irish had won nine national championships before Leahy's departure in 1953, and none since.

Now they had just concluded their fifth straight season without a winning record.

There was no end to the sadness. Northwestern had defeated Notre Dame four straight years. After dominating Navy for decades, the Midshipmen had taken five of the last eight. Only twice in the last eight years had Notre Dame finished with a winning record.

Now the players faced the grim prospect of yet another season with Devore.

"We really thought Hughie would be back for the 1964 season," Maglicic said. "Our administration was determined to keep a Notre Dame man in the head coaching position, and there was nobody else out there."

Time was running out for the fabled football program.

Chapter 6

THE CHASE

Amid the clacking of typewriters and the clattering of the teletype and wire service machines, Joe Doyle, a rotund man with a flattop and Irish features, hunkered over his desk inside the cramped offices of the *South Bend Tribune* and reached for his black, rotary-dial telephone.

Doyle had a plan. He was calling upon a strategy that had been a real potboiler in the days of Ring Lardner. Oddly enough, the famous sports columnist and noted author had begun his newspaper career at the *South Bend Herald* in the early 1900s. Given all of the broken-down furniture scattered about the place, Doyle figured he might be sitting in Lardner's former chair.

Doyle slowly dialed the office of Father Edmund P. Joyce, the priest who oversaw Notre Dame athletics. A gut feeling told him Notre Dame was already looking for someone to replace Hughie Devore, and why not? It was time to fix the problem.

Doyle's angle was to read off a list of possible candidates to Father Joyce and wait for his response. One by one, Doyle clicked them off, and, one by one, Father Joyce shot them down. Now the reporter had the priest exactly where he wanted him.

"Ara Parseghian," Doyle said.

After a long pause, Joyce tried to change the subject. Then he hung up.

"It was kind of like detective work," Doyle remembered. "I found out pretty quickly who they were going after."

Word on the street was that Ara Parseghian was unhappy as the head coach of Northwestern and ready to move on. He felt underappreciated after eight seasons in Evanston. Moreover, he was tired of always fighting with the shortest stick. Northwestern was a wealthy private university— the only one in the Big Ten. Year after year, the football team was forced to meet academic standards and scholarship limits unheard of at places like Michigan and Ohio State.

"During that time, Michigan ran the Big Ten in every regard," Doyle said. "It was very political, and Ara couldn't stand that."

Parseghian's Northwestern roster was as skinny as his players. Because most of the big studs were choosing large public universities with top 10 pedigrees, Northwestern normally got the leftovers.

"Big Ten regulations stated that I could take only thirty-nine players on road trips," Parseghian said later, "but I only had thirty-three." During his second season in Evanston, the roster had shrunk to twenty-three players, leaving him with barely enough to hold a scrimmage.

When Parseghian assumed the head coaching job in 1956, the Wildcats had endured four straight losing seasons, while winning just one of their last seventeen games. Athletics director Stu Holcomb had fired head coach Lou Saban and all of his staff, including a lanky, freckle-faced assistant coach named George Steinbrenner. Years later, when Steinbrenner owned the Yankees and Holcombe was the general manager of the Chicago White Sox, Steinbrenner got revenge at the annual owners' meeting by shooting down the Sox's television deal.

From the 1956 season through 1963, Parseghian had compiled a record of 36-35-1, a body of work that might have gotten him canned at universities with bottomless financial resources and huge, hungry alumni bases that clamored for national championships. But this was Northwestern, for God's sake. Coaches who compiled winning records in Evanston were about as rare as D-minus students. It was said that Northwestern was kept around by the Big Ten teams to pad their won-loss ledgers. Each season, there was talk that the Wildcats would bolt the Big Ten for a less competitive league.

Parseghian, with the exception of a winless season in 1957, actually enjoyed a terrific run at Northwestern, all things considered. Who could ever forget the Ohio State–Northwestern game of 1958? The Buckeyes were coming off an 8-1 record in 1957 and a No. 2 ranking, while Northwestern was trying to rebound from an 0-9 season. At the time, the Buckeyes, working on a fourteen-game winning streak, stood at No. 3 in the Associated Press poll.

The previous season, Ohio State had slaughtered Northwestern 47-6.

"Woody rubbed our noses in it," Parseghian remembered. "There is no question about it. He told the newspapers the day after the game that he substituted freely against us. That is not the truth. He didn't start sending in the subs until the last three minutes of the game."

The week leading to the Ohio State game at Evanston in '58, Parseghian reminded his players of how Ohio State embarrassed them. They remembered and they listened to their coach. By the time the Wildcats trotted out of the locker room, they were worked into a frenzy. Northwestern controlled the game from start to finish and won 21-0.

A year later, Oklahoma, a three-time national champion in the 1950s, opened the season at Northwestern. By the third quarter, the Sooners were getting so badly whipped that Parseghian sent in the reserves. The 45-13 defeat was Oklahoma's worst in fourteen years, and the victory propelled Northwestern to No. 2 in both wire service polls, where they stayed for over a month before faltering down the stretch.

Yet nothing in the history of Northwestern football could compare to the first six weeks of the 1962 season. The Wildcats opened the season by defeating South Carolina 27-7, Illinois 45-0, and Minnesota, the defending Rose Bowl champ, 34-22. Minnesota's other eight opponents that season would not score 34 points combined.

Next up was the Big Ten defending champion, Ohio State, at Columbus. Hayes's team was steamrolling toward yet another undefeated season and, once more, held the top ranking.

Hayes, emerging as one of the country's true high-profile coaches, was also known as a bully. During the 1968 season, Ohio State would hold a 42-14 lead over the hated Michigan Wolverines late in the game when Hayes chose the 2-point conversion. Asked why he had gone for 2, Hayes said, "Because the rules wouldn't let me go for three."

NATURALLY, PARSEGHIAN'S HEART was filled with anticipation as the '62 game against Ohio State approached. Parseghian had a terrific game plan for Woody and the Buckeyes. That day, he kept Ohio State off balance with a short pass into the flat that was driving Hayes mad. If the defensive end lined up tight, Parseghian would call for the short pass. If he lined up wide, the quarterback would run between the end and the tackle.

Further maddening to Hayes was that Parseghian was signaling the plays in from the sideline—an act strictly prohibited in the rule book.

"Yoo-hoo, Mr. Official," Hayes would yell. "That coach over there is signaling in the plays. Why don't you throw a flag?"

The officials were duly aware that almost every coach in college football was signaling in plays and getting away with it. Why should they penalize Parseghian when everyone else was doing it? So Hayes's words fell on deaf ears.

Parseghian was actually two steps ahead of the competition. For years, his quarterbacks had been audibilizing at the line of scrimmage. He learned this tactic from Paul Brown during his playing days at the Great Lakes Naval training center. Northwestern quarterbacks were allowed to change the play at the line of scrimmage on almost every play, and this left Hayes's defense guessing.

The Northwestern–Ohio State game rocked back and forth for fifty minutes. Every time the Buckeyes scored, Northwestern answered. Ohio State, with less than a minute to play, led 14–10. From the 3-yard line, halfback Steve Murphy leapt past Ohio State defender Gary Moeller for the winning touchdown. Northwestern made the 2-point conversion. Following the 18–14 victory, more than two thousand brave Northwestern fans rushed the field at Ohio Stadium and carried Parseghian off on their shoulders. Meanwhile, Hayes walked slowly to the locker room with tears rolling down his cheeks.

A week later, Parseghian's Wildcats defeated Notre Dame for the fourth straight year, this time by the embarrassing score of 35–6. It was the worst defeat for Notre Dame in the twenty-five games played between the schools.

A 26–21 victory over Indiana the following week was costly as the Wildcats lost five starters to injuries. You could almost see the air escaping from the Northwestern balloon. If there was one team that separated Parseghian from his dream, it was Wisconsin, next on the schedule. Year after year, Wisconsin caught Northwestern in the seventh week of the season, and each time, the Badgers beat down the Wildcats fatigued, welterweight roster with players who were 20 to 30 pounds heavier. The Badgers kept their starters fresh by substituting with entire units. Big teams with padded rosters were able to cripple the Northwesterns of college football by destroying them with fresh legs. Wisconsin was the typical Big Ten team of big, cornfed farm boys. Late in the season, Northwestern could not compete with the powerhouse teams, as Parseghian had to dip into the second and third strings to replace injured players.

The euphoria of the 1962 season ended with a thud against Wisconsin. A 37–6 defeat in Madison was followed by a 30–7 whipping by Michigan State. The Wildcats did win the final game against Miami, and the season record of 7-2 seemed sparkling in relation to the overall history of Northwestern football.

It was therefore both surprising and disheartening when Parseghian picked up the *Chicago's American* few days later and read a column written by Roy Olson. According to sources, Parseghian's contract would not be extended past the 1963 season.

Parseghian did not need to be Dick Tracy to identify one of those sources. The next morning, he walked into the office of athletics director Stu Holcomb and plopped down in the seat in front of his desk.

"So, Stu, what did you think of Roy Olson's column yesterday?" he asked.

Holcomb cleared his throat and studied the wall behind Ara's head.

"You know, Ara, you can't coach forever," he said.

"Why not?" Parsehegian shot back.

Holcomb did not respond.

"So what are you going to do, Stu? Give me tenure and stick me in a back office with the old professors?"

At age thirty-nine, Ara Parseghian was a vibrant, ambitious man and he was not about to leave coaching. The former college halfback worked out with his players and still could outrun a few. No one in the game conducted more rigorous practices, and the valiant effort put forth by his Northwestern teams every Saturday reflected his enthusiasm. His black eyes burned with passion. Outside of Paul "Bear" Bryant at Alabama, college football did not know a more driven coach. When Parseghian had tasted a national championship in 1962, it just made him all the more hungry.

At that moment, however, he was mad as hell.

"Tell you what I'm going to do, Stu," Parseghian said. "I'll serve my final year and get out of here. You can count on that. I will not be coming back to Northwestern."

Remembering that frustrating moment some forty-five years later, Parseghian said with a furrowed brow, "I took them to the top of the polls in 1962, and that was not good enough for Northwestern. That is very sad."

The day after Notre Dame's loss to Syracuse to end the 1963 season, Parseghian had picked up the phone and called Edmund Joyce.

"Father Joyce," he began, "I just want to make sure that Hughie Devore was your interim coach. I am not calling for the purpose of taking away another man's job."

"You are not, Ara," Father Joyce replied. "We are indeed looking for a new football coach."

Parseghian could feel his heart thumping in his chest. He wanted the Notre Dame job more than anything in the world. He knew he was qualified and that he could lead Notre Dame back to glory, but he also felt like an outsider. All of the coaches since Rockne had been both Catholics and ex-Irish players. Rockne had converted to Catholicism in 1923. Parseghian was neither Catholic nor a "brother of Notre Dame." He was an Armenian Presbyterian.

Parseghian and Father Joyce talked about the job opening for fifteen minutes. At the end of their conversation, Father Joyce said, "Ara, I will be getting back to you." Parseghian did not know what to think when he hung up. Father Joyce had seemed a little distant. He doubted that Notre Dame would deviate from its tradition to hire an outsider. One thing was certain. He needed a job. Even if Holcomb offered him a new contract, he was not going back to Northwestern. Hell would freeze over first.

Parseghian did have one head coaching offer waiting for him in the Florida sunshine at the University of Miami, where his longtime friend Andy Gustafson had recently been promoted from head football coach to athletics director. Gustafson had assured him that the job was virtually his if he would come down for an interview. Parseghian could roll the dice and hope that Notre Dame wanted him, or he could hedge his bets and catch a plane to Miami.

Moments after he hung up the phone, his wife, Katie, walked into the room. "How did it go with Father Joyce?" she asked.

"A little chilly," he replied.

So Ara packed his bags and, on the way out the door, turned to Katie. "On my way to Miami, I have to make a connection in St. Louis," he said. "When I get there I'll call you. I am hoping that Father Joyce will have called by then."

Parseghian contemplated his situation all the way to St. Louis. He knew that if Miami offered the job, Gustafson would expect an answer within hours, not days. Gustafson needed a new head coach on board to start recruiting the high school seniors. The University of Miami was on an upswing, thanks to three great seasons provided by quarterback George Mira, and this was an attractive job, but Notre Dame, *my god,* was the chance of a lifetime.

As he stepped off the plane in St. Louis, Ara checked the connecting flight information to Miami. He said a little prayer. Then he stuck several dimes into the pay phone. After one ring, she answered.

"Katie, did Father Joyce call?"

"Yes, honey, he did. He wants to meet with you."

Parseghian jumped on the next plane back to Chicago.

JOE DOYLE WAS now busy with the chase. He had connections in Chicago, some ninety miles away, among the five newspapers thriving there.

The sportswriting fraternity was one of the oldest anywhere, and when the boys got together, they loved to drink and swap stories. This was old-school networking long before the Internet or ESPN. Newspapers still ruled the world.

What Doyle knew by keeping his eyes and ears open was that Parseghian was finished with Northwestern. Northwestern, located just twelve miles north of downtown Chicago in Evanston, was well within the tentacles of the big city sporting press. The Chicago writers did not cover Northwestern with the same zeal as they blanketed Notre Dame, but the scribes kept tabs on Northwestern. As they said in the Biz, Parseghian was good copy.

The buzz about Parseghian making the leap to South Bend was growing louder by the minute. So Doyle was going to have to move fast. He picked up the phone and dialed Parseghian's home number in Evanston. After answering the downstairs phone, Ara said, "Hold on, Joe. We're having a party and I need to go to the upstairs phone."

As he climbed the stairs, Parseghian wondered what the hell this guy wanted. He was familiar with Doyle, having coached against the Irish for four straight seasons. In 1959, when Northwestern signed the four-game scheduling agreement with Notre Dame, Parseghian was invited to speak in South Bend at the spring football banquet. He could tell by the way everyone treated Doyle that he was a big man around town. He got a chuckle when Ed Sullivan, the biggest name in television, introduced Doyle to the audience. He just wished that someday he could be as high profile as a sportswriter. This evoked a smile.

Parseghian grabbed the phone and said, "Okay, Joe, what can I do for you?"

"I hear you're taking the Notre Dame job," Doyle said.

This is impossible, Parseghian thought. Only three people—his wife, Katie, along with Edmund Joyce, and Theodore Hesburgh, knew what was cooking. Parseghian had not even told Gustafson why he had aborted the trip to Miami.

"There really isn't anything that I can tell you," Parseghian said.

"Is it true? Are you taking the job or not?"

"There really isn't anything I can tell you, Joe," Parseghian said. I wish I knew more. But . . ."

Parseghian was not telling Doyle that he already had met with Father Joyce twice, once in Chicago and once in New York during a National Football Foundation convention. Parseghian felt certain that he was the top candidate for the job, but he also was aware that Missouri coach Dan Devine was in the running. Devine had compiled top 20 finishes the past five years and was one of the hottest young coaches in the business. It did not hurt that Father Joyce was a close friend of Devine's brother, a Catholic priest.

When Parseghian hung up, Doyle knew he had the story nailed. This was a "non-denial denial," from Parseghian, as they called it around the newsroom. Doyle was further amused that both Father Joyce and Parseghian were doing so much dancing. Now it was time for Doyle to waltz with the story.

The next night, Doyle was wearing his detective hat at the annual Rockne Memorial dinner in Chicago. It was an affair held every December and sponsored by the Chicago Club of Notre Dame. Mayor Richard Daley always attended, along with the Big Cigars that kept the football program rolling, but following a 2-7 season, there were a few empty tables.

Doyle's job was to keep an eye on Father Joyce. Hesburgh was not in attendance and that was not surprising since his heart was with academia. The big-shot priest was tired of hearing other big shots complain about the scaling down of football. Father Joyce, on the other hand, had no choice but to attend. Football factory or football follies, it was still his watch.

Doyle was working on his rubbery chicken and cold peas when across the room he saw Father Joyce leave his table. Father Joyce turned and walked away without saying anything to anyone. Doyle was quickly on his feet. He knew that he was probably following Father Joyce to the restroom. In a matter of seconds, though, Father Joyce seemed to vanish. Doyle hustled around a corner next to the men's room and saw the elevator door closing. He could not tell if Father Joyce was on board, but he could take no chances. Doyle was a little overweight, thanks to the nature of his business, but he hurried through the door marked STAIRWAY and began descending. With every step, Doyle asked himself, *How in the hell do you lose a priest?*

At the bottom of the stairwell, he burst through a door into the cold Chicago night and saw a taxicab pulling away. Doyle strained his eyes to see who was in the backseat. Aha! Father Edmund Joyce was going somewhere, and he was going somewhere fast.

There were no other taxis in sight, and, besides, Doyle was a little hungry. So he rode the elevator back to the banquet level and located a pay phone. He had memorized Parseghian's number. Katie answered.

"No, Joe, Ara isn't here," she said. "I don't know when he'll be back."

Joe hung up, stepped back, and took time to think.

"Let's see," he said out loud to no one. "If I put two and two together, will I come up with seven?"

THE MEETING WAS set for eight o'clock at the Ambassador East Hotel on the near North Side, just outside the Loop.

This time, Father Hesburgh was the one with the plan. He had been checking up on Parseghian. He had made phone calls around Chicago to people who knew things. He found out that Parseghian was as clean as a nun's whistle. He had never committed an NCAA violation, nor had he ever come close. His players graduated on time, some with academic credentials that launched them to the best law schools and medical schools in America. Father Hesburgh could find no one who did not like Ara, and this seemed impossible in the dog-eat-dog world of big-time college coaching. For crissakes, the guy had made a hard run at the national championship in 1962 with thirty-two players, and a good percentage of them would have been better suited for Slippery Rock College. Furthermore, he had beaten Notre Dame *four straight seasons.*

Inside the lush suite, Father Hesburgh looked across the table and his eyes firmly locked onto Parseghian's.

"You can coach for several years at Notre Dame and have mediocre teams," Father Hesburgh said, "but if you cheat, I will *personally* fire you."

At that moment, Parseghian knew he had the job. While his expression remained the same, his heart was now clipping along at a rapid pace.

"Yes sir," he said. "You can count on me, Father Hesburgh."

Joyce barely entered into the conversation that night and Parseghian knew why. Father Joyce was still considering Devine, but with Father Hesburgh now leaning toward Parseghian, the decision was basically made. This time around the block, Father Joyce's voice would not be heard. Father Hesburgh was the head honcho at Notre Dame. He would go on to counsel four popes and seven presidents and earn enough honorary doctorates to fill a garage. His work for civil rights alongside Dr. Martin Luther King had kept him in the headlines. (A photo ran in 1964 in newspapers across the country of Father Hesburgh holding hands and singing with King and several other activists.) Father Hesburgh, in that period, was the closest thing to a pope that America had ever known. This time, he was picking the coach. He was sick and tired of listening to the alumni complaints and watching donations go south.

In less than forty-eight hours, Father Hesburgh would need about three seconds to convince the athletic board to approve Parseghian.

BRIGHT AND EARLY on the morning after the meeting at the Ambassador East Hotel, the phone rang at the Parseghian home in Evanston.

"Coach," Doyle began, "tomorrow, you are going to be approved by the Notre Dame athletic board as the next head coach."

"Oh," Parseghian said. "I didn't know that, Joe."

"Yep."

"When are you going to publish this story?" Parseghian asked.

"Tomorrow."

"I'll tell you what, Joe. You call me a little later at my office at Northwestern and read me the story that you are going to write."

"You got it, Coach."

Parseghian was sitting at his desk when the phone rang. It was what the coach had expected—a report attributed to sources that Parseghian would be approved with ease. Doyle noted that Parseghian held the total support of Hesburgh and Joyce. The story left little doubt that Parseghian was leaving Evanston for South Bend.

"If you print that story," Ara said, "all hell is going to break loose."

"Well, I'm going to print it."

"Why?"

"Because it's true. Because it's news."

"Maybe it's not completely true."

Doyle should have listened to the exact wording of that answer. Parseghian had something on his mind that was troubling him.

EACH MEMBER OF the athletic board held a copy of the *South Bend Tribune* the next morning. Some were not pleased with Doyle's story.

"The timing of this is terrible, and it makes the entire university look bad," one said.

The board members were sitting at two tables with a space in-between. Father Hesburgh walked into that space, and with a stern expression, said, "It does not matter. We are here today to hire Ara Parseghian and it's time to get it done."

Another member cleared his throat. "This story in the *Tribune* makes it look like Joe Doyle is running the university."

Father Hesburgh was known for his peaceful demeanor and his thoughtful manner of speaking. He was the visage of a pope. But the look that came over his face at that moment was of a man going to war. He spoke in a voice just a decibel below thunder.

"We have come here today to hire Ara Parseghian," he said. "Now show me the vote."

Every hand in the room went up. The deal was done. In the next hour, Parseghian received a phone call from Father Joyce. "The job is yours, Ara, congratulations," he said.

"Great," Parseghian said and hung up.

The next morning, Parseghian made the drive from Evanston through Chicago and into the cornfields of Indiana in his Pontiac. The last time he had made this trip driving his own car he was so nervous about addressing the Notre Dame football banquet that he failed to check the fuel gauge, and ran out of gas. This time he was equally as nervous, but also agitated.

This deal had come together too fast. He and Father Joyce had never discussed the amount of money he would make, or the length of the deal, nor had the subject of assistant coaches ever been broached. "I think the fact that I wanted the job so badly made them think I would jump at the offer," Parseghian remembered, "but the more I thought about it, the more I realized that we really didn't have a deal." Fathers Hesburgh and Joyce were now rushing him into a marriage he could not accept.

That afternoon, flashbulbs popped in his face and blinded him as Parseghian marched into the room where the press conference would be held. It was so packed with reporters and photographers you could barely breathe. Parseghian had trouble making out the face of Father Joyce, now smiling. They shook hands, and as the priest was heading toward the lectern, Parseghian tapped him on the elbow and said, "Father, let me first have a word with the press."

Parseghian's expression as he approached the lectern was stern and businesslike. The reporters who had known him over the years had not seen such a serious face. Oh, he could be deadly serious on game days, or when scolding players at practice, but Ara was normally a back-slapping, jovial guy when he was around the boys in the press. He could share a drink and deliver a punch line with the best of them. Today, however, those coal black eyes were burning.

He stepped to the microphone and said, "I think everyone who came here today was expecting that I was all ready to take the Notre Dame job, but that is not the case just yet. There has been so much speculation about me coming to Notre Dame that I just had to put a halt to it."

He paused as the room fell silent. Joyce looked even paler than usual.

"I asked Joe Doyle not to write the story he wrote the other day in the *South Bend Tribune*," Parseghian continued, "but he said he was going to write it anyway. It was premature. There is no deal at this moment that will bring me to Notre Dame to be the next head coach."

Everyone in the room turned and looked at Doyle. He turned up his palms as if to say, "What the hell did I do?"

Parseghian rushed off the stage, out the door, and was driving away in the Pontiac before the reporters could react and catch up with him. He was long gone back to Evanston.

DOYLE WOKE UP the next morning and walked onto the front porch to retrieve the newspaper. What he found instead was a FOR SALE sign on his front lawn. The folks in South Bend were not too happy that Notre Dame had lost such a fine coach because of a newspaper story. The sign might have been a neighbor's prank, but it still sent a chill up his spine.

"People were really, really mad at me," Doyle remembered. "I caught a lot of hell over that. Ara put all of the blame on me. I kept wondering why."

As Doyle was contemplating the sign in his front yard, Parseghian was in Evanston, thinking. At first, he had wanted the Notre Dame job so badly that he could almost taste it. Now his engine was traveling so rapidly in reverse that he could not find the brakes. The fact that a contract had never been negotiated made him feel a bit exploited. How dare Fathers Joyce and Hesburgh assume that he would come waltzing down Notre Dame Avenue without some form of financial security.

There was yet one more bothersome issue about Notre Dame that Parseghian had never dicussed with anyone beyond his inner circle, and it involved his late father, Michael Parseghian. Born in the late 1800s in Moosh, Armenia, Michael almost never made it out of the Middle East with his life. Moosh, bordering the eastern edge of Turkey, was a city that dated all the way to the sixth century and was the early center of Armenian civilization. Michael, an ambitious fourteen-year-old with many of the qualities and traits he would pass along genetically to his son, traveled by camel caravan all the way across Turkey to the western port city of Smyrna to enroll in the American studies program at the Border Mission School. He soon learned to speak English, along with French, Italian, Greek, Turkish, and Arabic. His number one goal in life was to reach America.

His first years in Smyrna were peaceful, but an order came down from the Ottoman Empire to deport all Armenians in the city. The Ottoman empire, established in 1299, was more than eighteen million strong and ruled on three continents. Interior Minister Talat Pasha had accused the Armenians of collaborating with Russian forces in invading Anatolia. Pasha cited the numerous Armenian volunteer units in the Russian army as proof of Armenian treachery. When the order went forth, the inhabitants of Smyrna flocked together and began forcing the Armenians out of Turkey.

In a dramatic scene, British, French, and Greek ships rushed to the port of Smyrna to pick up the desperate Armenians. Michael Parseghian boarded a long rowboat that headed out for one of the Greek ships. He managed to survive one of the first onslaughts against Armenians that would develop into a full-scale ethnic cleansing by April 24, 1915, when Talat Pasha ordered the deportation of all Armenians in the region. More than 1.5 million would die, during and after the war.

When Michael Parseghian reached America, he was grateful to be alive, but he carried with him a distaste for the Roman Catholic Church in Armenia. His perception was that the Catholic church had stood idly by during the Aremenian deportations. This issue would still be on Ara's mind almost four decades later as he pondered the opportunity at Notre Dame.

"What would my father think about all of this?" he told a friend with a close affiliation to the Northwestern football program. "My father hated the Catholics for what they did to the Armenians."

Parseghian told his friend that he was considering going back to Northwestern. The friend alerted him that Stu Holcomb was on the verge of naming Alex Agase as the new head coach. All of this was complicated by the fact that Agase had been Parseghian's line coach during the past six years and was one of his best friends. At that moment, as he straddled the fence between Northwestern and Notre Dame, Parseghian did not know what to do. Just two days earlier, one of the wealthiest members of the Northwestern Board of Regents had called to tell him that Holcomb had been instructed to draw up another contract for him. This new contract would provide a substational pay raise along with more security. Yet just the idea of going back to Northwestern to work for Holcomb soured his stomach and, furthermore, it appeared to be no longer an option. If his friend was right, the door had already been slammed shut in Evanston.

"There was just something about Parseghian that bugged Holcomb," said long-time *Chicago's American* reporter Roy Olson. "Maybe it was Ara's independence. Perhaps it reflected the "old guard" feeling at

Northwestern. There were former athletes and big contributors who did not like him."

Parseghian picked up the phone and called Father Joyce. They started to hammer out a contract that would provide Parseghian a salary of about $20,000 in 1964, along with the freedom to hire one of the best coaching staffs in college football. What few people realized is that if this deal had not been struck quickly, another man might have been soon occupying the head coach's office at the Rockne Memorial Center. Notre Dame was within a few days of offering the job to Devine, who eventually would become the head coach of the Fighting Irish in 1975.

On December 14, eleven days after making the initial call to Father Joyce, Ara Parseghian officially became the new head football coach at Notre Dame. A couple of hours later, a kid with a flattop and a pair of Polish gym shoes jumped on the hood of a '53 Chevy and started chanting the name: "Ara Parseghian! Ara Parseghian! We finally got our coach! Notre Dame is back!"

Tony Carey was not the only Domer celebrating on that day.

Chapter 7

THE SECOND COMING

In December of 1963, everyone at Notre Dame knew Edward "Moose" Krause, one of the most beloved icons in the history of the most historic football program. Moose never seemed to have a bad day. He was a three-time All American in football, beginning in 1930 under Knute Rockne, and the only athlete elected to the university's hall of fame in football and basketball. A poor boy from the Chicago stockyards, he rose to the position of athletics director. Moose was known for his terrific one-liners.

On December 14, 1963, when Parseghian finally agreed to a contract, Krause drew deeply on his signature stogie and released the smoke slowly. He smiled.

"Parseghian should be here for a long time," he said. "He took the job twice."

With the news of Parseghian's second acceptance, the entire town of South Bend was electrified. According to the 1963 census figures, South Bend boasted a population of 134,556, and practically everyone liked Parseghian. The football program was in good hands once more. South Bend needed something to celebrate around Christmas of that year, because word floating on the wind was that the Studebaker factory was shutting down. Studebaker had fed the local economy for more than a century. In the past fifty years, it had rolled out tens of thousands of automobiles.

Now the burden of hope at Notre Dame rested on the shoulders of a raven-haired man who roared through life like a small locomotive. You could feel Parseghian's energy the moment he walked into a room. This man did not come to Notre Dame for the pursuit of mediocrity. This was no Kuharich or Devore. Here was an intelligent, ambitious man with a heavy dose of savvy mixed with cunning and guile.

The hiring of Parseghian was an about-face for university president Rev. Theodore Hesburgh. By changing his unrelenting position on the moderation of football, Father Hesburgh had managed to shed an annoying label. No longer would he be called "the Grinch who stole Notre Dame football." Father Hesburgh had finally been willing to hire a coach who engendered hope.

Father Hesburgh believed Parseghian would run a clean program, and this allowed him to take the handcuffs off Notre Dame football. Hesburgh was now admitting that world-class academia could coexist with football greatness. Fathers Hesburgh and Joyce were willing to increase football scholarships by almost ten annually to thirty-four. Maybe the Fighting Irish would soon be back.

The morning after signing his new contract, Parseghian aimed his Pontiac down Notre Dame Avenue and was overcome with a powerful emotion. He gazed up at the recently gilded Golden Dome. Then his eyes shifted to the spectacular steeple of the Basilica.

Parseghian, more than forty years later, would recall his feelings that day. "The answer to the question is yes, I felt anxiety about coming to Notre Dame. I was concerned over the religion issue. I discussed this at length with Father Joyce, and he told me, 'We are not concerned with your religion. We want to hire you as a football coach to represent the University of Notre Dame.' "

Parseghian pressed the gas pedal and started driving again, all the way to the Rockne Memorial Building, where the coaches offices were located.

"That is when I got excited," he remembered. "That is when I felt that surge of electricity up my spine. Because I suddenly realized that I had taken on a huge responsibility for upholding this wonderful tradition at Notre Dame. I had grown up during a time when Notre Dame football was held in the highest esteem. I listened to all of the games on the radio. I knew just how great Notre Dame football could be again."

Striding up the steps to the building, Parseghian said to himself,

"Oh, my God, you've got Rockne and Leahy here, and I am walking into a national institution."

In the foyer, he spotted the bronze bust of Rockne in the corner. He approached it, placed his hand on Rock's head, and said, "You are responsible for starting all of this, you know."

Even before setting up his desk, or making sure the phones worked, Parseghian's most pressing duty at that time was calling a team meeting to explain his philosophy on just about everything. Many changes needed to be made, and the faster the better. He knew the team had basically quit on Hughie Devore late in the 1963 season, and the hangover might be lingering.

He did not know exactly what he would say, or where he would begin. He put nothing on paper. Instead, he thought about all of his years in football, going back to grade school, and all that he had learned. It was time to bring the team together.

The next day, they gathered in the auditorium inside the Administration Building beneath the Golden Dome. Parseghian first introduced the recently hired coaching staff to the players. This was probably the best group in college football: Paul Shoults (defensive backs), John Ray (linebackers), Joe Yonto (defensive line), Tom Pagna (offensive backfield), Doc Urich (offensive line), Dave Hurd (offensive line), John Murphy (prep team), and George Sefcik (freshmen).

Pagna had played for Parseghian at Miami of Ohio and coached under him for three years at Northwestern. Effectively, Pagna was the offensive coordinator in an era when no such designation existed. John Ray had been the starting center on Notre Dame's 1944 team before joining the war effort as a paratrooper. His past five seasons had been spent as the head coach at John Carroll University in the greater Cleveland area, and his teams in 1962 and 1963 went undefeated. He would coordinate the defense.

After introducing the coaches, each player was asked to stand up and give his name, position, and hometown.

Then it was time for Parseghian to embark upon the speech that everyone had been waiting to hear. He felt a chill rushing down his spine as he stepped to the lectern.

"I have been around football all of my life," he began, "and I will tell you that the only condition I have is that you listen to me, and you listen to the coaches. If you do that, I promise you, *we will win.*

"You know what it takes to win. Just look at my fist. When I make a fist, it's strong and you can't tear it apart. As long as there's unity, there's strength. We must become so close with the bonds of loyalty and sacrifice, so deep with the conviction of the sole purpose, that no one, no group, no thing, can ever tear us apart. If your loyalty begins to fade, it becomes a little easier to go out and have a beer, to slack off a little in practice, to listen to someone who will tell you that you should be playing on the first string in front of someone else. If that happens, this fist becomes a limp hand.

"How do we accomplish success? You have to make a believer out of me that you want to be football players! And I must make you believe I am the best capable leader for you! What will I promise you? I will promise you that you will be the best-conditioned football team that Notre Dame has ever had. You will have absolutely the best strategy in football. I will constantly study and update our techniques. I will also promise you that my door will always be open to you and I will talk to you about anything. I will work as hard as I can. I promise never to criticize you publicly, but I expect the same in return. I will be fair with you, as will each member of this staff, but I insist that you respect us. I don't want you to put any of us on a pedestal. Call us by our first names if you like."

For more than an hour, every eye on the room was riveted on the new coach. No one so much as sneezed. After Parseghian finished, nobody moved. He had captured their attention and spoken the football gospel like no coach since Rockne.

At the end, Rassas turned to Carey and said, "Boy, if he'd just come along a few years earlier. We might've won some games."

Carey shook his head and smiled. "I already know that I'd run through a brick wall for him."

As they walked out of the meeting, Parseghian was slapping backs and smiling.

"I cannot wait to get these guys in pads," he told Pagna. "I can't wait to see this team in action. I can't wait for the first day of spring practice."

THE ROCKNE MEMORIAL Building, a.k.a. "the Rock," was constructed in 1938 to provide offices for the athletic staff, along with an intramural gymnasium in the back available to the entire student body. When the two-story edifice was finished, no one would have guessed that this beautifully proportioned brick building was an athletic facility. It hardly resembled the Old Fieldhouse. With its arched loggia and Gothic entrance, it looked more like a liberal arts building. What else would you expect? This was a monument to Rockne and grandeur was required.

A month after Parseghian arrived on campus, the staff was working late one night, watching film and grading the players from the previous season. Others were reading up on Notre Dame history at the behest of their new coach.

"I want you to read everything you can get your hands on," Parseghian told the coaches. "I want you to know Knute Rockne from top to bottom, from the inside out. Same with Frank Leahy. I want all of us to know everything possible before we start the 1964 season."

Parseghian's office in the Rock was situated in the corner with a view of the South Quadrangle from one window and Mary's Lake from the other. It was spacious yet hardly fancy. A long table extended from Parseghian's desk and that is where the staff meetings were held.

One night in mid-February, the phone rang at Parseghian's office and the voice on the other end of the line belonged to Frank Gaul, the senior member of the pep rally committee.

"Coach Parseghian," Gaul began. "We were wondering if you would mind coming over to Sorin Hall for a pep rally. The students would really like to see you." Parseghian could not believe what he was hearing.

"A pep rally in February?" he said. "You've got to be kidding me. We are not even close to the football season yet. It's still basketball season."

"That's right, Coach," Gaul said, "but the kids are pretty hungry. You know that we haven't had a winning season in quite a while."

Parseghian hung up and again was reminded of his enormous obligation to Notre Dame and all of its fans. As each day passed, the pressure mounted, and every time he walked across the campus, he could see the desperation in their eyes.

Through the snow, Parseghian trekked across the campus with Tom Pagna by his side. They were surprised to find more than three thousand students standing in front of Sorin Hall, located next to the Administration Building. The band was playing and the students, standing in ankle-deep snow, were going wild. They were already building human pyramids and chanting, "We Want Ara! We Want Ara! We Want Ara!" Parseghian smiled and turned to Pagna, who winked at him.

"Looks like you'd better talk to those kids," Pagna said. "I don't think they're going away."

The columns of students seemed to stretch forever. Parseghian strode up the steps of Sorin Hall and turned to face the worshiping masses. They bellowed and called out his name and, when Parseghian lifted his right hand for silence, they got louder. Finally, he raised both hands and bent forward as if he were bowing. The noise began to subside.

"I came to Notre Dame to renew the winning tradition," he said. "I really believe that we will win again."

That was enough for the roar to resume. They were jumping and screaming and, in spite of the heavy layer of snow, they were building more shoulder pyramids again. This was as close as free men could come to a prison riot. After several more minutes, Parseghian managed to quiet them down once more.

"I don't know how long it's going to take for us to look like one of those great old Notre Dame teams again," Parseghian said, "but I don't think it's going to take as long as some people think. *We will win again.*"

By now, the cheering was so loud that Parseghian gave up. He turned, waved good-bye, and headed back to the Rock. On his way to the stairs, he stopped and looked Rockne in the eye.

"I told you," he said. "You were the one who started this mess."

THE NEXT MORNING, Nick Rassas had an idea. This was not unusual for someone whose brain never stopped working. It was the reason that Rassas had hung on for almost three years on the "Shit Squad."

"Look, I've got a game plan," he told Tony Carey. "I thought this up when I was at the pep rally at the Rock."

"Slow down just a little, Nick," Carey said. "You worry me."

"Actually, I think this will work. Coach told us at our first team meeting that his door was always open. That he wants to hear from us."

"He's been here a month," Carey said. "We haven't even put on the pads yet. I kinda doubt he wants to hear from anybody just yet."

"Just go with me," Rassas said. "Longo's already said he'd go."

Tom Longo for the past three years had been in much the same boat as Rassas and Carey. Recruited as a quarterback out of New Jersey, he had been knocking around the past three seasons on the Shit Squad, too, with little hope. In 1963, the coaches had tried him as defensive back. He knew that his best hope under Parseghian was on defense.

When the three arrived at Parseghian's office, Rassas turned to Carey and Longo and said, "You guys let me do the talking. Just stay out here on this bench and I'll let you know how it goes."

When the receptionist told Nick the coach was ready to see him, he practically sprinted into his office.

"So, Nick, how are you doing?" Parseghian asked. "You're a lot bigger than the last time I saw you in high school."

"Coach, I've gained almost forty pounds and I'm rarin' to go," Rassas said. "That is the biggest reason I'm here."

"Okay," Parseghian said with a broad smile.

"Let me get right down to it. What if I told you that I've been here three years and I actually started a game last season, and I don't even have a scholarship?"

Parseghian's jaw dropped. "Are you kidding me? You start for Notre Dame with no scholarship!" He picked up the telephone and called the office of Father Edmund Joyce. "Father Joyce, I'm sitting here with Nick Rassas and he tells me he doesn't even have a scholarship. I think he should have one." Parseghian gave Father Joyce time to respond and said, "Okay, okay. So you'll take care of it. I really think he should be on scholarship since he started the Syracuse game last year."

Parseghian hung up the phone, turned to Rassas, and smiled again.

"Okay," Rassas said. "I really appreciate it. Now I have another situation. Tony Carey is sitting out there in the hallway, you see. Did you know that he missed his entire sophomore season because of a separated shoulder? Tony's never even suited for a game. I bet you could get him another year of eligibility."

Parseghian nodded and picked up the phone again. "Father Joyce, Nick Rassas here tells me we might be able to get a medical redshirt for Tony Carey. It would give him another year of eligibility. . . . Okay, you think you can handle it?"

Parseghian smiled again and said, "Okay, Nick, what else can I do for you?"

"Well, Coach, Tom Longo is also sitting out in the hall with Tony. Tom had a broken wrist two years ago and didn't play a single down. Never even suited up. I just bet you could get him another year of eligibility."

Again, the coach reached for the phone and started dialing.

"Father Joyce, I'm learning all kinds of things from Nick Rassas today. He says that Longo didn't play two years ago because of a broken wrist." Parseghian paused to hear the answer. "Thank you, Father. All of these moves could help us quite a bit."

The coach looked across the desk at Rassas, who held his hands up.

"That's all I've got, Coach," Rassas said.

"Well, that's certainly enough."

Rassas shook hands with Parseghian and hustled through the door. Back in the hallway, he waved at Carey and Longo. He slapped his two friends on the back as they walked away.

"Looks like we're all going to be playing for Notre Dame for a long time," he said, "and I just bet we'll all be starting in the same secondary."

Chapter 8

ARA THE BEAUTIFUL

There was a time when only a miracle might have allowed football to enter the life of Ara Raoul Parseghian. He was born May 21, 1923, in Akron, Ohio; his father an educated, multilingual, and ambitious man, his mother a fearless woman, orphaned at age nine, one who took great risks to reach America from her native France.

Michael Parseghian fled Smyrna, Turkey, at the age of sixteen on a Greek ship to Athens, where he spent two years as an accountant.

At the onset of the Armenian deportations from Turkey in 1915, Michael fled from Greece to Paris, where he boarded a ship for the United States. Weeks later, he managed to reach Akron, Ohio, which boasted a large Armenian population and, months later, he was drafted by the United States army and sent to France to be a liaison between French and American officers in War World I. Upon his return to Akron after the war, he met a young French woman who showed him pictures of a beautiful lady she had recently met in Paris. From the photos alone, young Michael fell in love with the Parisian and soon began writing to her in Paris.

Amelia Bonneau had overcome many struggles in her life. Her mother died of typhoid fever when she was nine and her father was unable to care for Amelia and her three siblings. So she was sent to an orphanage until her sixteenth birthday, whereupon she became a seamstress and a nanny for a wealthy family. She soon learned that her brother Jean Batiste had been killed in World War I. Her two sisters lived in distant places, so Amelia felt quite alone in Paris.

She was a bit overwhelmed at the passion of the letters she received from Michael Parseghian. But before long, she agreed to marry him and was soon on a ship to America to meet him. Michael boarded a train for New York, where he met his bride-to-be and soon they were on their way to Ohio.

Michael and Amelia had three children—Gerard, Isabella, and Ara— the latter named after a mythological Armenian king named "Ara the Beautiful." So homesick was Amelia for her homeland and her sisters that she took the kids back to Paris when Ara was four years old. They stayed for six months, long enough for Ara to learn some of the language, and long enough for Michael to wonder when they were coming home. Husband and wife were not at odds and enjoyed a loving relationship. Soon, Amelia and the kids were on their way back to America, and Michael was overjoyed when they returned.

So protective was Amelia of her youngest son, Ara, that she kept him in dresses until he was six. By the time Ara got his hands on a pair of pants, he was sneaking off to the sandlots of Akron to play tackle football. Amelia could never imagine her little boy playing a game as violent as football with the neighborhood kids. The only way she could get him home was with a sawed-off broomstick she utilized to stir the family wash.

"I think one of the reasons she was protective is that she had never seen a game like football that had so much contact," Ara remembered. "The only sport she had ever seen in France was soccer."

Amelia Parseghian was so concerned about her son's safety that she would not allow him to take a job delivering newspapers for the *Akron Beacon Journal*—until she realized the job might have some educational value.

"Ara, you can throw the newspapers," she said, "under the condition that you will read the paper from front to back before you complete your route every day."

Playing football, and throwing hundreds of newspapers, was the way Ara Parseghian liked to live. He was a child with an itch for action. It was not long before the other kids tabbed him the toughest kid in school, and by the eighth grade, the Board of Education had confirmed this fact. There were so many vandals breaking into the school in those days that Ara was hired to patrol the grounds at night. His checks came straight from the Board of Education, which, according to his brother, Gerard, brought a sense of great satisfaction.

His mother grudgingly gave in to the notion of him playing football for the junior high team, but upon attending the Akron South High School games, she spent the afternoon under the stands praying for his safety. Her son might have been smaller than the other boys, but he won most of the battles. His high school coach Frank "Doc" Wargo remembered a game against Steubenville High, a team composed mostly of miners' sons.

"Ara was tough, but Steubenville had a tough fullback, too," Wargo said. "On the first play from scrimmage, the two of them met head-on, and you could hear the helmets crash. Both boys went down. After a few seconds, Ara jumped up and they carried the big ol' fullback off the field."

During the late thirties and early forties, a coach named Paul Brown was making a name for himself at Massillon High School, some twenty miles from Akron. The Massillon games were played on Friday nights and South High School normally played on Saturdays, so Ara would jump in his car late Friday afternoon and drive down to Massillon.

"I was so impressed with what I was seeing that I couldn't believe my eyes," he remembered. "The precision of that team was just unbelievable. It was all due to Paul Brown. Their behavior on the field was beyond comprehension. Boy, would I have loved to play for those Massillon teams."

Brown coached the Ohio State Buckeyes to a national title, then led the Cleveland Browns to seven pro championships. Not many people knew he was the master of high school football. Winning 89 percent of his games, Brown transformed Massillon into one of the biggest high school powers in the country. One year, Kent State asked Brown if he would consider playing an exhibition game in the spring as a kind of tune-up for the college team. Massillon defeated Kent State to the tune of 35–zip.

After graduating from high school, Parseghian initially enrolled at Akron University, but World War II was raging in both Europe and the South Pacific, and he was soon drafted. Within weeks, he was assigned to the Great Lakes Naval Training Center north of Chicago. Much to his surprise, and delight, he learned that during his spare time from training his football coach would be Paul Brown.

At age thirty-five, Brown was still eligible for military service, but like many of the notable coaches of the day, he was kept in the United States to coach a military team, just as Chicago Bears coach George Halas had done during World War I. Brown's team was stocked with talent, and he instantly took a liking to a small halfback with plenty of guts.

"That experience was priceless," Parseghian said. "Paul Brown would go to the blackboard the first day of practice and tell us what the goals of the team would be. He would write them down—one, two, three, and so on. Then he would make us write them down. That way we always remembered the basics. He told us we would be successful if we did these things. And you know what? He was right."

In the war years, the Associated Press included the military training centers in the top 20. That season, Great Lakes finished with a 9-2-1 record and ranked No. 17 in the country. Now the name Paul Brown was gaining status in coaching circles.

"Paul Brown was not a big guy, but he could scare the hell out of anyone," Parseghian said. "The biggest players of the day were about 250 pounds, and he was scaring the daylights out of them, too. We all carried around notebooks so we could memorize the things he told us. If you could not comply with what Paul Brown wanted, you were out of there."

With the end of the war, Parseghian enrolled at Miami of Ohio, a small school with an uncanny knack of producing great coaching talent—names like Army's Earl Blaik, Paul Dietzel, Woody Hayes, and Weeb Ewbank. The latter led the 1958 Colts to the NFL championship and the New York Jets to victory in Super Bowl III.

At Miami during the 1946 and 1947 seasons, Parseghian was coached by Sid Gillman, one of the greatest offensive innovators in the history of football. This was a period when football was still a brutish and untamed game, and most coaches wore sweatshirts with chili-dog stains on the front. Gillman was one of the first to treat football as an intellectual game, a chessboard with the players acting as the pieces.

Ara Parseghian would pay attention and digest every word from Gillman's mouth. In the years after the war, the T formation became all the rage in both the colleges and pros. It had been introduced by George

Halas in 1940 and as a result the Chicago Bears became a terror, beating the Washington Redskins 73–0 in the NFL championships.

In the year preceding the T formation, football was mostly a running game from the single wing. Now, with the quarterback under center, offensive football became more balanced.

At Miami University in 1947, the Redskins boasted a tough halfback wearing the number 70. "Hardnose" was the name that Paul Brown had given him at Great Lakes. It was the way the 193-pound halfback slammed into tacklers and bounced off. Brown was interested in Parseghian when he came spinning off the Miami campus after graduating in the spring of 1948. Parseghian wanted to play so badly for Paul Brown that he could taste it. He signed with Cleveland, a member of the newly formed All-American Football Conference, and was one of the first to show up for training camp, notebook in hand. He was the Browns' regular halfback that first season in spite of a bad hip.

"He'd hurt that hip and then we would take him out of the game," Brown remembered. "And the next thing you know, he's limping up and down the sidelines until he could walk on it again. Then he'd beg me to put him back in."

In a game against the Baltimore Colts the next season, as he shot through an opening in the line, Parseghian cut to avoid a linebacker and sprawled headlong onto the ground. He felt a sharp pain in his right hip. Doctors would later explain that he had suffered frayed cartilage. Parseghian thought that a little time in the whirlpool would cure this injury, but every time he made a quick turn, or was hit from the side, the pain would flare up.

"At first, I think the Cleveland doctors thought I was faking it," he said. "I think the coaches thought I was faking it, but I just couldn't go like I used to." (Over the next sixty years, Parseghian would undergo five major hip surgeries and three more on his left knee. Both injuries were suffered playing football.)

By the end of the 1949 season, Parseghian's football career was over. The injured hip was already degenerating. Ironically, this is what he had said to his brother, Gerard, about the business of coaching: "There is no way I will ever coach. That profession is for the birds."

That said, when his alma mater called, Ara did an about-face. He was contacted by Miami head football coach Woody Hayes, who offered the suggestion that he coach the freshman team while working on his master's degree. Then he could decide what he wanted to do with the rest of his life. Parseghian was officially hired by athletics director John Brickles.

Hayes took off for Ohio State for the 1951 season, where he would win five national championships (three were consensus) and thirteen Big Ten titles over the next twenty-eight years. Hayes's departure led to Parseghian being elevated to the head coaching job at Miami. Brickles had been that impressed with him as the freshman coach and his 5-0 record. Now Parseghian was hooked on coaching, and why not? He would compile a record of 39-6-1 that would bring Northwestern calling for the 1956 season.

What he never got out of his blood was playing football. Few people knew that Parseghian walked away—actually limped off—from Cleveland in a state of frustration. His future had seemed bright with an up-and-coming team and their brilliant coach. He had expected to start at halfback for several years in Cleveland. In 1950, the Browns moved into the National Football League and reached the championship game each of the first six years, winning three of those. Parseghian was left to watch and wonder.

One day, Parseghian and Pagna were walking across the Miami campus when Ara suddenly stopped and kicked a pile of rocks. His face turned red.

"God, I wish I was still playing football," he said. "I know that I could still be playing football if I hadn't gotten hurt. Tommy, I know in my heart that I could have been a really good player."

That fire in his belly would be converted into coaching energy. At Notre Dame, he was going to need every ounce of it.

Chapter 9

CHESSBOARD

I must be in the huddle. I must be in the line. I must be in the action—I must.

—ARA PARSEGHIAN

Ara Parseghian prowled the practice field that first day of spring drills like a husky cat on an empty stomach. A sense of urgency burned in his dark eyes. In a recent interview with *Sport* magazine he had said, "Seems I'm always in a rush. Don't know where I'm going, but I'm always in a rush."

Now the masses were filing into Cartier Field as team managers tried to restrain the crowd. *How is this possible?* Parseghian kept asking himself as he watched more than five thousand fans march into the rickety old stadium built in 1889. *What are they expecting from me? This is spring practice!* The clock was already ticking—five months and counting until the start of the 1964 season.

What the starved faithful of Notre Dame football witnessed that warm April afternoon was a man who would never be compared to Joe Kuharich. Parseghian was starched and pressed and cleanly shaved. His dark, wavy hair was precisely trimmed. He wore a blue sweatshirt with NOTRE DAME emblazoned across the front in gold letters trimmed in white. A crease was ironed into his slacks. Even his coaching shoes shined like mirrors. Kuharich was known for his five o'clock shadow and rumpled suits. Parseghian was snappier in a sweatshirt than Kuharch in coat and tie.

Upon seeing Parseghian for the first time, *Los Angeles Times* columnist Jim Murray wrote, "They told us he was another [Knute] Rockne. The nerve of them! Why I checked personally and his nose was straight, he had all his hair, and he doesn't speak like a Gatling gun. He doesn't wear hats that look like he found them under a truck. Ara would have to stay in makeup for two days to look as bad as Rock. If they made Ara's story into a movie, they could use Hugh [O'Brien] instead of Pat O'Brien."

Everything about Parseghian seemed straight and orderly and properly filed. Some wondered if he counted his chews during breakfast. Practice was so precisely planned that everyone knew what they were doing from one minute to the next. Parseghian was a coach, father, priest, general, and cheerleader rolled into one. More than anything, he was a master organizer.

The coaching staff already operated like a finely tuned military outfit. From Northwestern he had brought three close friends—Tom Pagna, Paul Shoults, and Doc Urich. The others—John Ray, Dave Hurd, Joe Yonto, George Sefcik, and John Murphy—were ex-Notre Dame players. Everything seemed symmetrical under Parseghian.

Pareseghian was jacked up from the moment he hustled onto the practice field. He trotted to the front of the calisthenics formation and began clapping his hands. He then led the team in side-straddle hops.

"Let's go!" he yelled at the players in his raspy voice. "Pick it up! You guys are already lagging behind. You are wasting my time!"

Then he jumped straight up on legs that seemed spring-loaded. He kicked up his feet in midair and touched his toes with his fingertips. It was an acrobatic act you would expect from an overcaffeinated graduate assistant, not some forty-year-old coach, father of three.

"Jeez!" Ken Maglicic said to Tony Carey. "This guy is in better shape than us."

At the end of calisthenics, Parseghian instructed the players to form a circle around him.

"This is all I'm going to tell you before we get started with spring practice," he said. "Everybody is going to be treated equally. I'm going to give everyone a fair chance to win a starting position. At this moment, no one—and I mean no one—owns a starting job. Is that clear?"

"Yessir!" the players shot back. They clapped their hands as practice began.

Changes were coming at Notre Dame and they were happening fast. From dawn until late at night, six days a week, the coaching staff had labored to design a new blueprint. Parseghian wanted the roster torn down and rebuilt—like a car engine. No one would recognize this team when they were finished. That was the best news anyone around Notre Dame had heard in a long time.

Kuharich's coaching concepts from 1959 to 1962 had been both antiquated and dysfunctional. On offense, Kuharich leaned on the "Elephant Backfield," pounding the ball between the tackles with two backs, Paul Costa and Jim Snowden, who weighed more than 240 pounds each. It was a pro-style attack that mirrored what the best NFL teams thrived on—hammering the ball down the field. The best example was Paul Hornung and Jim Taylor in Green Bay. Cleveland, on the verge of winning another NFL championship, was led by powerhouse running back Jim Brown. A battering ram named Bill Brown had turned Minnesota into a contender in the Western Conference.

Yet none of the aforementioned weighed 240 pounds.

In the college ranks, Parseghian knew it was simple to defend a slow, overweight backfield. He had accomplished this four times with a basic formula at Northwestern. Because Kuharich persisted with his "Elephant Backfield," Parseghian sent his linebackers blitzing up the middle on practically every play in what amounted to a "run blitz."

"All we had to do was plug up the holes with our linebackers and we had them," he remembered. "Their backs didn't have the speed to get to the outside."

Kuharich's offense, straight from the dark ages, had wasted the great passing arm of Daryle Lamonica for two seasons in 1961 and '62. Parseghian later coached Lamonica in an all-star game, and this was his assessment, "Daryle Lamonica is one of the best passers I've ever seen in college football. Period. I cannot believe what happened to him at Notre Dame. He should have thrown for thousands of yards." Under Parseghian, Lamonica would have been everybody's All American.

In 1964, with gunslingers like Alabama's Paul "Bear" Bryant, Texas's Darrell Royal, Arkansas's Frank Broyles, USC's John McKay, and Parseghian leading the way, college football stood on the brink of a revolution. For the first time in more than a decade, teams would enjoy free substitutions during timeouts. New rules that season would also allow two substitutions with the clock running. Instead of a core of eleven players, teams would now need twenty-two starters. College football was finally coming out of a fog; the best and the brightest minds would be the benefactors.

The game was changing faster than anyone could keep track. Around the country, smaller and faster players were at a premium now that the multiple offense was all the rage. The advent of two wide receivers was turning it into a vertical game. The last few years at Northwestern, Parseghian had operated one of the most wide-open offenses in the nation. Quarterback Tommy Myers threw the ball all over the field as Northwestern rose from the bottom of the Big Ten to a Rose Bowl contender.

Parseghian had come under the tutelage of several great coaches. These chessmasters taught Parseghian that football was more than a game of elephant backfields and paper-thin playbooks. He soon discovered that X's and O's could dance all over the chalkboard—and all over the field. Offensive football was now off the leash. It was time to turn the game over to quarterbacks like Joe Namath at Alabama, Roger Staubach at Navy, Bob Griese at Purdue, and possibly even John Huarte at Notre Dame.

Job one on that first day of practice was to break up the Notre Dame backfield. With that done, Parseghian's next move seemed a bit radical. He reassigned all three running backs—Pete Duranko, Paul Costa, and Jim Snowden—to the defensive line. When news spread across the Midwest that Parseghian was converting running backs to tackles, everyone shook their heads. Had Notre Dame already scrambled poor ol' Ara's brain? To Parseghian, it made perfectly good sense. Duranko, Costa, and Snowden were among the biggest players on the team. Why shouldn't they be in the line?

"I really don't know what Joe Kuharich was trying to accomplish with that elephant backfield," Parseghian remembered. "It was one of those coaching decisions that you don't see every day. The only thing I could think of is that Kuharich had a pro influence and he wanted Notre Dame to look like a pro team. I will say that Kuharich's teams did not seem prepared or organized. They didn't seem to have the fundamentals to be a winning team."

What Parseghian inherited was chaos, disorder, and despair. From top to bottom, the roster was out of whack. Players were lining up at the wrong positions, and some of the most talented players had no position at all.

That first day of practice, Parseghian's eyes traced a high, spiraling punt that fell into the arms of number 27—Nick Rassas, who caught the ball on the run and split the coverage unit like a jackrabbit bolting through a herd of standing cattle. Rassas was one of the fastest players on the roster.

Eyes widening, Parseghian turned to Pagna. "Tom, I didn't know Rassas could do that."

Pagna smiled. "Ara, I think there are a lot of things about Nick that we don't know about yet."

With a furrowed brow, Parseghian watched a smiling Rassas hustle back up the field.

"This is what I don't understand," he said to Pagna. "How is it possible that the previous coaching staff didn't see the talent in this Rassas kid?"

"I think there were a lot of things the old coaches didn't see," Pagna said. "They couldn't agree on much. A lot of backbiting, you know."

Parseghian pulled a notebook from his back pocket and placed a check mark next to Rassas's name. Then his eyes scanned the position changes, moves he had contemplated night and day. A few days earlier, Parseghian had delivered this speech to his coaching staff:

> Here is the X factor of coaching. Say you have fifty players. It becomes the job of the head coach, and the assistant coaches, to recognize and to evaluate the talent where they can best help the team. That is what coaching is all about. If you misplace them, or you have talented players sitting on the bench, then the coach is not helping the team. A coach has to know what is the best thing for the team. That is coaching. That's what makes the difference between winning and losing.
>
> As coaches, we are going to go out there on the practice field and throw everything at our players but the kitchen sink. I want them to

wonder what is coming next. I want them to know that things are changing around here. We are going to make serious changes with this football team—fast changes.

Following the breakup of the entire offensive backfield, the next priority was a senior-to-be, Jack Snow, a player who had labored the past three seasons as a halfback in a backfield that did not suit his talents—or size. Snow weighed about 210 pounds, so he did not qualify as an elephant back. Standing beside Duranko, Costa, or Snowden, he looked like, well, a wide receiver.

Snow's history in Kuharich's pedestrian offense had been limited. Six passes were thrown his way in 1963—all in one game—and he caught each one. What impressed Parseghian on the game film was that Snow possessed big, soft hands and could run after the catch.

Little did Parseghian know that Snow had been cut off at the pass during the 1963 season. In the first game that season against Wisconsin, Snow, lining up at wingback, dashed 24 yards down the right sideline for a touchdown that gave the Irish a 7–0 lead. Oddly enough, Huarte kicked the extra point, but Huarte and Snow were quickly back on the bench as Wisconsin rallied in the second half for a 14–9 victory.

The next week against Purdue in West Lafayette, Snow caught passes all over the field, but the Irish lost again. Snow's 6 catches that day still brought new hope to the Notre Dame faithful, but when the Irish returned to South Bend after the game, Devore delivered some bad news.

"Jack, we've got a little problem here," he said. "You know who they're pushing for All American around here—and it's not you. It's Jim Kelly."

The previous season, Kelly had compiled remarkable statistics on a team with a stodgy offense. Daryle Lamonica rarely got the green light, but he still completed 41 passes to Kelly, who set the Notre Dame season record for catches. Kelly finished with 523 yards and 4 touchdowns. In a 43–22 victory over Pitt, Kelly set a single game record of 11 catches for 127 yards and 3 touchdowns. He made the All-American first team while Lamonica was voted to the third team.

The Notre Dame public relations machine was known for spinning out All Americans at a rapid pace, even in bad years. One example was the magical powers of PR director Charlie Callahan in luring the Heisman Trophy to Notre Dame in 1956 when Paul Hornung had a so-so season and the Irish finished 2-8.

One of Devore's toughest tasks was explaining to Snow why he was going to the bench.

"Jack, you know how it works around here?" he said. "I've got to make sure the ball is thrown to Kelly. When you're on the field, our quarterbacks want to throw the ball to you."

"Say what?" Snow asked. "You're going to bench me so Kelly can make All American? Again!"

"That's exactly what I'm telling you," Devore said.

Snow threw his helmet to the ground.

"Kiss my ass, Hughie," he said as he stomped away.

Week after week during the 1963 season, Snow and Huarte stood on the sideline and witnessed one of the most futile passing offenses in the country. They felt like a couple of ghosts. Meanwhile, Notre Dame averaged just 60 passing yards per game, encouraging opposing defenses to stack the line to thwart the running game. Huarte and Snow watched quarterbacks Sandy Bonvechio and Frank Budka miss open receivers time and again, and when the quarterbacks hit the receivers, they normally dropped the ball.

During those frustrating times, Snow would walk up to Huarte and pound his fist on the quarterback's shoulder pads.

"God, John, we could have made that play," Snow would say. "If they would just give us a chance. Maybe someday, Johnny."

One of the most maddening games of the past few seasons was against the Parseghian-coached Northwestern Wildcats. That day, quarterback Tommy Myers shredded the Notre Dame defense by throwing pass after pass to Paul Flatley in a 35–6 victory.

After each completion, Snow would point to the field and say, "Just look at that, Johnny. That could be us. God, if they would only give us a chance."

In the final minutes of the Michigan State game, Snow and Huarte were biding time on the bench when Devore sat down between them. Bonvechio was having a terrible game, and the Fighting Irish were trailing

12–7. Devore had promised Huarte that he would start the Michigan State game, then changed his mind minutes before kickoff. At this point he needed a comeback in the worst way.

"Look guys," he said. "The offense needs a boost. If I put you guys in the game, will you promise me that you won't screw up? Will you promise me that you'll win the game?"

They both looked at the coach incredulously.

"Eat shit, Hughie," Snow said.

Snow walked away, followed by a silent Huarte.

Notre Dame lost 12–7.

SNOW WAS A stoutly built player with wide shoulders, and as one of the few weight-lifters at Notre Dame, he held most of the school records. His neck was bull-like. Based on his physique alone, it was hard to envision Snow as a wide receiver. On team picture day, he was more easily grouped with the likes of linebackers Jim Carroll and Ken Maglicic.

Gut instinct told Parseghian that Snow would excel at the wideout position. He certainly possessed an air of confidence that belied his second-string status. Snow never thought twice about swaggering into Parseghian's office without an appointment and smiling confidently as he shook hands with his new boss. Meanwhile, walking behind him, was slump-shouldered third-string quarterback John Huarte. While Snow radiated self-assuredness, Huarte exuded an air of defeat.

"Coach," Snow began. "You might not know it, but I am the best. Don't look at the films because you'll find only 5 or 6 catches by yours truly, but I can assure you that I am the best receiver on this team. On top of that, this man right here beside me is John Huarte. He is the best damn quarterback on this team."

Huarte looked down and shrugged his shoulders.

As they left the office, Huarte turned to Snow and quietly asked, "Jack, do you think we should have done that?"

Snow laughed. "I don't know, Johnny, but at least he knows who the hell we are."

Even before the start of spring drills, Parseghian had his eye on Huarte, and this had nothing to do with film study. Huarte rarely showed up in the films because he was usually on the bench. That first day, Parseghian's eyes began to track the passing drills of three quarterbacks— Dan McGinn, Bonvechio, and Huarte. Bonvechio, with his strong arm and quick feet, started most of the 1963 games. Still, Parseghian's assessment of him was hardly flattering. "He's a nice kid from Ohio." McGinn possessed a strong left arm, but lacked experience. Huarte? Well, there was something about Johnny Huarte. Granted, he was lacking in self-confidence. You rarely heard his voice on the practice field—in fact, you rarely heard his voice at all—but the kid could wing the ball.

"I really think that John Huarte has some talent," Parseghian told Pagna. "I just need you to build on that confidence the best you can."

That first day of spring practice, as Huarte threw strike after strike to his wide receivers, Pagna approached the quarterback.

"Look, John, I can barely hear you calling the signals. You need to speak up."

"What do you mean, Coach?"

"I mean I want you to yell '*Hut! Hut!*' so everybody on this damn field can *hear* you."

"Got it, Coach," Huarte said a little more loudly.

Reasons abounded for Huarte's lack of confidence. The previous two seasons, he had recorded a grand total of forty-five minutes on the field—roughly 3 percent of the possible playing time. To earn a monogram, or letter jacket, a player was required to play at least sixty minutes per season. In 1963, the Fighting Irish had suited up five different quarterbacks, and most of the time Huarte was listed as either fourth or fifth string.

Even more insulting, four Notre Dame quarterbacks picked up their monograms at the end of the 1963 season—Sandy Bonvechio, Frank Budka, Tom Meagher, and Dennis Szot.

Needless to say, Parseghian was shaking his head when he saw Huarte for the first time in a practice situation. He threw spiral after spiral. He drilled the receivers between the numbers. Granted, he threw the ball a little side-armed, and Parseghian would have preferred a more over-the-top delivery, but who cared? Johnny Unitas's delivery was no work of art. Huarte's feet were quick and his passes accurate. Parseghian and

Pagna found it almost impossible to pry their eyes from this newfound prize.

As they walked off Cartier Field together one afternoon, Parseghian turned to Pagna and asked, "Why the hell did John Huarte sit on the bench the past two years?"

"Good question," Pagna said. "I hear they yanked him out of the games for the tiniest mistakes. He would practice all week with the first team and then they would slap his butt back on the bench. I think his confidence is shot."

Parseghian watched Huarte trot off the field. "I don't know if John Huarte will ever be a great leader. He seems pretty shy, but maybe he can be our shepherd."

"Do you think he can be our starting quarterback?" Pagna asked.

"Damn right," Parseghian said with a smile.

Chapter 10

THE SHEPHERD

John Huarte did not know what he was walking into that first day at Notre Dame back in September of 1961. Suddenly he was standing before the orneriest man in the history of the university.

Jack "Black Jack" McAllister stood only 5'3", yet his bark and mad-dog stare could scare the dickens out of a freshman walking into the locker room for the first time.

McAllister's tenure as the football equipment manager at Notre Dame had dated to Knute Rockne. He seemed practically invincible and usually acted like it. Standing behind the long steel counter, where the socks, jocks, and gear were passed to the players, Black Jack looked like a gray-stubbled grinch. He was the caricature of the tough little Irish guy who got drunk and picked bar fights. At Notre Dame, he operated a small fiefdom—often with an iron fist. If he wanted you to have a sturdy pair of shoulder pads and a solid helmet, you were in luck. Otherwise, good luck.

"What can I do for you, sonny boy?" McAllister asked Huarte.

"Sir, my name is John Huarte and I am here on a football scholarship. This is my first day of practice."

McAllister picked up his clipboard and flipped through a three-page roster. Then he looked up at Huarte with a menacing glare. "Get the hell out of my locker room, pissant. You're not allowed in here. You are not on *my* list."

Huarte handed him an envelope containing a letter that would verify his football scholarship.

"I don't care about no letter, pissant," McAllister said. "If you're not on my list, you're not on anybody's list."

Huarte walked away mumbling to himself. "Looks like I came a helluva long way for nothing. Nothing at all." All the way from Anaheim, California.

This run-in with McAllister was unnerving for a quiet young man of German-Basque ancestry, one who did not drink, smoke, or cuss, and who got along with everyone. His teachers back at Mater Dei High School in Santa Ana said he was the nicest boy they had ever met. Fathers around town prayed he would date their daughters.

Huarte was the All-American kid. From the moment he could walk, he was always wearing some kind of sports uniform. His father, Joseph Huarte, was a minor league shortstop player dating back to the Great Depression. The elder Huarte had never made it to the major leagues, but he was invited to play in two off-season exhibition games with Babe Ruth and Lou Gehrig. At that point in his life, Joseph Huarte was hooked on big-time sports. He hoped his sons would feel the same.

Five boys were born to Joseph and Dorothy Huarte, and this was quite fortunate for a family of farmers. The Huartes harvested oranges, lemons, and avocados on a sixty-acre spread near Anaheim. When the boys were not playing sports, they were working the farm through the week. Then, during the downtime on Saturday, the five boys and their father would sit in the bed of a faded green 1957 Chevy truck and listen to the Notre Dame games on the radio. Little John's first hero was 1953 Heisman Trophy winner Johnny Lattner, the ultraversatile back who could run, pass, catch, punt, and return kicks. John also idolized quarterbacks Ralph Guglielmi and George Izo. He would never forget the Oklahoma–Notre Dame of 1957 when battering fullback Nick "The Greek God" Pietrosante powered his way down the field in the final scoring drive as the Irish broke the Sooners' 47-game winning streak, 7–0.

One of the top recruits in California, Huarte was hotly pursued by Kuharich in the spring of 1961. On a West Coast recruiting swing, Kuharich spent two days making his sales pitch. Huarte finally signed, and the Notre Dame coach was ecstatic.

Most quarterbacks with his credentials would have swaggered onto campus expecting a starting job, but not Huarte. He couldn't even get his hands on a jock strap.

Finally, one of the coaches instructed McAllister to give him a uniform. With trepidation, Huarte returned to the locker room to face Black Jack. The old man sneered at him and said, "I don't know who the hell you think you are, pissant. You ain't no Monty Stickles, that's for sure. I'll give you a uniform, but it won't be a good one."

Stickles, a two-time All-American end and placekicker from the late fifties, was McAllister's favorite player of all time.

The next day, as Huarte (pronounced *Hew*-ert) walked onto the practice field in full uniform, he heard someone yelling, "Hew-arty! Hew-arty! Where in the hell is Hew-arty?" It was Kuharich and he was trying to summon his new freshman quarterback. It took Huarte several moments to figure out that "Hew-arty" was actually him. Kuharich didn't even know how to pronounce his name.

When Huarte finally responded to "Hew-arty," the coach with the high, squeaky voice said, "What the hell is wrong with you, son? Don't you even know your name?" Huarte never corrected him.

Day by day, Huarte retreated into his shell. Some of the coaches did not know his name, and others could not pronounce it, so they referred to him as "that guy." It was not unusual in 1961 for a prize recruit to get lost in the Notre Dame system—if you could call it that. The freshman team did not schedule any games, and there was very little supervision. A common sight was the freshmen group breaking into a volleyball game.

"I got better coaching in high school than I did my freshman year at Notre Dame," Tony Carey remembered. "And we had a damned good freshmen class. We had guys from all over the country that could really play football. If we'd had any coaching, I bet the freshman team could have beaten the varsity."

The freshman class of 1961 was loaded with nationally recognized recruits, and many of them would thrive years later in the Parseghian scheme. Three from that freshmen class would become All Americans, and ten would start on the 1964 team.

Most of the players who were being shoved to the background in the

Kuharich years learned to bide their time. They somehow believed that a better day was coming, but not Huarte.

"I thought I was invisible," he said. "I felt like I didn't exist and it wasn't much fun. I knew that they had no intentions of ever playing me, so I often questioned why I was there. Only one coach during my first three years ever even talked to me—called me by my right name. Coach [Don] Dahl actually taught me to do some things. He paid attention to me and I appreciate that. But one day I looked and he was gone."

Dahl was fired after the 1961 season.

During the 1962 season, Kuharich had no interest in throwing the ball in spite of the presence of Daryle Lamonica. He worked his butt off recruiting the strong-armed kid, but Kuharich never intended to change his conservative offense, and that doomed Huarte from the start. Huarte would labor on the Shit Squad, along with the likes of Nick Rassas and Tony Carey. Rassas knew he was going to stick it out, regardless of the odds. On the other hand, Haurte had endless doubts. He was determined to get his degree in business finance, but football, as the seasons passed, mattered less and less. He was not mentally equipped like Rassas to endure the disappointment.

"Players like John Huarte went through some really tough times," Parseghian remembered. "Many of them were demoralized, and I noticed it right off the bat. Plus, everybody was bitching at everybody else. I actually identified with John because I had been treated the same way at Northwestern. John Huarte was a nobody for three years at Notre Dame."

In his book, *Era of Ara,* Pagna later referred to Huarte as "quiet, introspective, lonely, and reserved."

Rassas said that Huarte went around for days without saying a word. The coaches thought he simply did not care. The less he exerted himself, the farther he fell down the depth chart.

"We used to say that Johnny Huarte was the most laid-back kid we'd ever met," said Nick Rassas. "We used to tell him that he got too much sun back in California. Some people thought he wasn't playing with all of his marbles. I knew better. I went to finance classes with him. He might have been a little flakey, but the guy was sly like a fox."

Huarte was not a battler like Rassas and he lacked the perseverance of Tony Carey, who came back to Notre Dame after being kicked out of school. Carey had once been denied a pair of clean socks by McAllister. Instead of walking away, he jumped over the steel counter and chased the frightened little man all the way through the back door.

Huarte was never going to be Rassas or Carey, but with the arrival of Parseghian and Pagna, he at least had someone to talk to.

"I want you to bring him along slowly," Parseghian told Pagna. "Every day, I want you to work with him. Every day, I want you to rebuild him."

Chapter 11

THE COMEBACK

Tony Carey weaved his way through the crowd at Cartier Field as another day of spring practice approached. Life was good. He had been promoted to first-string cornerback.

Two years earlier, Carey never expected to be standing where he was that day. Suspended from Notre Dame during his second semester, he was certain his football days were over. He returned to school for the following fall semester and stuck it out. Not once did he suit up for a game that season. Yet he swallowed the hurt and went on.

Carey's life had been depressing until the arrival of Ara Parseghian a few months earlier. At this point he awoke every morning ready to knock down walls.

As he approached the practice field, wearing a wide grin, Carey felt his emotions suddenly switching gears. Anger rushed up through his spine and exploded into his brain. His face turned beet red as he wheeled around to look at two men carrying on a conversation about Notre Dame football. Both were wearing Bermuda shorts and golf shirts that did not match—of course, checks and stripes never do.

"Ara Parseghian will never make it as the Notre Dame football coach because he's not Catholic," one man said.

"I can't believe they hired the Armenian rug-maker," the other said. "Hell, Rockne'd roll over in his grave."

"At least the Rock converted to the Catholic faith. I hear that that Parseghian plans to remain a god-damned Presbyterian."

Carey stepped toward the men.

"Why don't you dumb old farts move on?" he said. "We don't need your kind around here."

In 1961, when Carey enrolled at Notre Dame, he weighed 160 pounds. Now he stood 6'1" and tipped the scales at 200. From head to toe, he was nothing but lean muscle. He looked imposing wearing a full football uniform with the number 1 stitched to his jersey. Carey could be easygoing. Even so, his teammates knew about his Irish temper that, at any moment, might set the woods on fire.

This was one of those moments, and he kept staring at the men. "Either you support Ara, or you get your asses out of here," he said.

"Okay, okay," one of them said. "Maybe Ara can coach—"

"Damn right Ara can coach," Carey shot back. "You better believe it."

As he walked away, Carey thought about the bozos and their stupid opinions. Then something occurred to him: They might not be alone. Was there a public undercurrent working against Parseghian? Was there a backlash because he was not Catholic? How many Domers felt this way?

To Carey, this made no sense. How could anyone question a man with this kind of dedication and commitment?

Carey stepped back to consider the situation. Maybe they all had something to prove.

TONY CAREY'S DOWNFALL began on a Friday afternoon back in the winter of 1962. His hometown of Chicago, some ninety miles away, was calling. Maybe it was homesickness. In truth, it was the lure of his former high school, Mount Carmel, playing Leo High for the Chicago Catholic League basketball championship, and he was not about to miss it.

Carey knew that leaving campus was about as easy as obtaining a prison furlough. Notre Dame was basically a military academy without the guns, the ammo, or the uniforms. Ken Maglicic once described the place as "an army camp on the north side of South Bend."

You could leave town on Saturday following classes after filling out papers, but you were expected back bright and early Sunday morning without lipstick on your collar or whiskey on your breath.

Carey's problem was getting out of South Bend on a Friday afternoon and catching a train without being noticed. He needed to be at the Mount Carmel gym in South Chicago by the 7:30 tip-off. He would need someone to cover for him.

That someone was linebacker Ken Maglicic, Carey's best friend and perhaps the most loyal guy on the Notre Dame campus. Maglicic was a cutup himself, always into pranks, and he knew the importance of somebody watching your back.

"I can handle it," Maglicic said. "I have a plan. I'll make sure that the dorm rector doesn't know a thing. You go on back to Chicago and have a good time. You can count on me."

To a total stranger, Maglicic could have seemed like a bookworm with his round face and studious eyes. Despite that, his teammates knew him as the kid living on the edge of trouble. His sense of humor worked overtime, and he was the master of pinning a nickname on anyone. Until it backfired on him.

That first semester at Notre Dame, his parents came for a visit from Cleveland and during a conversation with Carey, they let it slip that Ken's childhood nickname had been "Binks" because of his obsession with a teething ring known as a Binky. Most kids grew tired of their binky, but not Ken, so everyone in the family and around the neighborhood and around his schools began calling him Binks.

His teammates at Notre Dame would never let him live it down—Binks this and Binks that. No one could remember anyone calling him Ken Maglicic again.

That night, Maglicic would entertain Tom Coughlin, a high school football recruit from his hometown of Cleveland. After eating some pizza, and maybe drinking a couple of beers, they would return to the dorm before the ten o'clock curfew. At the dorm's security checkpoint, the recruit would sign in as "Tony Carey." He would sleep in Carey's bunk with the covers over his head just in case there was a bed check.

After Carey departed, Maglicic took the high school senior to Guiseppi's Pizza in downtown South Bend. Guiseppi's could be hopping on a Friday night, and a few fights might break out, but Maglicic was not worried. Not many people wanted to tangle with a Notre Dame starting linebacker.

They both ordered beers and Coughlin practically chugged his.

"Want another beer?" Maglicic asked.

"Damn right," Coughlin said. "That's why I'm here. To have some fun and see if I want to play at Notre Dame."

A small combo cranked up in the back corner, and the next thing he knew, Coughlin was asking girls to dance. He was also drinking every beer he could get his hands on. By then, the "townies" were all over him, and a couple of cute ones had invited him back to their apartment.

Never one to be bashful, Maglicic imbibed his share of beer and was loving every minute of it. After all, he was spending free money provided by the football recruiting fund. Maybe Coughlin would get plastered, and one of the townies would take him for a romp in the backseat of her car. Surely that would convince him to sign with Notre Dame.

Just before eleven o'clock, Maglicic almost panicked. They were within minutes of curfew.

"When we get back to campus," he told Coughlin, "you'll sign in at the front desk as Tony Carey. Got that?"

Coughlin slurred something that did not make any sense.

When they returned, a security guard was stationed just inside the front door of the dorm with a small lamp on his desk.

"Do not breathe," Maglic told the kid. "If you breathe, the guard will know that you're drunk."

Coughlin stumbled up to the desk and signed the register. Maglicic looked down and realized that "Tony Carey" was just a couple of squiggles.

"What is that?" the guard said, pointing at the messy signature.

"Oh, Tony broke his hand at practice today. He can't write."

The guard looked at the drunken high schooler, now wobbling around the foyer.

"That's not Tony Carey!" the guard said.

"Oh yeah, it is," Maglicic said. "He also broke his nose and his whole face at practice today. You just don't recognize him."

Maglicic hooked an arm around Coughlin's waist and they stumbled up the stairwell toward their room. He then shoved Coughlin under the covers and told him to hold his breath. Minutes later, there was a knock on the door.

"Come in," Maglicic slurred.

"Is that you, Kenny?" Father Henry Geuss inquired. "You don't sound well."

Maglicic leaned over the side of the bed and vomited.

"Touch of the flu," he said.

The priest shone the light on the lump under the other covers.

"Is that you, Tony?" the priest asked.

"No Father, it's Tom Coughlin from St. Edward's." A puzzled expression crossed the priest's face.

"So if you are Tom Coughlin from St. Edward's dorm, then why are you in Tony Carey's bed? You need to get back to your own dorm. Immediately."

"No, Father, I am Tom Coughlin from St. Edward's High School in Cleveland, Ohio."

"Don't get smart with me," the priest said, pointing out the window. "Get your butt back to your own dorm."

The priest shined the flashlight in Maglicic's eyes. "Okay, Kenny, please tell me where Tony Carey is."

Maglicic swallowed hard and threw up again. He knew they were cooked.

AT SIX THE next morning, the phone rang at the Carey home in South Chicago. Tony was sleeping on the downstairs sofa and heard his father answer.

Robert F. Carey paused and said, "Yes, Father, I will make sure that he's on the next train back to South Bend. Sorry for the inconvenience."

His father was silent again, and Tony could hear a tinny yet loud voice coming from the other end of the line.

"Yes, Father," Robert Carey said. "Tony has made a mess of things and he will take his punishment when he gets back to Notre Dame."

Never one to mince words, Robert Carey walked over to his son lying on the sofa and said, "You need to get rolling. They caught you." Then he walked away.

Carey had no money, so he hitchhiked back to South Bend. It was the longest trip he would ever endure from Chicago back to campus. When he walked into the dorm, Father Henry Geuss was waiting, standing with hands on hips, tapping his foot, and glaring at him.

Carey said, "Look, Father, all I did was go home. I didn't kill anybody. I didn't get drunk. I didn't do anything."

"So you went home without signing out, is that right?" the priest said.

"That is correct, sir, but that is the only thing that I did wrong."

"Why couldn't you wait until Saturday like all of the other boys? You know you also missed Saturday morning class."

"Because I wanted to see my high school play for the Chicago Catholic League championship in basketball."

"Oh, so there is more to the story. You didn't just go home to see mom and dad."

"That is right, sir."

Carey could see Hughie Devore walking down the hallway toward them, wearing the Spencer Tracey hat and a wrinkled London Fog overcoat. He walked straight up to the priest and removed his hat.

"So what is going on here, Father?" Devore asked. "I hear this boy has done nothing wrong."

"Come into my office, Coach," the priest said.

The faces of both men were red, possibly from drinking, and Carey found it ironic that the person in trouble was him. After the door closed, Carey heard loud voices.

"I will have this boy kicked out of school if it's the last thing I ever do," the priest yelled.

"For going home to see his parents, Father?"

"He also went to a high school basketball game last night. Without permission!"

Devore chuckled. "Now, Father, that is hardly criminal stuff. I mean, Tony Carey is a good boy and he's a damned good football player."

"Football is not as important around here as it used to be. You know that."

Devore cleared his throat. "But that is no reason to take it out on a good kid like Tony Carey. I know you priests hate football, but we've got a job to do here."

Moments later, the door opened and Father Geuss walked toward Carey. His voice was like the crack of a whip. "Go home and don't come back till we call you, and that might not be for awhile. Good-bye, Tony."

Tears burned in his eyes, but he refused to cry. Devore walked toward Carey and pulled his hat down snug. Before he could speak, Carey said, "Coach, all I did was go home."

In the deep gravelly voice, Devore uttered words Carey could barely fathom.

"Tony, let me give you some advice," Hughie said. "The only place you confess around here is at confessional, and you'd better watch your ass there, too."

Carey almost burst out laughing. Nevertheless, he held it until he got outside and felt the cold wind slicing down from the north. Stepping outside right behind him was Ken Maglicic.

Carey smiled at his friend. "Binks, how in the world did you guys manage to get my ass kicked out of Notre Dame?"

"It was the kid," Maglicic said. "I let him get too drunk. Then when we got back to the dorm, all hell broke loose."

Carey put his arm around his friend's shoulders and smiled again. "I will never trust another Croatian for the rest of my life, Binks." They both laughed as Maglicic reached into his pocket and pulled out a wad of one-dollar bills.

"Here's train fare back to Chicago," he said. "I expect to see you back at Notre Dame next semester."

Carey's smile melted into a look of sadness. "I don't know, Kenny," he said. "That priest's got a hard-on for me. You heard the part about him kicking me out of school if it's the last thing he ever does."

Maglicic put his hand on Carey's shoulder. "The problem here, buddy-boy, is there's not a coach on this campus with any balls. There's nobody to go to bat for you."

The two shook hands and Maglicic walked back into the building.

Still, Maglicic's troubles were not over. Father Geuss demanded that he write a letter home to his parents about what he had done—"Dear Mom and Dad. I am very embarrassed to tell you this, but . . ."

Binks felt horrible about the entire situation. He had just lost his best friend to a suspension. Moreover, writing the letter home had been one of the most difficult assignments of his entire life. Growing up in the Depression, both of his parents were forced to quit high school and go to work by age sixteen. They never had a chance to attend America's Catholic shrine to education. Binks was offered advantages that others before him never had. To make matters worse, according to the punishment doled out by Father Collins, the prefect of discipline, he would be restricted to campus for the rest of the semester—and that was almost like being locked up.

AS CAREY WALKED away from the dorm, he looked to the heavens.

"Heavenly Father, I can't believe what just happened to me," he said. "I can't believe what Hughie Devore just said to me, but I will promise you this. I promise that I will be back."

It was the longest and coldest walk to the St. Mary's train station that he could ever remember. He would be taking the South Shore Railway back to Chicago. Notre Dame students liked to call it the "Vomit Comet" because of all the beer consumed, which caused many upset stomachs. Once the train pulled out of South Bend, leaving behind the hawk-eyed priests, the Domers started popping tops on their favorite beverages— Schlitz, Old Style, Budweiser, Hamm's, Miller, and Old Milwaukee. Soon, the beer cans would be everywhere. The South Shore made frequent stops, especially as it got closer to Chicago. As the train pulled into the station, hundreds of beer cans would roll to the front of each passenger car. As it pulled away, the cans rolled to the back.

As Carey entered the second car and searched for a seat, he did not believe his eyes. Sitting there on the third row with his normal scowl was Black Jack McAllister.

"What the hell you think you're doing, pissant?" McAllister said. "You ain't supposed to be leaving school."

Carey dropped his head. "Black Jack, I might be leaving Notre Dame for good. They're kicking me out."

For the first time, Carey saw a look of concern cross the old man's face.

"They can't do this to you, pissant," he said. "I mean, you ain't no Monty Stickles, but you're a helluva football player, son. I know that I've never told you that, but you really are."

It was the first time Carey could remember words of encouragement at Notre Dame. Not since he had walked away with a big victory at the 1960 Chicago City Championship had he felt wanted. It was funny. Once there had been a time when everyone wanted to see Tony Carey play. They once called him the next Johnny Lujack. In truth, Carey knew how good he was, and how good he could be.

Now he would go home and think about that.

BACK AT THE family's house in Chicago, the phone was already ringing. The first call came from Bob Devaney, the head coach at Nebraska. Then Jack Mollenkopf called from Purdue, followed by Andy Gustafson at Miami.

Each coach wanted Carey to transfer to their university that very day. Each one had recruited him out of Mount Carmel and was disappointed he had signed with Notre Dame. All three offered a free airline ticket with the promise he would suit up and start on the varsity for the 1962 season. These were tempting offers.

Tony sat down to discuss it with his father.

"Dad, I'm leaning toward going back to Notre Dame," he said. "I already miss the guys back there. I really would like to take some time to think about it. I'm not so sure that I'm ready to give up on Notre Dame."

His father's expression never changed. He still looked like a man who had been punched in the gut. "Then you will have to get a job," he said.

Carey knew that his father was devastated by the suspension. After all, his father had launched his successful law practice after earning his degree at Notre Dame. He was involved in the alumni groups. His brother Tom had played quarterback for the Fighting Irish in the early fifties.

Silence was Robert Carey's way of punishing his children. Tony had experienced it many times over the years. Day by day, Robert Carey did not talk to his son. Day after day, Carey sank into a deeper depression.

Tony went to work for the Gus K. Newberg Construction company in South Chicago. Newberg, a 315–pound Swede, had started a small carpenter's business that bloomed into one of the largest construction companies in the country. Carey was a laborer who cut and welded the paving forms for the East-West Freeway. They also finished up some of the public housing buildings on the east side of the Dan Ryan Freeway. Watching the workers filter in and out—hired one day, laid off the next—taught him one of life's great lessons: Go back to school and stay there.

Time away from Notre Dame was spent reflecting on just how good he'd once had it. He was blessed that Tom Carey had been elevated to head coach at Mount Carmel just as he was reaching the varsity team. How lucky could a kid be to have his big brother watching over him every day, teaching him the intricacies of the quarterback position? Then at night, after the dishes were cleared, they would stay at the dining room table and pore over the playbook.

Remarkably, Tom Carey was coaching the Mount Carmel team on the side. His real job was completing his degree at Northwestern Law School.

Nothing in the history of Chicago high school sports was bigger than Mount Carmel. The pipeline between Notre Dame and Mount Carmel was erected all the way back in the mid-1920s. Among the great Notre Dame stars that made the trek were All-American tackle Ziggy Czarboski and All-American end Dan Shannon. Elmer Angsman from the Mount Carmel class of 1942 had scored the winning touchdown in the 1947 NFL championship game won by the Chicago Cardinals by the score of 28–21 over the Philadelphia Eagles.

Expectations at Mount Carmel were always through the roof. The school had every resource imaginable, even the old Notre Dame uniforms. An all-private Catholic institution, Mount Carmel was a kind of Notre Dame Junior. Football was pushed not only by the coaches but by the priests. Winning was everything, and this was evident by long tradition. How many high school football teams held preseason camp in another country? Each August, the Caravan took off for a ten-day training camp in Canada. They boarded a bus on Sixty-third Street in South Chicago that carried them through Detroit and Windsor, Canada, en route to Niagara, Canada, not far from the Falls.

"This was no honeymoon," Carey remembered. "The coaches worked our tails off. We were actually out there in the middle of a farm in the middle of a hot, humid summer getting our butts kicked and toughened up for the start of the season."

They stayed at the Carmelite Seminary, that the Carmelite nuns help run. The Carmelites are a Roman Catholic religious order founded at Mount Carmel in Palestine in the twelfth century. At the seminary, the boys endured the Spartan conditions of dorms that featured steel bunks. The meat they consumed was from the seminary ranch as the cattle were slaughtered and the meat processed and prepared on site. It normally gave the boys diarrhea the first couple of days. In spite of all that, the camp was a springboard to several city championships, and the Caravan played in three straight all-Chicago championships at Soldier Field from 1958 through 1960, with Carey on the roster.

In the fall of 1960, Tom and Tony Carey were in hot pursuit of yet another city title. When the brothers huddled at night, Robert Carey sometimes hung in the periphery but rarely said a word. Robert was a reserved man who kept his distance. Track, not football, had been his sport at Notre Dame, but he still knew football. The brothers also knew he was listening to their conversations.

During the season, Mount Carmel practiced each day on the shore of Lake Michigan at Jackson Park, next to the Nike Missile Site C-41. The Hercules and Ajax missiles were positioned there to protect Chicago during the Cold War and the Cuban Missile Crisis of the early 1960s. The swordlike guided missiles stood in grim contrast to the pastoral setting of Jackson Park. Still, as the *Chicago Sun-Times* reported, "Chicago has become the best defended city in the Midwest against enemy air-to-ground attacks."

On the west side of Mount Carmel's practice field was a stand of trees, along with a long hedge. Tom and Tony were convinced that a spy was watching their practices, for in America in the early 1960s, a conspirator seemed to be hiding behind every bush.

During their nightly meetings, Robert Carey would occasionally speak up when he heard something that piqued his curiosity.

"That option play you guys are running really looks good," he said one time. "That's working for you."

The brothers laughed when he walked into the other room. Tom then whispered to Tony, "See, I told you he's been watching practice. We've never run the option in a game. He's the one hiding back behind the bushes."

They laughed and then got back to work.

So intimate was Tony Carey with the Mount Carmel offense that he was allowed by his brother to audibilize on any play. This was unheard of in 1960, especially at the high school level.

The Caravan were a quick, small, rugged, and well-coached band of kids, as most of the players were sons of steelworkers. At Western and 79th Street, the Carey neighborhood somewhat resembled the United Nations—Italians, Irish, Armenians, Poles, Czechs, Croatians, and Jews, blacks, Mexicans, and Serbs. U.S. Steel on the South Side was the biggest employer around Mount Carmel.

Tony Carey, with his Irish joviality and his Irish temper, quickly found his niche in the tough neighborhood. He was from a family that prided itself on manliness. His grandfather, Thomas Carey, was an Irish immigrant who was forced to comply with indentured service in the 1800s. Because his passage from Ireland to the United States was paid for by a Chicago brick mason, he was required to work for the man until his debt was paid off. He rode the rails from Boston to Chicago and went to work. A man with boundless energy, Carey worked twelve hours each day as a bricklayer, then finished off his workday at the Hawthorne Race Course.

He managed to start his own company—Carey Brick. When Hawthorne hit upon troubled financial times in 1909, Carey had saved enough money to bail out the racetrack. Before long, he owned it.

He soon moved into politics and was elected as a Chicago alderman from the South Side.

Years later, another Chicago politician would take a liking to Thomas Carey's grandson. Mayor Richard J. Daley, elected in 1955, loved the Chicago sports scene and had a front-row seat for Mount Carmel–Taft in 1960.

One of the perks for winning MVP honors was sitting in Daley's box for the high school championship game. At first, Tony Carey felt disarmed by the power of Daley and his piercing blue eyes. Despite that, they soon were carrying on a conversation, and the mayor learned of Carey's setback at Notre Dame.

Weeks earlier, Tony had received a letter from Notre Dame that stated he could resume his academic work, but he would not be allowed to play in the varsity games during the fall of 1962. According to NCAA rules at the times, athletes were required to complete two straight semesters before gaining eligibility for the third.

As Carey was saying good-night to Daley, the mayor set his hard, blue eyes on the young footballer. "So, Tony, tell me where you are going next?"

"Mayor, I'm going back to Notre Dame. I said I would never give up and I never will. They will have to kill me this time."

At last, Tony Carey was on his way.

Chapter 12

MAKING OF A TEAM

The players were dressing for the biggest spring training practice of 1964 when Ken Maglicic looked into the eyes of Tony Carey and saw someone he did not recognize.

"What's wrong with you, Topcat?" Maglicic said. "You look like you're about ready to kill somebody."

The nickname "Topcat" was courtesy of secondary coach Paul Shoults, a big supporter of Carey. In the two years since returning to Notre Dame, Carey had gone from the doghouse to Topcat. The past few months, Shoults had become attached to Carey and his hard-hitting ways. From the start it was clear that Shoults knew what he was doing as the coach of the secondary. Shoults and Ara Parseghian had been together longer than anyone on the staff—going back to 1946 and 1947 when they were the starting backfield at Miami. As a coach, Shoults had been with Parseghian every step of the way, beginning in 1951 when he took over as the head man at Miami. They were two of the most intense men you would meet in the coaching business. Shoults was not as demonstrative as Parseghian, but he left little doubt that he was equally as tough. Shoults possessed both the quiet voice and the big stick.

At the moment, Carey was staring straight ahead with eyes that belonged to a serial killer.

"I'm going to be okay," Carey told Maglicic. "Just a little juiced. This is the biggest day of my life. This is make it or break it. This is the day when I officially make the starting lineup. This is the day that I show the bastards who I really am."

After several days of drills and roster moves, it was time for Notre Dame's first scrimmage of the spring under Parseghian. Seventeen players were now in new positions. One of the biggest changes had occurred in the defensive secondary, where Nick Rassas, Tom Longo, and Carey were all starters for the first time.

As the players were stretching, Shoults walked between the long rows until he found Rassas.

"I still can't believe they wouldn't give you a scholarship, little fellow," Shoults said. "Kuharich must've been a real knucklehead. Why, you play as hard as anybody on this team. You could start for me any day."

Rassas grinned and said, "Coach Shoults, do you think I can go both ways this year?"

"Whoa now, little fellow," Shoults said. "One thing at a time. You're gonna have to ask Coach Parseghian about that one."

Again Parseghian, with his nervous energy at full speed, was leading the calisthenics. He spotted a smiling Pete Duranko in the first row.

"Hey, Pete Duranko, how do you like it over on defense?" he said.

"Lovin' every minute of it," Duranko hollered. "Thanks a lot, Coach."

Spirits had not been higher in a decade at Notre Dame. Practices were pure drudgery in past seasons. No wonder so many players had been quitting the team, but now the fight was back.

Defensive coordinator Johnny Ray was standing over Alan Page, stretching on the ground. The sophomore defensive end was the biggest man on the playing field at 6'6" and 230 pounds. When Ray looked at Page, he saw greatness, although, at the moment, he was standing over a nervous, lisping eighteen-year-old. Ray said, "Alan Page, you need to get your butt in gear, and you need to get your butt in gear *today*."

Head down, Page said, "Yessir, Coach."

Parseghian possessed the most commanding presence on the practice field, but Ray was hard to overlook. Mostly it was the deep, gravelly voice that grabbed everyone's attention. The voice was the product of chain-smoking Camels for several years. It was so deep that it seemed ready to fall straight out of his throat.

Parseghian was the new messiah of Notre Dame football. Ray, on the other hand, was a persuasive man whose words would be heard and respected. He was bringing his version of the split-six defense to Notre Dame, and coaches around the country could not wait to study the films of the Irish defense. Ray called his version the 4-4-3 defense: four down linemen and two outside linebackers, who were basically stand-up ends, two inside linebackers, and three defensive backs. In college football, the pass offense was growing more sophisticated every year with the addition of a second split receiver. Old-schoolers like Ray, however, still believed you could defend the pass with three defensive backs. Many years would pass before the coming of the "nickel package"—five defensive backs on passing down.

Ray believed in attack, attack, attack, which meant blitz, blitz, blitz.

"The best way to stop the pass is to make sure the sonofabitch doesn't get the pass off," he told the players. "If I call a blitz, I want you to get that damn quarterback."

Like Parseghian, Ray was always pacing, moving, making himself heard. He already knew he had the horses to play an action-oriented defense. The Notre Dame linebackers—Jim Carroll, Ken Maglicic, Jim Lynch, and Tom Kostelnik—were born hitters. In addition, the secondary he had chosen for the opening of spring practice—Longo, Carey, and Rassas—were a little band of fighters. Ray was amazed that the three had virtually no playing time under their belts.

Ray gravitated to Carey because he knew the tall, lean cornerback would knock you into never-never land and never blink. Yet, Carey needed to adjust his thinking. One afternoon, Carey intercepted a pass and trotted back up the field.

"That is not what I want," Ray bellowed. "You intercept the damn pass, and I want you to take that sonofabitch all the way to the house."

Parseghian had been waiting for this day since hitting town back in December. It would be two hours of hard combat. Their hard work would pay off today, or they would be working double overtime until the start of the season. Parseghian's expectations were fairly high, as he told the coaching staff, "If we are lucky, I think we can go 6-4. If we are really lucky, we can go 7-3."

That would be a major turnaround from a 2-7 season. Most of the fans were trying not to get greedy—not after five seasons without a winning record. The new mantra among the alums was "Six and four in '64." That would be almost Rockne-esque.

The biggest surprise for Parseghian was that the overall talent was not that bad. For years, the press and the fans had battered Kuharich and Devore for lagging behind on recruiting. Their patented excuse was the dwindling scholarships. The problem with Kuharich and Devore is that neither knew if a football was blown up or stuffed. College football had moved into the modern era of passing and pinball scoring, and neither coach wanted to leave behind their stodgy ways.

For years, the Chicago newspapers had blamed the Notre Dame decline on a breakdown in the pipeline between the Windy City and South Bend. They wrote that the top prospects were choosing the bigger state schools that welcomed females and did not turn out the dorm lights at 10:00 P.M. Many of the highly ranked recruits were going where they could drive a convertible across campus with a pretty coed in the passenger seat.

To the contrary, Notre Dame was fairly well-stocked. You could still count fifteen Chicago players on the roster. The biggest surprise to Parseghian was the quality of the sophomore class, the ones recruited by Devore. The new head coach was already counting on three or four from that group to be starters in 1964, and a few others would play key roles. They were mostly on the defensive side—end Alan Page, linebacker Jim Lynch, tackle Tom Regner, tackle Kevin Hardy, and end Don Gmitter. Another sophomore that begged his attention was a silky smooth halfback from northern California named Nick Eddy, and he was already impressing the coaches with his speed and elusiveness.

In the spring of 1963, Devore had made the most of his final opportunity to round up talent. Because he was easygoing, and did not mind picking up a bar tab, high school coaches were drawn to Devore. He had reeled in some of the leading recruits in the country. To the good fortune of Notre Dame, it would now be up to Parseghian—not Devore or Kuharich—to decide who would play where.

After fifteen minutes of light drills, Parseghian stood in the middle of the practice field and blew his whistle.

"Okay everybody, this is it!" he yelled. "Everybody buckle their chinstraps. It's time to play some football."

The first-team offense lined up against the second-team defense. On the first snap, quarterback John Huarte used his quick feet to motor backward as he sidearmed a bullet over the middle to Jack Snow, running a quick post. Snow caught the ball on the dead run, split two defensive backs, and broke into the open field. Touchdown!

"How is it possible that Jack Snow seems to be getting faster and faster?" Parseghian asked Tom Pagna.

"I am wondering the same thing," Pagna replied.

Now it was the first defensive unit's turn to tangle with the second-string offense.

Quarterback Sandy Bonvechio had no sooner taken the snap from center when he was grabbed from behind by a pair of arms that were long enough to be tentacles. Page whipped him to the ground and then fell on him. As Page rose from the ground, he felt a forearm driving into his midsection, a powerful punch delivered by defensive line coach Joe Yonto. It was an expression of pure joy.

Yonto yelled, "Alan Page! Alan Page! At Notre Dame, you'll be all the rage!"

Yonto stood 5'6" and looked like a miniature Vince Lombardi. He even had the gap between his two front teeth. Like Lombardi, he was of Italian ancestry and as hyperactive as the Green Bay coach on the practice field. With his windbreaker zipped to the neck and his cap pulled low, Yonto at age forty-two could have been Lombardi's younger brother. Now he was acting just like him. He grabbed Page's jersey and bellowed, "That's the best damned play that you made all spring. You play like that, and you've got All American in the bag."

Page tilted his head forward and now looked almost straight down at his coach, who was almost a foot shorter. He smiled and said, "You're making me feel better, Coach."

Moments later, the first-team offense returned to the field. The screen pass is generally the most difficult play for a new offense, but Huarte ran it like Bart Starr. He retreated deeply into the pocket, waited for the on-rushing linemen to approach, and dumped the ball over their heads to running back Nick Eddy, who knifed through the middle of the line-backers for a 30-yard gain. No one expected Eddy to be this silky smooth as a sophomore, nor did they foresee his maturity as a running back. It was now almost certain that Eddy and Bill Wolski would open the sea-son as the starting backfield.

Before the end of the day, Rassas would return a punt 80 yards for a touchdown and Carey registered 2 interceptions. The second-team of-fense went nowhere against the first defense that had basically come to-gether overnight. Only two players—linebackers Jim Carroll and Maglicic—would hold on to their positions from last season. This was a new unit with an attitude that would make any coach smile.

On offense, Huarte threw one incompletion in 13 attempts. His ac-curacy thus far in the spring had been mind-boggling.

At the end of practice, the coaches sprinted back to the fieldhouse side by side with the players. The staff was as excited as the team. Parseghian led his men into the coaches' dressing room, where they be-gan to hoot and holler.

"Is the door closed?" Parseghian shouted. "I don't want the players to see this."

Yonto double-checked the door and then locked it.

"We're behind closed doors, Coach," Yonto said.

"Boys, this is one fine football team we've got here," Parseghian said. "I never thought we would get this good this fast."

Chapter 13

TURN OUT THE LIGHTS

They almost had to close down all the bars in South Bend when Ara got there.

—NICK RASSAS

W alking through the front door of the Flamingo Bar in 1964 was like drifting into a dark hole. The first person you encountered was a bouncer named N. T. Shine—the initials standing for New Testament, his real name. He stood 6'5", weighed 330 pounds, and, according to the Flamingo regulars, looked like "an overgrown Sonny Liston."

Liston, the heavyweight champion of the world for two years, was an ex-con with Mafia ties and a glowering demeanor. Trainer Jim Wicks was once asked if his fighter, Henry Cooper, would be interested in stepping into the ring with Liston. "We don't even want to meet Sonny Liston walking down the street," he said.

Liston, with his huge shoulders, sunken eyes, and massive arms, scared the bejesus out of the heavyweight contenders of the early 1960s. Until Cassius Clay came along in February of 1964—just two months earlier—and won a seventh-round TKO down in Miami Beach.

With his massive frame, N. T. Shine blocked out the light as customers entered the Flamingo. So dark was the bar that you heard his voice before you actually saw the man.

"I need you to behave tonight," he would say to a customer walking in, "or I will turn off your water."

Of all the bars in South Bend, the Flamingo was the safest and the most organized. Bar patrons said it was the presence of Shine, along with the quick trigger finger of the bartender, that kept the place nice and peaceful. The Flamingo also served the best fried chicken and barbeque in town, for the "Bird," as it was called, was an all-black establishment.

Northern Indiana at the time held as many orders of the KKK as the Deep South and East Texas. Black people were not allowed in South Bend's white bars, but everyone was welcome at the Flamingo, where, on many nights, the whites outnumbered the blacks.

One night, Jim Thornburgh, history major from the class of 1965, bumped into one of the regular patrons who lived in the workaday world of South Bend.

"So how is it, Thornburgh?" the man said. "How is it that the black people don't get to go to the white bars, but the white people get to go to the black bars?"

Thornburgh smiled. "I've been in South Bend all of my life. I went to St. Joe's High School. I know it can be a funny town, but I don't think it's as racist as you think."

The man eyeballed him even more closely.

"Okay, Thornburgh, then let me ask you this question. Why does the white man get to go to heaven and the black man doesn't?"

"I don't think that's true," Thornburgh said.

"It's true. It's true. And when you get there, I want you to tell them about me."

Thornburgh walked away briskly. As he approached the bar, one of the waitresses approached him. She was giggling and holding up her left hand that was decorated with a ring about the size of a baseball.

"Where in the world did you get that?" he asked.

"Big Daddy Lipscomb," she said.

"Whoa," Thornburgh said. "Big Daddy died over a year ago."

"I know," she said, "but one of his friends gave it to me. Said Big Daddy would have wanted me to have it."

She was wearing Gene "Big Daddy" Lipscomb's NFL championship ring from the Baltimore–New York Giants game in 1958. Many sportswriters called it "The greatest game ever played."

Lipscomb, a 6'6" 288–pound goliath of a man, was named All Pro three times but was better known for his nightlife and his big yellow Cadillac. He played his final two seasons with the Pittsburgh Steelers.

On May 10, 1963, after drinking with two women most of the night, Lipscomb was found dead on his kitchen floor, the victim of a heroin overdose.

"I don't know where my friend got Big Daddy's ring," the waitress said, "but I'm just glad to have it."

It seemed the stories never stopped coming from the Flamingo. Just a mile south of campus, cloistered inside a black neighborhood, the Bird was a sanctuary for black students from Notre Dame. Because the university was almost 99 percent white at the time, some of the blacks felt socially displaced, but not at the Bird, where the ribs and chicken were always hot, and so was the jazz.

The restaurant section of the Flamingo was large, with several tables. The real action, though, was in the back listening to the Rhythm Rockers—Billy "Sticks" Nix on the drums, Oscar "Baby" Jones on the xylophone, and Paul Renthros burning up the tenor sax. What really stirred the Bird were the nights when Junior Walker walked through the front door. A native of South Bend, Walker had been knocking around the South Bend bars, playing sax for a group called the Jumping Jacks.

Walker would change that name to Jr. Walker & The All Stars about the time the band moved to Detroit and signed a Motown contract. By 1965, their greatest hit of all time, "Shotgun," would climb to No. 4 on the *Billboard* charts.

The Bird was a magnet for the Notre Dame football players—black or white. It was a mile from the dorms and worth the walk, even in three feet of snow. The only other bars reasonably close were Guiseppi's and Frankie's.

Football studs since the days of Frank Leahy were known for the fast life around South Bend. In the spring of 1958, a Notre Dame scholarship baseball player watched in despair as the football players headed out to the bars for another long night of drinking.

"God, I wish I'd been a football player," Carl "Yaz" Yastrzemski said. "I think I would have a lot more fun."

A year later, Yaz broke into the Red Sox organization en route to a Hall of Fame career that included the last "Triple Crown" in 1967.

In the fall of 1963, months before Parseghian arrived, Tony Carey and Ken Maglicic swaggered through the front door of the Flamingo and grabbed a table. They waved at their friend and teammate, Dick Arrington, who walked across the room to shake hands, but quickly returned to his black friends from the neighborhood.

"I feel sorry for Arrington," Maglicic said. "I walk around Notre Dame for days and see only white faces. The only black faces I see belong to him and Jim Snowden. How would you like to go to a college where the only thing you saw were black faces?"

"I don't feel too sorry for Arrington," Carey said. "Looks like he's getting more than we are."

Arrington was sitting at a table with four women.

Carey and Maglicic were soon joined by Joe Kantor and Norm Nicola. Spotting the gathering of white faces, Flamingo owner Art Herd hustled across the room.

"Why, if it's not the Four Horsemen of Notre Dame," he said. "Glad to have you boys, but gotta ask you studs a question."

"Shoot," Maglicic said.

"Where did you boys learn to block and tackle?"

Like many fans, Herd could not get the 2-7 record of 1963 off his mind. He was not aware that Parseghian was quickly turning the thing around.

"We'd be doing okay if not for Hughie Devore," Carey said.

"Hmmm, Hughie Devore," Herd said. "He was in here the other night. You should've seen his bar tab."

The foursome would drink their cares away and then head over to Frankie's, a place made famous during the days of Paul Hornung. Frankie's was the hangout for both Hornung and Monty Stickles plus about half of the football team in the mid-1950s.

The top floor of Frankie's seemed fairly innocent as they walked in. The real trouble was the bottom floor, where the drinks and the beer flowed. As they descended the stairs, they could see a cloud of smoke that made the place look like an opium den. The players drank a few beers and then decided to head down to Giuseppi's.

"Giuseppi's is where the girls wear hula hoops for belts," Carey said.

"Yeah, but I don't want to walk all the way down there," Maglicic said. "It's too cold."

"Good enough," Carey said. "We'll hitchhike."

Hitchhiking was a way of life at Notre Dame. Students were not allowed to have cars until their senior year, so they had two choices—the bus or hitchhiking. At that time of the night, hitchhiking actually held its advantages. The townies usually hung out around the top of the circle near the Morris Inn, hoping to pick up the male students—or to at least give them a ride.

The football players spotted a brown Chevy Impala with four girls on board. They were waving.

"Looks like our carriage is here," Nicola said.

The players jumped in with the four girls, and as the car sped away a voice from the inside said, "Look at all of these hula hoops."

IN THE YEARS before Parseghian, every disciplinary case at Notre Dame was handled by the priests. The prefect of discipline was Father A. Leonard Collins, a man who tolerated very little. He loved to suspend the misbehaving students and to put them on the Vomit Comet back to Chicago. Priests, however could not keep an eye on 6,500 male students. They did not normally hang out at the Flamingo, or Frankie's, or Guiseppi's, or Rocko's.

The arrival of Parseghian changed everything. He was now law and order at Notre Dame. He had resources—the local police and a few spies on the side. In that first team meeting, he demanded that the players stop drinking and smoking, and most knew he was serious. Some took their drinking all the way downtown, farther away from campus. A few sought refuge at Billy's Chili and Hot Dogs at the corner of Michigan and LaSalle, thinking the coaches would never find them there.

That spring of 1964, Dave Pivec was a tight end with a bright future at Notre Dame. Two years earlier, he had earned a monogram as a sophomore, and he was a starter for most of the 1963 season. At 6'3" and 220 pounds, Pivec was destined to play a big role in the Parseghian design. Most of the players stopped hanging out at the local high-profile pubs, but not Pivec.

"Dave was in my dorm room one day when Jim Carroll walked in," Maglicic remembered. "Jim was our new captain and, like a lot of the seniors, he knew how important it was to be a leader. He was a very good leader."

Maglicic remembers a conversation between Carroll and Pivec thusly:

Carroll: "Dave, everybody knows that you've been going out drinking. We don't want you to get caught."

Pivec: "Yeah, I hear you. I'm not really worried."

Pivec liked to drink and fight. As his teammates said, "Dave likes to get on his beer muscle." Pivec had either slept through the first Parseghian lecture or did not believe him. Ironically, Parseghian had said, "I know there is one player in this room who will not listen to me, but I'm telling you. If you go downtown and get drunk and get picked up by the police, I *might* be willing to give you a second chance, but if it happens a second time, you are off the team."

The coach was determined to follow through on his promise.

"Pivec went downtown and got on a rounder and the police got him," Parseghian remembered, "I called him into my office and said, 'Dave, you know the rules. If you do this again, you are gone.' Then two weeks later, bingo! he does it again. So I had no choice. I called him into my office and told him that he was off the team."

Pivec's parents pled for mercy, but Parseghian would not budge.

"They wanted Dave to get another chance, and I told them about my speech to the team," he said. "I couldn't go back on what I'd said."

On the day that Pivec was kicked off the team, Maglicic walked through the halls and shouted, "Shake down the thunder! Dave Pivec is gone! Everybody better watch their asses!"

Parseghian knew that Pivec's departure would not solve team issues for all time. He also hated losing a player of Pivec's talent. "I knew that when you are dealing with kids that you can't stop all of them from drinking and smoking all the time," he said. "I just wanted to minimize it."

Hoping that Pivec's football career would not be ruined for all time, Parseghian telephoned one of his contacts in the Canadian Football League to arrange for a tryout. That summer, Pivec played one season in the CFL and, in 1965, was drafted by the Los Angeles Rams. He played four years in the NFL for the Rams and the Denver Broncos.

The Pivec episode changed the culture of the Notre Dame program.

"I hated to let a player like Dave go," Parseghian said. "He was a hitter and I could have used him. But kicking Dave off the team unified the team. I could see the players walking a little taller. They knew that we were serious as we could be about turning this team around."

That was the day the music died at the Flamingo.

Chapter 14

DISASTER

Ara Parseghian sprinted toward his fallen quarterback as calm turned to chaos on the practice field.

Seconds earlier, Huarte had been driven into the ground by an onrushing lineman. Notre Dame's future now lay in a broken pile.

Down on both knees, Parseghian whispered, "John, are you okay?"

"I don't know yet, Coach."

It had happened in the blink of an eye. Huarte glided back into the pocket, showing his normal poise, and was preparing to fire the rock to Jack Snow when—*bam*!

This scene was difficult to fathom. Parseghian knew in an instant that he should have provided better protection for his quarterback. Red jerseys signifying "no contact" were normally reserved for injured players. Huarte was not wearing a red jersey, and Parseghian now regretted it. His greatest hope for the 1964 season was now laid out on the ground.

The defensive lineman who dropped the hammer on Huarte was Harry Long, a hard-nosed kid from the west side of Chicago and a highly recruited player from Fenwick High School. Long was like Rassas—undersized for his position and underrated by all. He stood 6' and weighed only 200 pounds. He was always hustling to overcome what could be perceived as a shortage of talent. In plowing through the line and sacking the quarterback, he was trying to show the coaches that he deserved to play in 1964, but he exacerbated the situation by turning Huarte upside down and corkscrewing his shoulder into the dirt. At the moment of impact, Huarte felt something pop. Offensive line coach Dave

Hurd ran toward Long and grabbed his jersey. "What the hell do you think you are doing?" he yelled. "This man is our starting quarterback."

Long had barely gotten out "Sorry, Coach—" when Johnny Ray came running from the other direction.

"Get your hands off my player," he yelled. "This kid is just doing his job." Ironically, Ray and Hurd were friends. Hurd was on Ray's coaching staff back at John Carroll University. Nevertheless, Ray did not like anyone trespassing into his territory.

Seconds later, Parseghian roared in from the side and yelled, "Both of you coaches stop it. I'll handle this."

By that time, Parseghian and the entire team had encircled Huarte. Then he slowly got to his feet.

"I think I'm all right, Coach," he said, "but I think I'd better go to the locker room. I don't think I can throw the ball anymore."

The stabbing pain was centered in the right throwing shoulder. Huarte now walked slowly to the locker room, his right arm numb, his heart stuck in his throat.

Huarte removed his jersey and shoulder pads and took a seat on the training table. "I've never felt anything like it," he told the team trainers. "I mean, I couldn't go out there and throw the football right now, but I really don't know if I'm hurt that bad."

Only a week remained until the Old-Timers Game that would pit the alumni footballers against the current players. Spring football would end that day. One more lousy week and John Huarte would have been working out in shorts and a T-shirt, but here he was, sitting slump-shouldered on the training table. Phone calls were being placed to orthopedic specialists all over South Bend.

Over the next few days, Huarte would be examined by three doctors. Each one took X-rays and were quick to deliver the bad news. He would need surgery, and that would mean no football in 1964. His collegiate career was over. Huarte finally accepted his fate and decided it was time to tell Parseghian. Early one morning, he called the coach at his office.

"Coach, I'm going to have surgery and that means my football career is over. I'm sorry."

In a loud voice, Parseghian said, "No! Hold on, John. Don't do anything. You can call your parents if you like, but Tom Pagna will come by and pick you up in the morning. He'll take you to Chicago to see another doctor. It's a guy I know. I trust him."

Parseghian's voice sounded panicky. Huarte did not know what to think. Did the coach value his talent that much, or was this an attempt to put a Band-Aid on a serious injury?

Parseghian made an appointment with Dr. Dick Cronin in Chicago and then arranged for Pagna to drive Huarte the next morning. An hour before leaving on the trip, Pagna got a second call from Parseghian.

"Tom, this is pretty serious stuff," he said. "I don't want John to play next season if he's not physically able to, but if there is any way John can play, we need him. You know that as well as I do. If John can't play, we're hurting. We'll be going with Sandy Bonvechio. Who would you rather have at quarterback—John Huarte or Sandy Bonvechio? I think that you know the answer. We need John Huarte this season."

That morning, Pagna and Huarte rode mostly in silence the ninety miles to Chicago. Getting a decent conversation out of Huarte was like prying rosary beads away from a nun. Anxiety surrounding the injury caused him to retreat further inside himself. All of this was confusing to Huarte. Just a few months ago, no one could have cared less if he walked away and never came back. Instead, here he was, being treated like the second coming of Paul Hornung.

As the car rolled along the highway in silence, Huarte knew in his heart the coaches were only trying to salvage his final season—his only season, really. A surgically repaired right shoulder would end his playing days. Surgery would kill his last hope of accomplishing what he thought he was capable of—leading a team to a possible championship. Huarte knew that he could make this happen. This was his one and only chance—his last chance. It was like being promised the last dance of the night with the most beautiful woman in the ballroom, only to reach for her as the music stopped.

In reality, the injury did not hurt that much. Of the two possible shoulder separations, this was less severe, and it would heal faster. The separation had occurred where the collarbone met the shoulder joint. There was a chance he would fully recover without surgery. Then again, he might lose much of his velocity and accuracy. At the moment, he knew he could not fling a ball more than five feet.

Huarte and Pagna arrived at the offices of Dr. Cronin, and the quarterback took a seat on the examining table. Dr. Cronin felt the shoulder, turned it, twisted it, and probed it with his fingers. Huarte felt more depressed than ever. He was certain that Dr. Cronin's opinion would be the same as the others—an operation to fix the separation.

Cronin took X-rays of the shoulder and returned to the examining room about thirty minutes later. Holding up an X-ray to the light and putting on his glasses, he seemed to be checking every detail. He cleared his throat.

"John, I had this exact injury when I was playing football," the doctor said. "There is no question in my mind . . ."

Cronin paused and looked at the X-ray again. Huarte felt that bad news was coming.

"There is no question in my mind that I wouldn't let anyone touch this shoulder. You don't need surgery. Time is a great healer."

Huarte jerked forward off the table and almost fell face-first. Blood rushed to his head, he coughed, and his face was now pale.

"What's the matter?" the doctor said. "You don't seem well."

Huarte took a deep breath and exhaled. "I'm ok, doc. What you said caught me so off guard that I almost fainted. I never expected you to say that."

Dr. Cronin handed him a piece of paper with suggestions on how to rehabilitate the shoulder.

"What I suggest at first is a lot of swimming," he said. "It will strengthen the shoulder a lot. As you start to feel better, do more swimming. Don't start throwing the football for a few weeks. Start gradually and then build up. If you have any problems, or any questions, I want you to call me."

Huarte wiped perspiration from his brow.

"One more thing," the doctor said. "The worst thing that might happen is that you'll get a knot on that shoulder. Don't worry about it. The knot means nothing."

Huarte took another deep breath. "This is the best news I've ever heard in my whole life. Jack Snow and I have been talking about staying in South Bend for the summer to work out. I'll take it slow. I'll be ready for the season."

Pagna smiled broadly and clapped his hands twice.

"Come on, baby," he said. "Let me buy you a big ol' steak."

An hour later, at Big Bill's Steakhouse inside the Loop, the two sawed into T-bone steaks large enough to cover their entire plates. The sudden sense of relief brought a smile to Huarte's face. It was the first time Pagna had seen signs of happiness from his young quarterback.

"John, you know that everything is going to be all right," Pagna said.

"I know, Coach. It just seems that everything has gone wrong for me since I got to Notre Dame. Until about an hour ago, I thought I was through with football. I've been up and down, and all around."

Pagna smiled a knowing smile.

"Look, I haven't been around Notre Dame the last three years, but I know this place has been pretty crazy."

"Crazy is not the word," Huarte said. "Chaos might work better."

"They wouldn't let you play."

"Ah, they would let me in occasionally. I'd play one minute and be gone the next. Coach Devore said I was going to start against Michigan State. Then they pulled the rug out from under me."

"The coaching wasn't very good."

Huarte dropped his fork and his eyes met Pagna's.

"Look," Huarte said. "Hughie Devore was a good guy. He had a big heart. He just didn't know what he was doing. I felt sorry for the guy, if you can believe that. He took the head coaching job because Notre Dame needed somebody. He felt obligated."

"So what went wrong?"

"Nobody was behind him. The coaches weren't behind him. The players weren't behind him, and I doubt the administration was behind him, either."

"And he didn't treat you very well."

"Hughie had a lot on his plate. He was trying to run the same offense that Kuharich left behind, and I didn't fit very well in that offense."

"Ever think about quitting?"

Huarte smiled. "It was tough, but not really. I had a year left. So why not ride it out?"

Pagna placed his knife and fork on the table. The happy-go-lucky face turned sincere.

"Now, look, John. What if I told you that your confidence is shot? I'm not saying it's your fault, but this whole Notre Dame thing hasn't been good for you."

Huarte stared at his plate.

"There was only one coach at Notre Dame that ever talked to me, and his name was Don Dahl," he said. "And they fired him. I never sat down and had a conversation with Kuharich, and Hughie, you know, was always in a different world."

Pagna cleared his throat. "You can talk to me any time you like. You can talk to Ara any time you like. Let me tell you something, John. We believe in you. We just need you to start believing in yourself."

"That might not happen overnight, but I'll try."

On the ride back to South Bend, they talked like father and son. Huarte noticed that his shoulder did not even hurt anymore. When Pagna dropped him at the dorm, he felt a rush of energy—as if he were starting over.

"Take it slow, John," Pagna said, "and when you're ready to start throwing the rock, let me know."

Huarte waved and said, "I will, Coach."

That night, Pagna walked into Parseghian's office. He was smiling.

"The shoulder is going to be fine," Pagna said. "No surgery."

Parseghian jumped straight up and clapped. This time, though, he did not touch his toes.

"I had a feeling," Parseghian said. "While you were gone, I said a Hail Mary. Or two."

"John and I had a great talk on the trip," Pagna said, "but I think it's time you call him in. Sit him down. Tell him how you feel."

Parseghian calmly placed his hands on the desk. "I will do it tomorrow."

THERE WAS A light knock on the door the next morning and Parseghian said, "Come in."

Huarte walked in slowly and took the chair in front of the desk.

"John, they tell me that your shoulder is going to be okay. Do you feel that way?"

"Actually, Coach, it doesn't even hurt that much anymore."

With a furrowed brow, Parseghian said, "And the doctor told you to take it slow. I know you will."

"I will do some swimming. When it feels right, I'll start throwing the rock again."

Parseghian stood, walked to the side of the desk, and sat on it. He was now just a few feet from Huarte.

"John, I gotta tell you. I have been around you only a few months, but I already see a lot of potential in you."

Huarte smiled and looked down.

"Here's a story that I don't tell a lot of people," Parseghian said. "Did you know that I am the only coach to compile a winning record at Northwestern? That's right. Bet you didn't know that in 1962 I coached Northwestern to the top of the polls. That's right. And we only suited up thirty-two players that year. We lost a couple of games and didn't get to go to the Rose Bowl, but we had a great season.

"Do you know what Northwestern said to me at the end of the 1962 season? They said they weren't going to renew my contract. John, that really hurt. It told me that they didn't want me anymore. I didn't understand why, but it really did hurt. I know what you've been through, son. I went through the same thing. I know how it feels. Northwestern basically ran me out of town, and I felt like I did a good job.

"You haven't been treated fairly, either, John. Your Notre Dame experience hasn't been the greatest in the world, but you need to know that I'm going to give you every opportunity to excel. I think your time has come. If you get well—and I think you will—I want you to lead the team next season. What do you think about that?"

"I think I can do it," Huarte said softly. "Thanks to you and Coach Pagna, I'm feeling pretty good about things. Finally."

The two stood and shook hands.

"Here's to a new beginning," Parseghian said.

Chapter 15

WYOMING COWBOY

Three days out of Chicago and the high-revving aqua blue Pontiac GTO with a 389-cubic-inch, V-8 engine was still on the western edge of Nebraska. Early in the summer of 1964, the "Goat" was the hottest road machine on the market. It was America's first muscle car, with a massive engine crammed into the lightest body available. The Pontiac marketers worried it might not sell, for it was too fast with its triple double-barreled carburetor and deafening with its dual exhausts.

How wrong could they have been? Nick Rassas could not have been happier with his new car as he and Bill Kelly roared down the highway, sprinting toward the happiest summer of their lives. Every driver on the road was in envy as they flew by. The car sounded red-hot, thanks to the newly installed glass-packs muffler, which muffled nothing at all. The GTO growled like an angry bear loose on the two-laner.

A week earlier, Kelly had called Rassas from New York City to say that it was time for a road trip. At 6'5" and 230 pounds, the Notre Dame rugby player normally got his way. He and Rassas had been friends since meeting at Notre Dame two years earlier. Kelly flew into Chicago's O'Hare Airport, and away they went—charging west, not really sure where they were headed. Just what you might expect from a couple of free-thinking, twenty-one-year-olds with money in their pockets and energy to burn. It did not matter that neither had ever traveled west of the Mississippi River.

Before leaving Chicago, Rassas had packed all of his free weights and dumbbells in the trunk of the Goat. This was going to be two months of adventure *and* work—a final tune-up before the start of the 1964 football season. He would be in top shape for the ten-game grind. He wanted to run faster than a GTO.

Everyone knew that Rassas's engine revved faster than anything Detroit could roll out. What better place to turn it all loose than in the wild mountain country of Wyoming? Hands on the wheel, eyes on the highway, he loved the feel of the powerful engine and the sound of the rumbling pipes. In its first year of production in 1964, the GTO sold for $3,200. Pontiac executives were shocked when first-year orders were six times what they expected. Little did they know that Americans were starved for fast cars and faster lives. The postwar era was dead and gone and the pace was picking up. The GTO was built for the open road, and so were Rassas and Kelly. They could care less about clocks or road maps.

It seemed that every other song on the radio was "I Want to Hold Your Hand." Five months earlier, the Beatles had made the teenaged girls scream on the *Ed Sullivan Show* for the first time. The music revolution in America was on. The Beatles and the Rolling Stones, with tambourine-shaking Mick Jagger, were moving up the *Billboard* magazine charts. Elvis Presley, with the summer release of *Viva Las Vegas*, was still hot. Yet, thanks to the British invasion, Elvis and his kingdom were now on the ropes.

A new voice was stirring up the music industry, and his song "Happy Feeling" a.k.a. "Dance and Shout" was playing on the radio.

"Who the hell is that?" Kelly asked.

"Why, that is Little Stevie Wonder. I'm surprised you didn't know that."

"I would've known all about him," Kelly said. "If anybody at Notre Dame had a radio or a record player."

The freedom of the highway meant Notre Dame's handcuffs were coming off. No priests, no curfews, no mandatory Mass, and no shortage of women. Clicking along at eighty miles per hour, Rassas said, "Where the heck do you think we are? Never in my wildest dreams did I think Nebraska was this big."

"I never thought we were going to get out of Iowa," Kelly said. "Where the hell is Wyoming, anyway?"

The previous night, in the vast darkness of the Iowa plains, during a driving rainstorm, they could not find a hotel and decided to sleep in the car. The next morning, Rassas cranked the Goat and drove a half mile over the next hill, and there stood a Holiday Inn.

Now they were twenty miles from crossing into Wyoming and beginning the long and winding trek toward the Grand Teton Mountains. Their destination was a little town called Moose, about twenty miles north of Jackson Hole. They were traveling at the behest of another Notre Dame student, John Turner, a lacrosse player and the captain of the fledgling Notre Dame ski team. During the summer, Turner resided at the Triangle X Ranch with his mother, Louise, and two brothers. The Turner family worked the largest dude ranch in America, which amounted to about eighteen hundred acres on the floor of the Grand Teton National Park.

Rassas became curious about John Turner back at Notre Dame when he saw him behind the wheel of a 1952 Packard hearse painted green. The hearse, purchased at a South Bend used car lot, was Turner's everyday wheels, and much more. It served as the team bus for the Notre Dame downhill skiers when they traveled all over Michigan and Minnesota. Some of the trips took seven or eight hours, and it was not surprising that the ski team got a little cramped in the Packard hearse. The first time Rassas saw the funeral car, Turner was driving with six guys in the back. Rassas knew there was no room for a corpse.

Skis and poles had been tied haphazardly to the roof with frayed rope. More than once, Turner and the ski team were forced to stop along the highway to retrieve flyaway equipment. Even so, this fearless group never seemed to care. They were already showing up the competition across the Midwestern states. The entire ski team hailed from the mountainous and ski-fanatical region of Colorado, Utah, and Wyoming. These kids knew how to lay it down. Since there was no budget for the ski team, they had to pay for their own gas. When the money ran low, they decided to forego food for beer. Fueled by barley and hops, the boys in the Packard hearse made it all the way to the NCAA finals that first year. At this time they were thinking about a championship for the 1964–1965 season.

Rassas had met Bill Kelly and John Turner when he was a sophomore living in Zahm Hall, still suffering on the Shit Squad. Kelly and Turner were roommates on the fourth floor, not far from the elevator. Rassas liked these guys because they would let him vent. He would wait for them at the elevator each evening, and that is where the bitching and moaning would begin.

"You wouldn't believe what that dumbass Joe Kuharich said today," Rassas would say. "He said he didn't want any repercussions after the Oklahoma game. He was acting like we'd already lost the game. No wonder everybody calls him the Kook."

Much had changed since the departure of Kuharich. Rassas was now in the Notre Dame starting lineup. Nick was telling everyone that Notre Dame was going to compete for the national title in the fall. No one believed him, but that did not shut him up.

That summer, he was about to become a cowboy in his spare time. Turner had talked him into the trip to Wyoming and pledged to Rassas that he would be able to work out for hours each day and to get into top shape for the football season. There was also the promise of pretty girls and an interesting nightlife.

As the GTO roared toward the setting sun, Rassas suspected that his teammates back in South Bend were about to finish "voluntary" workouts. Each day, the Fighting Irish would file into Gate 14, where coach John Murphy would check them in. Murphy lurked in the shadows behind the gate and never allowed himself to be visible to anyone on the outside of the stadium—especially the guys wearing the NCAA emblems. Mandatory workouts in the summer were considered illegal. A coach supervising the players constituted a NCAA violation that might get the program in a jam.

That day, the players had run laps around the field at Notre Dame Stadium under the watchful eye of "Irish Mike," an angry Irish Terrier housed in a cage at the southwest corner of the end zone. Irish Mike had recently gained some notoriety by appearing on the cover of the *Notre Dame Dope Book*, a preseason football guide chock-full of team records, statistics, biographies, and an evaluation of the upcoming season.

Rassas decided to skip "voluntary" workouts and take off for Wyoming because he wanted to be in better shape than his teammates. After all, he had built himself from a 5'4" 96-pound weakling into a walk-on player at Notre Dame, and finally to a scholarship athlete and a two-way starter. He was living for the season. He could not wait to walk into Notre Dame Stadium for that first game and hear his name announced in the starting lineup. It was time to work his butt off.

As the GTO crossed into Wyoming, Kelly asked, "So where are these Grand Tetons, anyway?"

"Not sure," Rassas said, "but they can't be far. I feel 'em coming on."

Back at Notre Dame, Turner had used some powerful adjectives to describe the Grand Tetons, which stood 13,677 feet tall. He had worked the Triangle X Ranch since age five with his brothers, Donald and Harold, breaking horses and rounding them up in the morning for the city slickers to ride. The ranch stabled more than 150 head, and most were rented out for the trail rides each day.

In spite of growing up around Chicago, Rassas was no rhinestone cowboy. He knew how to handle a horse and was looking forward to being a regular cowhand. Few people knew about his experiences with horses back at summer camp in Algonquin, Michigan.

From the sixth through the eleventh grade, Rassas had traveled to Algonquin every June with his brothers George and Kevin. It was the ultimate sports camp—football, baseball, basketball, softball, badminton, swimming, kayaking, tennis, track, rifle shooting, and horseback riding. The counselors were either army veterans or athletes from Michigan or Michigan State. The kids rose to Reveille each morning and ate breakfast as fast as they could; when the meal ended, the games began. They played until the sun went down between nine and ten o'clock. Rassas was one of the best in every sport because he had been playing the games since he could walk. What he loved the most at camp was the horseback riding. The young boy already had a hankering to roam the Wild West. He was about to get his chance.

Rolling northwest on Highway 276, Rassas sensed that something dramatic was on the horizon. They had been driving three and a half days and surely they were closing in. Besides, the GTO had been climbing for more than an hour, and the highway signs said they were at 8,000 feet. The duo had been watching the mileage markers for more than thirty minutes and knew they were almost there. They had already crossed over the Wind River.

Rolling northwest, Rassas and Kelly came to the top of a butte, and in front of them lay a large valley. As far as the eye could see, there were no houses, cars, cattle, or creatures of any kind. All they could see were rocky hills in the distance. The highway now cut a line as straight as an arrow across the wide-open country that neither Rassas nor Kelly had ever seen the likes of. For more than a hundred miles, there had been no speed limit signs on the highway, so Rassas looked at Kelly and said, "Let's see what this monster can do." He put the pedal to the metal and the GTO took off like a rocket. As they reached 120 miles per hour, Kelly yelled, "Nick, I give up. I'm calling uncle!" Rassas took his foot off the accelerator, although the needle on the speedometer continued to rise all the way to 135.

The scene ahead was beautiful enough to make their hearts stop. The panoramic view of the forty-mile mountain range was a world they had never seen, or imagined. Standing almost 14,000 feet tall was a stunningly beautiful new mountain range of sculptured rock. Rassas's eyes focused on the Cathedral Group—Grand Teton, Montana Owen, and Montana Teewinot. The next thing he knew, the GTO was headed for the ditch. Nick yanked the steering wheel and pulled the car back onto the highway at the last instant.

"You drive the car and I'll watch the damn mountains," Kelly yelled.

"I can't help it," Rassas said, his eyes widening. "That's the most beautiful sight I've ever seen. I'm trying to get my jaw off the floor."

For more than two million years, the alpine glaciers had carved the jagged peaks that rose almost four thousand feet straight up. These peaks seemed to be pointing to the heavens. Much of the mountain face had been sculptured from an enormous westward-titled fault of metamorphic and igneous rock. The Grand Tetons are the youngest in the Rocky Mountain range. Experts say they contain a more simple architecture than most of the great ranges of the world. Still, you could not convince Rassas or Kelly of this.

"The only mountains that I've ever seen in my life are in Michigan and Pennsylvania," Rassas said. "And this is about ten thousand times better."

"The only thing I've ever seen in my life is the Empire State Building," Kelly said.

Because there were no foothills, the Grand Tetons seemed to spring straight up from the floor of the national park. The Snake River slithered down from Yellowstone Park into Jackson Lake and then continued south to Jackson Hole, before turning west into Idaho. Jackson Lake, with its aqua blue water, shimmered in the sunlight on the east side of the Grand Tetons—composing one monster of an oil painting.

Rassas looked down as the needle on the speedometer passed a hundred miles an hour. He tapped the brake. The car slowed down, but his heart continued to accelerate.

"I never thought we were going to get here," Rassas said. "Now that we're here, it seems like the whole trip was nothing at all. I've got enough energy to climb those mountains right now."

A half hour later, as the GTO turned into the Triangle X Ranch, John Turner met them at the front gate. He was dirty from head to toe and smelled like cow manure.

"This place is heaven," Rassas said.

"It might look like heaven right now," Turner said, "but I want you to tell me that after you've worked the ranch a few days. Actually, I'm glad that you boys are here. There's plenty of work to go around."

John Turner worked side by side every day with his younger brother, Donald, and his older brother, Harold. They were also covered in dirt and sweat.

Up the road on horseback rode the head honcho of the Triangle X Ranch. Louise Turner Bertschy was a beautiful woman with some Mexican ancestry that provided her with dark and silky skin and flowing black hair. Her smile was as radiant as the mountains, but when Nick looked into her eyes, he saw something surprising.

"Why, hello Nick and Bill," Louise said, smiling. "I've really heard a lot about you two. Actually, Nick, John tells me some pretty amazing things about you. He says your motor never stops running."

"It's true," John interjected, "but at least the coaches at Notre Dame are going to let him play some football this fall. Wait till you see Nick work out."

"He can work out all he wants," she said, "but we might need to do something about that overactive motor."

That night, as John and Bill were drinking a few beers, Rassas looked across the table at his two Notre Dame friends. Never one to partake in alcohol, Rassas was working on a sugar rush with his third soda.

"John, I gotta tell you that your mother is absolutely beautiful," Rassas said. "Looks can be deceiving, though. When I look into her eyes, I see Ben Cartwright."

John Turner laughed and almost spilled his beer.

"She's been running this place ever since my dad died from cancer when I was a kid," he said. "She has a big job. This is the largest working dude ranch in America. This is a job for a man, but deep down, my mom is a pioneer woman. She's never once let this ranch get to her."

At the crack of dawn the next morning, the first job was to round up the herd. The five wranglers—Nick, Bill, John, Harold, and Donald—crept down to the lake looking for the lowest-lying fog. The lake, even in the summer, was warmer than the air, and the result was a thick fog that looked like smoke on the water. The horses usually hid along the lake beneath the low, gray ceiling.

"What we need to do is find the bell mare," John said. "Just open your ears and listen. Once we find her, the others will follow."

The bell mare wore a large cowbell around her neck that clanged as she walked. The boys located her in about ten minutes, and soon the herd was being saddled for the day's ride.

For the wranglers, the day was filled with a lot of chores, such as leading the trail rides, chopping wood, and raking the stable area. When the ride ended late in the afternoon, the horses were fed and then turned out. That is when Rassas popped the trunk of the GTO and pulled out a football. He laced up his football cleats and started zigzagging his way around the ranch.

Moments later, Louise stepped out onto the front porch and shook her head.

The starting defensive secondary at Notre Dame in 1964; *(left to right)* Tony Carey, Nick Rassas, and Tom Longo. *(Courtesy of the Nick Rassas Collection)*

Nick Rassas trots down the field after scoring his first touchdown ever against Purdue. *(Courtesy of the Nick Rassas Collection)*

Nick Rassas rips down USC Heisman Trophy winner Mike Garrett from behind as Tom Longo moves in during a 1965 game at Notre Dame Stadium. *(Courtesy of the Nick Rassas Collection)*

Tony Carey (1) leaps for an interception over All-American wide receiver Gene Washington (84) of Michigan State as Nick Rassas(27) moves in. *(Courtesy of the Notre Dame Archives)*

Nick Eddy (47) leads Nick Rassas around left end against Michigan State as Phil Sheridan (83) also blocks. *(Courtesy of the Notre Dame Archives)*

1964 Notre Dame Fighting Irish

FRONT ROW — (left to right): Joe Farrell, Jim Snowden, John Huarte, Tom Kostelnik, Paul Costa, Captain Jim Carroll, Ken Maglicic, Joe Kantor, John Meyer, Dave Humenik, Jack Snow.

SECOND ROW — (left to right): Alex (Sandy) Bonvechio, Tony Carey, Norm Nicola, Dick Dupuis, Vince Mattera, Kevin Hardy, Vince Dennery, Tom Mittelhauser, John Atamian, Tom Harding, Tom Longo, Jerry Tubinis.

THIRD ROW — (left to right): Paul McCarthy, Manager, Don Gmitter, Dan McGinn, Bob Merkle, Alan Loboy, Nick Rassas, Bill Zloch, Bill Wolski, Nick Eddy, Pete Duranko, Tom Regner, Pete Andreotti, Harry Long, Dick Arrington, Mike Fitzgerald, Senior Manager.

FOURTH ROW — (left to right): Alan Page, Bob Papa, Pete Thornton, Denny Conway, Tom Talaga, Mike Webster, Arunas Vasys, Phil Sheridan, Ken Ivan, Mike Wadsworth, Tom Sullivan, Bob Meeker, Vic Paternostro, Paul Seiler, Al Frenzel, Manager.

FIFTH ROW — (left to right): Jim Garrison, Hugh O'Malley, John Lium, Larry Conjar, Jim DiLullo, Jim Lynch, John Horney, Bob Hagerty, Tim Wengierski, Ron Jeziorski, Joe Marsico, Dick Swatland, Dave Zurowski, Tom Rhoads, John Zenner, Harry Alexander, Ed Zewinski.

SIXTH ROW — (left to right): Joe Smyth, Mike Earley, Tom Klump, Jim Kelly, Allen Sack, Tim Devine, Larry Mauch, John Reisert, Bill Riley, Jerry Kelly, Fred Schnurr, Jack Meyer, Tim Gorman, Angelo Schiralli, Dick Sauget, Jim Smith, Mike Krach, Jim Brocke, Dave Odlaug.

BACK ROW — (left to right): Coaches Richard "Doc" Urich, Joe Yonto, George Sefcik, Head Coach Ara Parseghian, Dave Hurd, Tom Pagna, Paul Shoults.

The 1964 Team Picture. *(Courtesy of the Notre Dame Archives)*

Quarterback John Huarte (7) looks for an open receiver in Notre Dame's first game in 1964. Waving to Huarte is Nick Rassas (27). *(Courtesy of the Notre Dame Archives.)*

Quarterback John Huarte on the sideline. *(Courtesy of the Notre Dame Archives)*

Here come the Irish before the Iowa game in 1964. In the foreground *(left to right)*
Nick Rassas (27), Norm Nicola (50), Tom Kostelnik (52), and Ken Maglicic (62).
John Huarte (7) leads the second wave. *(Courtesy of the Notre Dame Archives)*

The defense gets ready for Purdue. *(left to right)* Tom Kostelnik (52), Tom Regner (76), Jim Carroll (60), and Nick Rassas (27). *(Courtesy of the Notre Dame Archives)*

John Huarte (7) winds and throws to Nick Rassas (27). *(Courtesy of the Notre Dame Archives)*

Tom Regner (76) with Ara Parseghian. *(Courtesy of the Notre Dame Archives)*

Author Jim Dent with Ara Parseghian in 2008. *(Courtesy of the Jim Dent collection, photo by Jonathan Michaels)*

Tackle Tom Regner. *(Courtesy of the Notre Dame Archives)*

Press box view of the Notre Dame defense in the opening game of 1964. *(Courtesy of the Notre Dame Archives)*

Jimmy Connelly, the unofficial "Mayor of Notre Dame," with Ara Parseghian outside of the Beverly Wilshire Hotel in 1964. *(Courtesy of the Jim Connelly collection)*

Tony Carey (1) returns an interception against Michigan State as Tom Kostelnik (52) leads the blocking. *(Courtesy of the Notre Dame Archives)*

The Notre Dame defense springs into action against Iowa. *(Courtesy of the Notre Dame Archives)*

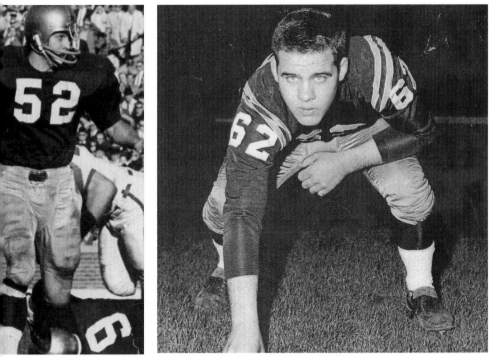

Linebacker Ken Maglicic. *(Courtesy of the Ken Maglicic collection)*

The All Americans: Dick Arrington *(left)* and Nick Rassas sign a football during the
Kodak All-American event ceremonies. *(Courtesy of the Nick Rassas Collection)*

(left to right) Nick Rassas, Bill Kelly, and John Turner at the Triangle X Ranch outside of Jackson Hole, Wyoming, in the summer of 1964. *(Courtesy of the Nick Rassas Collection)*

Tony Carey (1) defends a pass against UCLA. *(Courtesy of the Notre Dame Archives)*

Notre Dame president Father Theodore Hesburgh steps back from the microphone during a pep rally speech at the Old Fieldhouse in 1964. *(Courtesy of the Notre Dame Archives)*

The 1964 Notre Dame starting offensive and defensive lineups. *(Courtesy of the Notre Dame Archives)*

Purdue fullback Bill Harmon is driven into the ground by Tom Kostelnik (52), Don Gmitter (80), Tom Regner (76), and Alan Laboy (37). *(Courtesy of the Notre Dame Archives)*

Wide receiver Jack Snow leaping for a pass at picture day in 1964. *(Courtesy of the Notre Dame Archives)*

"Nick Rassas, what in the world are you doing out there?" she asked. Rassas was sweating and already breathing hard when he stopped and looked at her.

"Well, Mrs. B., this is a football drill that I made up. You see these sage bushes. Well, I treat them like would-be tacklers. That's why I'm darting and dodging all over the place. Trying to get away from these bushes."

Her right foot was now tapping.

"Nick Rassas, has anyone ever told you that you're crazier than a loon?"

"Well, in fact Mrs. B., they have. You can be sure that you're not the first."

"Nick, I want you to do something for me. If one of these bushes tackles you, will you please let me know?"

"You bet I will, Mrs. B.," Rassas said, grinning. "You will be the very first to know."

She shook her head and walked back into the house.

At night, the boys slept in a teepee. The next morning, Rassas was madly swinging an axe, and the pile of cut wood was now taller than he was. That is when he saw Louise walking toward him.

"Mrs. B., may I ask you what time it is?"

"It's 10:30," she said.

"What time is lunch?"

Louise put her hands on her hips. She gave him the same look from the previous afternoon.

"Why, Nick Rassas, all you want to do is rush, rush, rush. All you care about is what's next. I've been watching you and all you do is zip, zip, zip, zip, zip."

At last, the young man was speechless. For perhaps the first time in his life, someone had told him to slow down. Nick did not know what to say. It was true that he never stopped moving, twisting, shaking, hopping, and trying to get somewhere fast.

"Nick, put down that axe," she said. He followed her orders.

"Nick, I want you to sit down on that pile of wood," she continued, "and I don't want you to get up until you hear the lunch bell ring. I want

you to think about your life. I want you to think about where you're going in life. One of the reasons you came to Wyoming was to figure it all
out. I want you to sit there and watch those mountains grow." It was said
the mountains grew about five inches every century.

Nick followed orders and did not move for an hour. His eyes locked
onto the mountains and he thought about everything that had happened
since he enrolled at Notre Dame. He was about to start his first home
game for the Fighting Irish. For all that, he wanted so much more. The
more he thought about it, the more he wanted to get up and climb those
mountains. Thank God the lunch bell finally rang.

As the cowboys chowed down, Louise approached the outdoor table.

"Nick, are you feeling better now?" she asked.

"Actually, Mrs. B., I can't wait to get back to my wood-chopping," he
said. She rolled her eyes and walked away.

That evening, shortly before sundown, Louise was returning from
the market in the old Chevy truck when she spotted movement on the
racetrack. Straight as an arrow down the middle of the ranch was a two-
mile dirt road used for racing the horses. Sometimes the boys sprinted
the horses the length of the strip. Sometimes they won sizable bets.

This was no horse she was seeing on the racetrack, however. This
was a well-conditioned male athlete wearing football shoes and tearing
up the dirt. Rassas, running sprint after sprint, was soaked with sweat.

"Stop right there," Louise yelled. "I need to talk to you, Nick."

"Why, hello, Mrs. B.," Rassas said.

"What in the heck do you think you're doing?"

"Gotta get my wind sprints in," he said, pulling off his shoes. "Gotta
get ready for the season."

From the soles of his shoes, Rassas pulled out two leaded weights.

"Look, Mrs. B. I put lead in my shoes so my legs'll get stronger."

Again, with hands on hips, she shook her head.

"You've got weights in your shoes and rocks in your head," she said.

"A lot of people say that," he said with a grin.

WITH THE WORKDAY over, the boys took a bath beneath a garden hose
and got dressed. Then they piled into the green Packard hearse. Nick

had heard all about the Pink Garter Theatre and could not wait to get there.

The green funeral wagon trekked twenty miles down the snaking two-laner into Jackson Hole. The Pink Garter Theatre was where Broadway meets the West—literally. It was located at 50 West Broadway in downtown Jackson Hole.

The old theater was housed in the oldest frame building in town. It went up in 1916 and became Jackson Hole's first car dealership. Then it became the town's first bowling alley. When the bowling business went bad, it became a billiard hall, and then stood empty for a few years until a resourceful woman with a flare for promotions bought the place and converted it into a theater.

In the 1950s, Paula Jeffrey had intended to produce melodramas. One of the first was *Uncle Tom's Cabin* with a cast of white people wearing black makeup. Jackson Hole was a town of wooden sidewalks and cowboy bars and a Wild West spirit. It was not a town ready for melodramas. Soon, Western musicals became the rage, and it was not surprising that a bunch of cowhands riding in a hearse were now on their way to see *Annie Get Your Gun*.

Nick will never forget the moment he walked through the front door of the Pink Garter Theatre and set eyes on Hallie Bowes playing Annie Oakley, the quick-draw teenager who could outshoot any man in town. She was singing "You Can't Get a Man with a Gun." He thought his heart was melting until he heard the voice of Donald Turner.

"By the way, Nick," Donald said. "That girl up there singing. That's Harold's girlfriend."

Rassas looked like a man floating into heaven. "I don't care," he said. "Just as long as I can get one just like her." He had spent has last three years at Notre Dame without the scent of a woman. The rest of the time he spent working out. His sacrifices had turned him into an outstanding football player, but there was more to life than pounding the dickens out of other men.

Before the night was over, girls wearing tight-fitting Western wear and cowboy boots would sing and dance their way into Rassas's heart. They were mostly college coeds from places like Brigham Young, Utah, and

Utah State. When the night was over, the girls and the cowhands piled into the hearse and took off down Broadway. The Cowboy Bar at the Wort Hotel stayed open until 1:00 A.M. The cowhands and their dates would sit on the saddles that subbed for barstools. They would cowboy dance far into the night. The boys could care less that 6:00 A.M. would come early at the Triangle X Ranch. Sleep was irrelevant with Annie Oakley and the girls in town. What a great way to spend the summer.

By the middle of August, Nick knew it was time to load up the GTO and head back to Indiana. Fall practice was a couple of weeks away. Otherwise, he might stake a claim in western Wyoming and stay forever. Just looking at the mountains left him breathless. Thinking about the young actresses made him want to stay even more.

The gas tank was filled and the GTO was ready to go when Louise walked up to Nick and shook his hand.

"I know you've got to get going, cowboy," she said, "but take the time—at least occasionally—to sit down and relax."

Rassas knew it would never happen. He would consider her advice because she was an intelligent woman, but Nick Rassas was born to run. He nodded and smiled and kissed her on the cheek.

"You know, Mrs. B., if you'd come to a Notre Dame game, I'd score a touchdown for you," he said.

"I bet you would," she said, "and I might just take you up on that."

She watched Nick Rassas drive away as the dust boiled up from the dirt road. He was going slow, but before long, the GTO would be roaring down the highway with the mind of Nick Rassas going full tilt.

Chapter 16

THE UNDERDOG

Ara Parseghian is an impatient, determined man, convinced he can return Notre Dame to a position of dominance in college football, and this he undoubtedly will do one day—but not in 1964. This year, he will hope for the best, which could be a break-even season.

—SPORTS ILLUSTRATED, SEPTEMBER 1964

At 5:17 on a cool September morning, Ara Parseghian sat behind his desk and rapidly diagrammed plays with his left hand while flipping through the *Chicago Tribune* sports section with his right. His eyes shuttled from the playbook to the newspaper. He reached for a cup of steaming black coffee, his third of the last fifteen minutes.

Two hours before the sun rose over South Bend, Parseghian's brain was traveling faster than Richard Petty running away with the 1964 Daytona 500. This was nothing new for a man who could do several things at once without blinking. He put the newspaper aside, grabbed a fork, and began to eat breakfast with his right hand, still drawing plays with the left.

Sitting across the desk from Parseghian, digging through a pile of newspapers, was Joe Doyle, the Notre Dame beat writer and columnist for the *South Bend Tribune*. Doyle had covered Notre Dame football since 1949 and was an accomplished newspaperman, never afraid to chase the big story. Like most sportswriters of the day, he loved a play on words. His column headline was ACCORDING TO DOYLE, and it had taken him less than a month to call Parseghian's stay at Notre Dame the "Era of Ara."

Doyle and Parseghian were now fast friends, a major departure from several months earlier when the coach had created a public backlash by charging the sportswriter with jumping the gun on his hiring. The FOR SALE sign, placed in his front yard by a prankster neighbor, was gone and most of his friends and relatives were speaking to him again.

Back in December, on the day Parseghian accepted the job for the second time, the sportswriter had paid a visit to the new head coach.

"Joe, I've got to ask you where you got that story." Parseghian said, setting his dark eyes on him. "It caused me a lot of trouble, you know."

"Look," Doyle said in a booming voice. "I don't tell you how to run your football team, and I would appreciate it if you didn't tell me how to write my columns."

Parseghian stood, reached over the desk, and the two men shook hands. More than four decades later, Doyle still gets misty-eyed recalling his long friendship with Parseghian, and the day they made up.

Moments later, Parseghian poured his fourth cup and grew edgier. Fall two-a-day practices would commence in a couple of hours, and the season opener against Wisconsin was three weeks away. The Fighting Irish had much work to do and plenty to prove.

With breakfast now finished, the coach was immersed in a column written by Bill Gleason in the *Chicago's American*. He was still scribbling with his left hand when he looked up with a furrowed brow.

"Joe, why is everyone in the press down on our football program?" Parseghian said. "I mean, everybody is picking us way down the ladder."

Doyle smiled and his Irish eyes danced. "Don't know if you've checked lately, Ara," he said, "but Notre Dame has won fourteen games the last four seasons. That means you've lost twenty-five in the same period."

"I didn't lose any of them," Parsehgian said, his eyebrows arching. "Those games were lost by other coaching staffs. I wasn't even *here*."

Doyle's eyes turned serious. "Ara, I think that everybody has pretty much given up on Notre Dame. When Kuharich was here, a lot of the writers picked Notre Dame to make the top 20. Look what happened. They all got burned."

"But this is a new team—a new year!"

"Nobody is going to believe in you until you start winning again. Notre Dame has been losing too much lately. Besides, you barely won the Old-Timers Game in the spring."

"The heck we did, Joe," Parseghian said. "The Old-Timers offense scored one touchdown against our first-string defense."

"You won the game by a touchdown and the Old-Timers had the ball at the 16-yard line when time ran out."

"We won that game convincingly. They had two Heisman Trophy winners on their side."

"Yeah," Doyle said. "Johnny Lattner and Leon Hart. Both are over forty."

"You can't tell me that George Izo is not still a good quarterback. He plays for the Redskins. And Myron Pottios is still one of the best linebackers in the business. Red Mack is still a great receiver."

The Old-Timers Game had been dreamed up by Knute Rockne back in the twenties when Rock got tired of watching his boys banging heads against each other. So he invited the football alumni back for what would become an annual skirmish at old Cartier Field. So popular was this little spring scrum that several universities around the country had copied it. This was not surprising since the copycats devoured whatever Rockne was doing.

Coming into the 1964 game, the Old-Timers were 7-25-1 against the varsity. Naturally, the postgraduate players were not in the best physical condition. This Old-Timers team knew its strengths and weaknesses. Some of the guys were pot-bellied and over the hill. Others still had the fire, like Jim Kelly, a recent draft choice of the Steelers. That day, Red Mack would catch 4 passes for 96 yards and, at times, showed up the young secondary.

Twenty thousand fans had showed up at Notre Dame Stadium to see if Parseghian was starting to turn around the dismal program. They were impressed with Nick Rassas, who carried the ball 9 times for 64 yards and caught 1 pass for another 32. Parseghian told the press after the game, "Nick Rassas is a good, solid player for whom I have high hopes."

The fans were equally as impressed with Jack Snow, who caught five passes for 111 yards and 2 touchdowns. Sandy Bonvechio, subbing for the injured John Huarte, was 9 of 12 for 122 yards and 2 touchdowns.

After the game, though, the press and the public still were not convinced that Notre Dame was back. Parseghian could read it in the papers, feel it in his bones. They were ignoring his quote from the *Chicago Tribune* a couple of weeks earlier when he said, "It is my desire to have a 6-4 record my first season at Notre Dame. I want to start off with a winning record."

Parseghian looked at Doyle and held up a column written by Harry Sheer in the *Chicago's American*. "This guy is picking us to lose our first three games—*our first three games*, Joe." Sheer had written, "No one expects Notre Dame to win six games—except for the super-optimists."

Further down in the story, Parseghian found a troubling quote from Johnny Lattner: "This Notre Dame team hits hard. But they won't win many games."

He threw down the paper. There was no questioning this man's ambition. You could read it in the letter he had sent to the players just a few weeks earlier. It read in part, "Competing against the best is the only way we can develop a national rating. Seven of our opponents finished in the "Top 20" last year. Notre Dame is internationally known; people all over the world are aware of the Notre Dame tradition. In the short time that I've been with this great university, I have been impressed with the interest, dedication and loyalty of the alumni and fans. A great responsibility is ours."

No one appreciated the Notre Dame past as much as Parseghian. No one wanted to leave his stamp on the program more than he did. This was his destiny, he felt. At Akron South High School in 1942, the editor of the yearbook had written this caption below his senior picture: "Someday he will coach at Notre Dame."

As he tossed the *Chicago's American* in the waste basket, the coach peered across the desk at Doyle. "When I was a kid I listened to every game on the radio," he said. "I listened to Johnny Lujack play and I listened to Johnny Lattner play. You know how many national championships Leahy won."

"Yeah, I know. I was there—"

"That's right. It was six. Six national championships." Parseghian stood and gazed out the corner window at St. Mary's Lake, the blue water now shimmering beneath the first sunlight of morning. "I know they're not going to vote us into the top 10 right away," he said. "That's going to take some time. But I'll tell you, Joe, this is still the greatest football program in the country."

Not a single vote had been cast in either the AP (writers) or UPI (coaches) polls for Notre Dame to finish in the top 20 in 1964. Here was the writers' preseason poll, from one to ten:

1. Ole Miss
2. Oklahoma
3. Illinois
4. Texas
5. Ohio State
6. Alabama
7. Washington
8. Auburn
9. Syracuse
10. Navy

Teams rounding out the top 20 included Arkansas, LSU, USC, and Wisconsin. No one was giving Notre Dame even a distant shot of making it into the top 20 before the end of the season.

The polls frustrated Parseghian, but he also recognized the lack of attention might serve them better. In the past, opposing teams could not wait to line up the highly ranked Fighting Irish. This time they would not be quite as hungry.

One reason the press was doubting Notre Dame was the negative reports coming out of South Bend concerning John Huarte's injured shoulder. That suited Parseghian just fine. Let the writers think that Huarte's arm was shot, and the word would eventually reach the University of Wisconsin in Madison. If the Wisconsin coaches were not preparing for Huarte, they were in for a big surprise. All summer Huarte had been working out privately inside the confines of Notre Dame Stadium, or behind the large green tarpaulin that covered the ten-foot fence surrounding Cartier Field. Huarte and Jack Snow had been virtually inseparable for three months. When they were not attending summer classes, they were practicing together. In early June, Huarte could throw the ball no farther than 10 yards, but his range grew to 20, then 30 yards. Swimming in the morning and light weight-lifting in the afternoon was bringing the shoulder around. Huarte was starting to feel like his old self again. With preseason camp about to start, he was now firing the ball to Snow.

According to NCAA rules, Parseghian was not permitted to watch the workouts, or even get close to the players during the summer. He had his spies, however. He knew that Huarte was about ready to go.

As Doyle got up to leave the coach's office that morning, he smiled and pointed to the pile of unopened mail on the coach's desk. "The press might not respect you yet, but the fans obviously love you," he said.

Parseghian shrugged and said, "I don't have time to reply to all of this stuff. I must've gotten a thousand letters from the Armenians. They all think I'm rich. They all want to borrow money."

Parseghian knew from the day that he walked onto campus that Notre Dame was the gold standard of college football. The public adulation was beyond imagination. Most of the phone calls he had received at Northwestern were from small-town Illinois, or smaller-town Iowa. Now they were coming from all over the country—from the rich, the powerful, and the political. He heard from senators and movie stars and people who wanted to donate anything they could to help the program.

"I got a letter from a woman who lived about twenty miles from North-western," he told Doyle. "She wrote to say that we had the same name— Ara Parseghian. Imagine that, but here's the kicker. She lived that close to Northwestern and she never knew who I was. Then I move a hundred and twenty miles away to Notre Dame, and all of a sudden she's heard of me."

AT NINE THAT morning on the first full day of fall practice, Parseghian strode onto Cartier Field and felt the energy stirring. The players were deeply tanned and in better shape than three months earlier. The team was now on the muscle.

He certainly knew what kind of shape Pete Duranko was in. The strongman from Youngstown, Ohio, had started his career as a fullback and had recently been moved to defensive tackle. Parseghian was toying with the idea of making him a linebacker. He was one of the best all-around athletes on the team.

During the summer, Parseghian had entered Notre Dame Stadium to catch a glimpse of the "voluntary" workouts. He was amazed as he watched the 235-pound Duranko walk across the field on his hands, then start up the steps of the stadium, all the while singing the "Victory March" in Polish. He climbed all fifty-five stadium steps to the top. Not once did Duranko slow down for an extra breath. He did not grunt. He was barely sweating when he reached the top. It was an effortless trip and one of the greatest physical feats that Parseghian had ever witnessed.

Walking through the gate of the practice field, Parseghian knew the press would be waiting. A knot of sportswriters with pens and pads formed a circle around him. For ten minutes they had watched Huarte warming up, throwing bullet after bullet to Snow.

Bill Gleason of the *Chicago's American* asked, "Coach, what do you think of Huarte's chances of playing this season?"

Parseghian caught himself. He wanted to say, "I already know he's going to be just fine." Instead, he feigned surprise and said, "Gee, I hope he's going to be okay. We still don't know."

Just then, Huarte uncorked a 40-yard spiral that dropped nose-first over Snow's left shoulder and into his hands. As Snow trotted back up the field, Parseghian's eyes tracked the weight-lifter biceps. Snow would have been a dead ringer for a fullback if he had not changed his jersey number from 40 to 85. His muscles were bulging because he had been logging some serious time in the weight room.

"Jack," the coach said. "If you don't slow down on that weight-lifting, I might just have to put you in the line with Costa, Snowden, and Duranko."

"Hold on, Coach," Snow said. "You know I'm the best damn receiver on this whole squad."

"I know, Jack. You've already told me."

Parseghian was laughing on the inside as he chided Snow. He also knew the team had no better role model for conditioning. The coach never stopped preaching about the need to be the stronger team in the fourth quarter. Snow, it seemed, never stopped working out.

The gym where he was doing all of his weight-lifting was not located in one of the athletics complexes. It was a spartan 20 × 25–foot room situated in the back of Brownson Hall, far from public view. The cramped room

was filled with free weights, barbells, dumbbells, and the sounds of grunt-
ing men. It was run by one of the most remarkable men ever produced by
Notre Dame—Father Bernard Lange, C.S.C., a.k.a. the "Strongman
Priest." He had graduated from Notre Dame in 1912 with a Litt.B. degree,
and in 1924 received his M.A. Two years later, he was awarded his Sc. B.
In the 1930s, he would earn his Ph.D. in biology at St. Edward's University in Austin, Texas.

Father Lange had been both a contemporary and close friend of
Knute Rockne. While Rockne won a record number of games in the
1920s with his charm, guile, and wit, Lange built the Notre Dame players into physical specimens. He drilled Rock's boys like a Prussian field
marshal, motivating with a combination of fear and Teutonic discipline.
In the early 1920s, thanks to this quaint little gym behind the Golden
Dome, he was ranked as the fourth strongest man in the world. Pictures
of a shirtless Father Lange lined the walls of the gym, revealing bulging
biceps, a barrel chest, and huge thighs. Each thigh was as big around as
another man's waist.

In the 1920s, the Fighting Irish were among the first serious weight-
lifters in college football, so it was not surprising that Snow found his
way to Lange in the early 1960s. Now in his seventies, the priest drove
Snow to new heights as a weight-lifter. He would stand over Snow, yelling and inspiring him to give every ounce of energy.

Snow might have been cocky, but no one was more dedicated to the
sport of football. He already handled himself like a professional, and his
teammates admired him for it. He was determined to put his first three
years behind him and move forward. He still believed that Notre Dame
could compete for the national championship. The All-American team
was not far off his radar. After graduating, he planned to set his sights on
the pros. The AFL and NFL were just beginning their bidding wars,
and there was big money on the table.

Snow liked to tell a story from the summer of 1964 when one of the
nuns, wearing a habit, walked into Lange's gym. Women were strictly
prohibited from entering for any reason. When Lange saw her, he threw
a 10-pound weight in her direction and yelled, "Hey, sis, we don't allow
women in here."

Lange was a legendary figure for many reasons—including his antics. He was Charles Atlas before Angelo Siciliano changed his name to Charles Atlas in 1922. Before weight-lifting became popular, he did hundreds upon hundreds of push-ups and strengthened his quadriceps by leg-pressing Model A Fords. As a student at the Notre Dame Preparatory School, Lange one day decided to show off his muscles by climbing to the top of the Golden Dome and wrapping his right arm around the Virgin Mary. The police were summoned and a frantic chase ensued through St. Edward's Hall and all the way down to St. Mary's Lake. Lange dove into the frozen lake and managed to swim all the way across under the ice before emerging on the other side and sprinting into the woods.

The astounded witnesses could barely imagine how the kid had survived the swim. They were not aware that he often greased his body with animal fat and swam the lake, even on the iciest days of winter.

If not for his dedication to his studies, Lange surely would have been kicked out of school for climbing the Golden Dome. He was a man of so many talents that it was difficult to keep track. His wood craftsmanship was more than art; it bordered on genius. In his leisure time, he crafted a model of a French Gothic cathedral. It was accurate to its most minute detail—one inch representing six feet. He used ink and watercolors to get the stained glass effect.

In the process of earning his Ph.D. at St. Edward's, he helped construct the Grotto. When Lange was not constructing grottos or cathedral models, he was building football players. One of his greatest pieces of work was Jack Snow.

Parseghian now noticed that the sportswriters were also admiring Snow's physique as they walked away. Moments later, Nick Rassas trotted through the front gate of Cartier Field and past his coach. Over the summer, he had added ten pounds of muscle and a beach bum's tan.

"Jeez, Nick," Parseghian said. "What'd you do on summer break? Bust broncos?"

"Pretty close, Coach," Rassas said. "Spent the summer working at a dude ranch in Wyoming. Even watched the mountains grow."

As Rassas made his way onto the field, his teammates began a chant they had concocted back in spring training:

Rassas! Rassas!
Knock 'em on their asses!

To make sure his team reported in good shape, Parseghian had hand-delivered every pair of football shoes to the lockers on the last day of the spring semester. Inside each pair was a note that read, "Take these shoes with you this summer. Have them broken in when you return."

The message: Fall drills would be exhausting and blisters could not be tolerated. They would be running until their tongues hung out. Notre Dame players were already accustomed to physical abuse after years of Joe Kuharich and Hughie Devore. Kuharich had pushed his team through punishing practices, and many of them still resented him for it.

On the first day of fall practice, with players in full uniform for the first time since the Old-Timers' Game, Parseghian allowed a few of the newspaper photographers into Cartier Field for a quick shoot.

He lined up the starting offensive unit from left to right. Front row: flanker Jack Snow, tackle John Meyer, guard Dick Arrington, center Norm Nicola, guard John Atamian, tackle Bob Meeker, and end Phil Sheridan. On the back row was the starting backfield of Rassas, Joe Farrell, John Huarte, and Bill Wolski.

Parseghian, still trying to decide whether to put Rassas on offense, said to Tom Pagna one day, "I might just use the little rascal all over the place—offense, defense, and kicking teams. How did I get so lucky?"

Pagna smiled. "We're all lucky that he hung around for as long as he did."

It was time for Parseghian to blow his whistle and gather the players around for the start of the first day of practice.

"We will be on this field for an hour and fifty minutes each practice," he said. "That is all. Surely you can handle that. All of you will be staying in the same dorm the next three weeks before school starts. There were will be no coaches in those dorms. You will be on your own, and I expect you to behave and act like Notre Dame men. Team managers will be doing the bed checks."

A smile creased Ken Maglicic's face. "Oh, boy," he said to Tony Carey.

"Looks like we'll be hitting downtown South Bend every night. Man, I can already taste those golden needles in the back of my throat."

Practices that day were organized, meticulous, and timed to the second. The movement never stopped. Players ran from station to station, from drill to drill. Maglicic became a little confused in the maze of drills and sought the help of Doc Urich. "Coach, I've got a question," he said.

"Kenny, we don't have time for questions," he said. "We've got to keep moving. You can ask questions at the skull session."

That evening after dinner, Carey walked into Maglicic's dorm room and found him sprawled on his bunk. "Okay, Binks, let's go to Rocko's," He said.

"Topcat, I'm so sore and tired that I can't even move. I thought I was in shape. I never even had time today to catch my breath. I'm pooped."

Carey smiled. "Just think about all the fun they're having at Rocko's. School's out and the party's on."

Maglicic shook his head. "Good thing there aren't any girls around. I'd hate to miss them."

Carey laughed. "Oh, they're out there, Binks. They're out there."

Seconds later, Maglicic drifted off and began to snore.

ONE OF THE first things you heard each morning from the north end of Cartier Field was the thwacking of footballs against the hands of the quarterbacks. Three quarterbacks and three centers would work for more than fifteen minutes on snapping and receiving the ball without fumbling.

"Victory will be our reward," Parseghian always yelled. "But not if you jugheads don't learn how to center the ball."

Parseghian was master of the most minute detail. That is why his teams had made so few mistakes at Northwestern and why, in spite of a thin roster, the Wildcats won so many games.

A week later, when the contact drills started, Maglicic and the others lined up for hitting drills while the centers continued to snap the ball to the quarterbacks.

One day, Maglicic said to Nicola, "Man, I sure wish I could be a center. You guys don't do a damn thing but snap the ball in practice."

"Binks, it's not my fault," Nicola said. "Parseghian is the biggest fundamentals coach I've ever had in my life."

Little wonder that Parseghian was obsessing over minutia. His roster had been completely torn down and rebuilt, and now the only three players in the same positions from the 1963 season were linebacker Jim Carroll, tackle John Meyer, and Nicola. Joe Farrell was still a starter in the offensive backfield, but he was moving from left halfback to fullback. Dick Arrington was moving one door down, from tackle to guard.

The entire secondary was new with Nick Rassas, Tom Longo, and Tony Carey as the starters. Four sophomores were breaking into the lineup—linebacker Jim Lynch, end Alan Page, defensive tackle Tom Regner, and halfback Nick Eddy.

The entire elephant backfield had been dismantled and moved to the defensive side with Paul Costa at end, Jim Snowden at tackle, and Duranko at linebacker. Duranko was basically a stand-up defensive end who would do a lot of blitzing from the 4-4-3 alignment.

At that moment in Madison, Wisconsin, the Badgers coaches were wondering if John Huarte would even be able to play in the opener. Parseghian was keeping a lid on it. Out-of-town sportswriters would be allowed into Cartier Field for warm-ups, but were asked to leave before practice started. The only fans allowed to watch practice were the ones with ID proving they were students at Notre Dame, or those with a degree. Only the loyalists would be able to catch a glimpse of the new blueprint.

Wisconsin coach Milt Bruhn had yet to uncover one ounce of insider information on Notre Dame, and this was clearly weighing on his mind. He had beaten Parseghian as the Northwestern coach six of eight times, but this time the cards were facedown on the table.

"I know the man," Bruhn told reporters during preseason drills. "But I don't know what he's got or what he's doing with it. It was easier to figure him out at Northwestern. He's at a new school with a lot of new faces and he's been playing around with something down there since last spring. South Bend is a very tight place. We can expect anything, just about anything."

Observing Huarte one day during practice, Parseghian turned to Pagna and smiled. "I think that John Huarte is throwing the ball better than before he injured his shoulder. I guess we're lucky that we took him to another doctor."

"Very lucky," Pagna said.

"I think the people in Madison have got a little surprise coming their way."

They both laughed.

AT THAT MOMENT, Parseghian did not know that he was walking around with a new nickname—"Bossy the Cow." The players were never going to call him that to his face, but around the locker room, the dorm, and some of the outlying bars, he was no longer "Coach Parseghian."

"Look at that Bossy the Cow." Fullback Joe Kantor was the first to say it. "All he wants to do is boss, boss, boss—boss everybody around. He even bosses his own coaches. I bet they're getting tired of that."

Parseghian prided himself in delegating authority, and each of his coaches covered their own territory. Nevertheless, he was also known to look over everybody's shoulder at some point during the day. The head coach was not afraid to dress down an assistant coach—right in front of the players. He might say to offensive line coach Dave Hurd, "You know, Dave, you're killing us. That technique you're teaching our players is the complete opposite of what we talked about in the coaches' meeting."

During a driving rainstorm that September, coach Paul Shoults said to his boss, "Ara, maybe you ought to call practice off."

Parseghian set his dark eyes on him. "Paul, we are not out here to practice. We are out here to accomplish things. I am the one running this operation and you are going to do what I say."

The silence was deafening.

Three weeks of preseason practice might not sound like much, but the long days and nights of early September were becoming nerve-wracking. Parseghian was like a firehose aimed at a blazing building. He never let up, even when the fire was out.

Yet unlike the other hard-nosed coaches of the era—the Bear Bryants and the Duffy Daughertys—he rarely raised his voice. It was not necessary. All he had to do was cock his head and fix his dark stare on you. That was when you started looking for a hole to crawl into.

During the 1967 season, fullback Rocky Bleier fumbled during a critical stage of the Notre Dame–Michigan State game. Before trotting to the sideline and facing Parseghian, he said he actually checked around the stadium to see if there were any open gates to exit through.

In the heat of that September 1964, the players were getting worn down mentally and physically. Plus, the coaches were starting to snipe at each other. Parseghian's plan from the start was to create this gnawing tension that would simulate game conditions in the fourth quarter of a tight game. As he often said to his assistant coaches, "I want you to throw everything at them but the kitchen sink. I want them to be ready for everything when it comes time to play the games."

Some of the players were starting to get fed up with the pressure. "Bossy the Cow is starting to push too hard," Kantor said one day. His teammates nodded in silent agreement.

"I knew that I had that look with my eyes and I had their attention," Parseghian remembered. "I didn't have to yell at them, but I did have to stay after them. I was always saying, 'No fumbles, no penalties, no mistakes.' Maybe I wore them down a little bit at first. I didn't believe in wearing them down physically, but sometimes I had to be relentless in what I was trying to get across."

Fortunately, Parseghian knew when to turn off the water. A promise made by the coach to his team back in December was about to be fulfilled: They were going to have some fun. Parseghian believed in painstaking preparation, but he also enjoyed a few laughs. The players had never seen Parseghian in a social situation, such as a cookout with cocktails at the family's house, where he could become the life of the party in about three seconds.

So the next-to-last night before the end of two-a-day practices was set aside as "Rookie Night." It was a cross between stand-up comedy and skits dreamed up by the sophomores. Because freshmen were not eligible in those days, the sophomores were considered the rookies.

First up on the stage were Alan Page, Jim Lynch, Don Gmitter, and

Tom Regner. They had scripted a scene at the Parseghian family break-fast table. The players asked their audience to imagine that Parseghian's three kids—his son, Mike, and two daughters Kris and Karan—were sitting among them.

Regner, mimicking the coach: "Okay, Mike, you've got ten seconds to finish that orange juice. Now, go . . . ten, nine, eight . . . two, one."

Lynch: "Okay, Karan, you've got ten seconds to finish that piece of toast. Ready go . . . ten, nine, eight . . . two, one."

From the back of the room came the loudest laughter—straight out of Parseghian's mouth. The players could not have been happier to learn that their drill sergeant possessed a sense of humor. Even the assistant coaches were almost rolling on the floor.

Binks Maglicic, a senior in 1964, was known as a prankster and a bit of a ham. He was not about to be left out of the show. Seizing the moment and the microphone, he launched into his best impersonation of Joe Kuharich.

Hands stuck in his back pocket, Maglicic screeched, "I know we can't beat Michigan State. I know we can't beat USC. I know we can't beat Iowa. But why do I have to take all the god-damned blame?"

They roared with laughter.

"Everybody says we've got the best talent in the world," Maglicic/Kuharich continued. "Where do they get that crap? I'm here to tell you guys one damned thing—you guys stink!"

They laughed until they were almost out of breath, but Maglicic was not finished.

"Where is that quarterback they call Hugh-arty?" Maglicic looked around the room and found John Huarte. He waved and smiled. "Come here, Hugh-arty. Ara's filling you up with bullshit. If it were up to me, your ass would be back to fifth string. No letter jacket for you, dumbass."

Laughter eased the tension. Players were slapping each other on the back as they walked out of the room. They now knew that Bossy the Cow had another side. They just wished they could see it more often.

Wisconsin was only three days away.

Chapter 17

A HIT OF CONFIDENCE

Days earlier, Tom Pagna had cracked the code.

Over the summer, while Jack Snow and Huarte had worked on endless pass routes, a code had emerged. Before the snap, Huarte would turn his head toward the flanker and then turn the other way. If Huarte glanced at Snow a second time, the code was in effect—THE FOOTBALL IS COMING TO YOU.

Huarte could normally tell within a few seconds after checking the defensive scheme if Snow would be open. During a light practice on a breezy day at Cartier Field, Pagna walked up to Huarte and winked. "I'm onto you."

"What do you mean, Coach?"

"I figured out your signal," he said. "When you look at Jack Snow a second time, you're going his way."

Huarte opened his mouth, but before words could tumble out, Pagna threw up his right palm.

"Shush," Pagna said. "Everything is fine until the defense figures it out. And when they do, we're going to have to quash it. Dig?"

Pagna walked away, then casually turned back toward Huarte.

"I don't think Ara's even figured it out yet," he said. "Let's see how long it takes."

An hour later, Huarte was walking back to the fieldhouse when he heard footsteps from behind. Someone was running toward him—fast. It was Parseghian, and Huarte knew what was coming.

"John, I need to talk to you about something pretty important," Parseghian said.

Huarte stopped and looked into the eyes of his coach.

"John, you need to know something right here and now," he said. "You are my starting quarterback Saturday against Wisconsin. You are going to be my starting quarterback even if you throw five interceptions—even if you throw six interceptions. Believe me, you are not coming out of the game."

Huarte nodded and said, "I believe you, Coach."

"Look, John I know what they did to you in the past around here. They yanked your chain. I am not going to do that to you."

Never one for chitchat, Huarte nodded again.

"That is great news, Coach."

Before the two parted ways, Parseghian said, "I know all about your little signal with Snow. I don't know if Pagna's even noticed it yet. But if the defense picks up on it, we'll have to cut it out."

Huarte actually smiled.

"You got it, Coach."

FRIDAY MORNING BEFORE the trip to Madison, Parseghian walked to the middle of the practice field and instructed the players to kneel around him.

Don Hogan, now a student assistant coach, sensed what was happening, and he walked away. This was going to be an emotional scene and he wanted to be somewhere else.

There was a time when everyone held high expectations for Hogan. One of the top recruits out of St. Ignatius High School in South Chicago, Hogan had led Notre Dame in rushing during the 1962 season with 90 carries for 454 yards. He was named honorable mention All American. He certainly possessed the talent to become one of college football's great running backs. He was equipped with both speed and elusiveness, along with the power to carry between the tackles. Hogan was almost unstoppable in short-yardage situations.

His teammates were impressed with his talent and work ethic. Hogan was the first one to class in the morning and the last to leave the library at night. His goal in life was to become a lawyer, and no one doubted he would succeed. He always made himself available to tutor his teammates, and they appreciated it more than he would ever know. They loved him as a friend. They also enjoyed the quirky aspects of his personality, like the fact that he rarely tied his shoelaces.

Driving on the ice-coated Dan Ryan Expressway on Christmas Eve of 1962, Hogan lost control of his car and it slammed into an abutment, killing his sister. Both of his hips were crushed, and doctors told him that his football career was over. He would be lucky to ever walk again without great pain.

Notwithstanding, Hogan valiantly rehabilitated his hips and tried to make a comeback in spring practice of 1963. In spite of a limp, he still managed to gain some yardage in the scrimmages. Still, doctors and trainers knew it would be impossible to rebuild his hips to full strength. There was too much damage.

One day at practice, Hogan collapsed in the middle of the field. He was helped to the sideline by the trainers and then to the locker room. His good friend Tony Carey offered sympathy along with a dose of reality.

"Don, I just don't think you're going to make it," he said. "You've tried as hard as you possibly can. You're still not the same."

That is when the realization set in that a comeback was out of the question. He decided to leave the team. But when Parseghian was hired, Hogan became swept up in the excitement like everyone else. He asked Parseghian for another shot. Instead, the new coach offered him a chance to work on the coaching staff as a student assistant. To an extent, it satisfied what Hogan was trying to accomplish in helping the team, but he was always haunted by the memory of that Christmas Eve when his life changed forever.

As the 1964 season approached, Hogan decided to sit down and compose a letter to his ex-teammates. He wanted them to know just how much he cared.

That letter was in Parseghian's back pocket. "Gentlemen," the coach said, pulling it out, "this was written by your great friend Don Hogan.

He wants me to read it to you. Understand that he very badly wants you to have a great season. He wants to be with you. He just can't. But I can assure you that Don Hogan is going to be with us in our hearts every step of the way this season. This is what he wrote:

" 'If ever a practice seems too long, or you get tired along about the third quarter, just think for one second that a guy named Hogan would give anything to trade places with you, and if he could, he would never give up. Give that second and third effort. Bring Notre Dame football back to where it belongs.' "

A misty-eyed Parseghian looked around at his players. Some had tears in their eyes. Most were looking at the ground.

"Now if this isn't enough to inspire you, I don't know what is," he said. "Practice is over. The season starts tomorrow. Let's go beat Wisconsin for Don Hogan."

Chapter 18

POKER FACE

The sun rose over Madison—or did it? Ara Parseghian could not be sure as he opened the drapes inside his hotel room. He gazed at the low, black clouds and the rivers of rainwater that criss-crossed the parking lot. A cold wind made it feel more like mid-November than late September.

"I wonder if John can throw in this kind of weather," Parseghian said to Tom Pagna.

"How can we possibly know?" Pagna replied. "They never let him play—come rain or come shine."

The headline in the *Chicago Sun-Times* that morning read, IRISH WILL GRIND IT OUT AGAINST WISCONSIN. Parseghian smiled when he read it. How could anyone expect a coach named Parseghian to grind it out when his teams had thrown the ball all over the lot at Northwestern? Pounding the ball was never going to be the Notre Dame style with a healthy John Huarte at quarterback.

On the record, this is what Parseghian had told the *Sun-Times*: "A possession game? That is not the way I like to play. But if John Huarte and Jack Snow cannot give us that passing threat for a more diversified offense, why, sure, we'd play ball control and depend on the defense."

The sporting press still did not know if Huarte's shoulder had completely rebounded from the injury in the spring. Parseghian had never fully discussed it, leaving everyone to guess. Basically, he had urinated around the campfire when he was pressed on the matter.

Sportswriter Bill Jauss was one of the many writers who did not know what to expect. This is what he wrote a few days before the season opener: "There does not seem to be a home-run punch in the Irish attack. The Irish, like the 1963 Chicago Bears, might have to grind everything out. They might have to rely on their defense and capitalize on mistakes by the other team."

As Parseghian looked out at the driving rainstorm that morning, he worried about Huarte and the Notre Dame passing game. Could Huarte throw a slick football? No one knew, and according to the radio weatherman, the rain was not going to let up. In the dim light of dawn, it was coming down in buckets.

Parseghian sighed. He had prepared nine months for this day, and now there was more uncertainty than ever. To complicate matters, he had never had much luck against Wisconsin. The team with the red W stamped on the back and front of the white helmet was like the ghost he could not vanquish. Six times in eight years, the Badgers had broken his heart. In 1962, riding a 6-0 record and a No. 1 ranking in both polls, Parseghian's Northwestern team laid an egg against Wisconsin. No one could quite understand how the Wildcats could tear through the schedule and lose to Wisconsin by the score of 37–6. It was the most calamitous loss in his thirteen-year coaching career—the very reason that athletic director Stu Holcomb decided not to renew his contract. It also cost Northwestern its first shot at the Rose Bowl since 1949 and ruined any hope of the Wildcats finishing in the top 10 for the first time since 1941, when quarterback Otto Graham was the greatest all-round offensive threat in college football. So talented was Graham that at halftime of home games, he would rip off his shoulder pads and helmet and play the cornet in the marching band.

As the countdown began to the Wisconsin season opener, Parseghian had grown edgier by the day. Pagna worried about his best friend. He had been limping around for a couple of weeks with a swollen big right toe that doctors attributed to gout. They also said it could be caused by a case of nerves.

At breakfast that morning in Madison, Parseghian seemed as nervous as a cat. The hotel had prepared a high-protein breakfast that included steak and a baked potato.

Parseghian had a million things on his mind and he was now walking from table to table, delivering last-minute instructions.

"Look at Bossy the Cow," Joe Kantor said. "I wonder if he does that stuff at home."

"I'm not sure that he goes home," said Ken Maglicic. "From my dorm room, I can see the lights burning at the Rock every night, all night. You just don't know how much this game means to him. Half the world is praying he turns Notre Dame around. The other half is waiting for him to fall on his Protestant ass."

In spite of his Protestant beliefs, Parseghian attended Mass with the players every chance he got. It was his strict order that a priest be brought from campus to say Mass in Madison. He frequently said a Hail Mary, and crossed himself around the Catholic coaches and players whenever he felt like it. An outsider who had never heard of Parseghian would have never guessed he was not Catholic.

Even after Mass that morning, he seemed edgy, and why not? One of the best measuring sticks over the years had been Notre Dame's success-failure ratio against the Big Ten. Knute Rockne's record had been 24-2-1. Frank Leahy went 28-3-4, but since 1953, Notre Dame was 12-26 against the Big Ten. Reasons abounded for these failures; the most prominent theory was the subpar recruiting. Parseghian knew the reduction in scholarships had taken its toll, but the coach also knew that many players were out of position. By late September of 1964 all of the pegs seemed properly placed.

It was time to board the bus to the stadium. Just as Parseghian was starting to relax, the banquet room door swung open and the players walked into a lobby jammed to the hilt with fans. Parseghian's mouth flew open and Pagna heard an "Oh, no!"

Pagna caught up with his boss and said, "Better get used to it, Coach. We're not in Evanston anymore."

For the most part, the Fighting Irish fans restrained themselves. The team quickly filed onto the bus and was rolling through downtown

Madison a few minutes later, en route to a stadium filled with fans dying to see them lose—again.

AS THE PLAYERS finished dressing and sat down in front of their lockers, Parseghian was pleased at how they looked in their new uniforms. He had redesigned the uniforms for a more streamlined look and feel. Gone were the stripes around the shoulder pads, along with the dull-looking helmets, now keyed to the metallic gold of the Golden Dome. The pants matched the helmets. White jerseys with blue letters were snugly pulled over shoulder pads that were lighter and smaller. Hip pads and thigh pads were more compact. Parseghian's goal was to accent team speed with a lighter uniform.

What the coach saw that day in the bowels of Camp Randall Stadium was a brand-new Notre Dame football team. After nine months of work, the Fighting Irish finally fit all the trends of the fast-changing college game. The days of plodding football were over. It was now fashionable in college football to line up with two wide receivers instead of one. The elephant backfield was about as out of date as McCarthyism. Quarterbacks were now letting it fly in an era of the thinking man's game.

Teams at this time were expected to look sharper and play smarter. Even the coaches were starting to shave for the television cameras. The conservative 1950s were long gone and it was time to polish the overall image. College football by this point was in a horserace with the pro game. The colleges had dominated the sport until December 28, 1958, when the Baltimore Colts defeated the New York Giants 23–17 in a game broadcast nationally and decided in overtime. Late that afternoon, as the shadows crept across the dusty field of Yankee Stadium, an entire country got a chance to see just how great football could be. John Unitas completed a remarkable 17 passes to Raymond Berry, and Alan Ameche plowed over from the 1-yard line as Baltimore won the game.

The NFL product was on the move. When he took over as NFL commissioner in 1960, Pete Rozelle was determined to seize the lead from the colleges. A man with an eye for glitz, Rozelle arranged a marriage between television and sports. He convinced the owners to share the

TV money, and between 1962 and 1964, those revenues tripled to $14 million per team. Until the late fifties, pro football owners were afraid of TV. They believed that if every game was piped into every home, the fans would stop buying tickets and coming to the games. Instead, Rozelle rewrote the road map to success and showed everyone the money.

The time had come for the collegians to play catch-up and to embrace the little glass box in the living room. The college game needed to be revamped and modernized. Uniforms were being redesigned all over the country. Men like Bear Bryant at Alabama, John McKay at USC, Darrell Royal at Texas, and Parseghian were ready to saddle the fast pony and ride.

Sports in America were beginning to reflect the fast-changing public attitudes. The sixties were picking up speed by the minute. Pop music was changing, and the sexual revolution was on. Americans were driving fast cars and living faster lives, spending money like they never had before. The baby boomers of the 1940s were now in college.

The change could be felt in all of sport. Boxers, once raised in shotgun shacks, were now driving the biggest Cadillacs on the road. Heavyweight champ Cassisus Clay was a classically constructed athlete who was glib and articulate. In baseball, a slugger like Mickey Mantle could no longer walk into Toots Shor's without men shaking his hand and women trying to touch him. Arnold Palmer possessed charisma and a crazy golf swing that landed him on the cover of *Sports Illustrated* about every third week.

In the fall of 1964, every American sport was going from black-and-white to color, as were thousands of TV sets across America. It was time to entertain.

Parseghian was the right man for the times—smart, handsome, and well trained under Sid Gillman and Paul Brown. He was cutting-edge. Most important, Parseghian knew he possessed the tools to thrive in these transitory times. That was why Notre Dame would be faster, sleeker, and more intelligent than the competition. Fans would blink twice when they saw the new product trotting onto the field. An entire nation would be amazed. The Wisconsin game was being broadcast from coast to coast by ABC. What a great time to reintroduce Notre Dame as a major player in the grand scheme of sports.

As he looked around the locker room, Parseghian knew why the players were so charged up. They were chewing gum a hundred miles an hour and pounding each other on the shoulder pads. They were excited because Notre Dame football had been overhauled. The Kuharich–Devore era was six feet under. The Irish had been rebuilt from the ground up. With hope renewed, the adrenaline was finally flowing.

Soaking up the atmosphere, Parseghian smiled. Then he looked up into the windows that were situated in a long row just below the ceiling. He could see the Wisconsin faithful arriving in long raincoats and toting umbrellas. The pestering rain would not go away. Passing the ball 40 times in this weather would be insane.

The coaches' smile completely melted when he looked down. Lying on the floor, sound asleep, was his starting quarterback.

He walked over to Pagna, who was trying not to smile.

"What the hell is wrong with Johnny Huarte?" Parseghian snapped.

"Actually, Ara, I think it means he's relaxed. You took the worry right out of him. You said he could throw 5 interceptions and stay in the game. I think he's got his head on straight. He's ready to go. He just doesn't look like it."

Parseghian shook his head and walked away.

THE FIRST THING the Notre Dame players noticed as they roared down the tunnel and onto the playing field was that the Wisconsin fans had no faces. They could see 54,000 people without eyes, noses, and mouths. Umbrellas were pulled down so low that you could barely see necks and shoulders. They wanted nothing to do with the pouring rain. More depressing, the ceiling was low and gray with the promise of more showers.

Parseghian watched Huarte throwing the ball to Snow along the sideline and was surprised at the crisp spirals that found the target. Maybe it was the sidearm delivery that allowed him to control the wet football.

The players huddled around Parseghian, whose brow was tightly knitted.

"Fellas, this is where it all begins," he hollered. "This is where Notre

Dame starts its comeback. It's all up to you. It's like I said in the locker room. Give me sixty minutes and we can beat this football team."

On the first possession, Huarte completed 2 quick passes to Snow over the middle, but the Fighting Irish could not string together more than three first downs and had to punt. In spite of a howling wind that ripped the stadium flags, Huarte did move the offense to the 14-yard line late in the first quarter and on the final play of the period, Ken Ivan kicked a 31-yard field goal and Notre Dame led 3–0.

Two weeks preceding the game, Parseghian had demanded that Snow lose eight pounds.

"Jack," he said, "you're just not going to have the breakaway speed weighing 220 pounds. You look more like a fullback. I need you as a deep threat."

Snow lost ten pounds and was looking more like a wide receiver every day. With the ball at the Irish 39 after two nice gains by Bill Wolski, Huarte-to-Snow was about to be introduced into the American consciousness. As Huarte slid his hands beneath center Norm Nicola, he looked to his left at Jack Snow. Then his eyes slid across the field to the right cornerback. Then just before saying "Hut-hut," his eyes returned to Snow. The code was now in effect.

On a post pattern, Snow had little trouble running past cornerback Gary Pinnow, but safety Dave Fronek was waiting for him at the 50. So Snow kicked it into another gear as Huarte's long spiral began to descend. At full stride, he caught the pass at the Wisconsin 30. By now, there was no chance Pinnow or Fronek could catch him. It was a work of art in the eyes of Parseghian. To celebrate, he ran down the sideline pumping his right fist. He could not remember being more excited.

Ivan kicked the extra point for the 10–0 lead. A few minutes later, after Wisconsin was stopped after three plays, Ivan would add a 30-yard field goal for a 13–0 halftime lead.

The players could see the sense of urgency in Parseghian's eyes as they gathered in the locker room. Everyone knew what the critics were saying. Opponents always came from behind to win in the second half because the Notre Dame players were not in shape. Look what had happened at the end of the Syracuse game last November.

"Defense is playing great," Parseghian shouted. "You guys are all over their quarterback. Stay after it. Offense, we've got to be more consistent. We are going to need more than 13 points to win this game."

In the first half, tackles Tom Regner, Don Gmitter, and Mike Wadsworth had broken through the line time and again, sacking quarterback Harold Brandt 4 times and causing several of his passes to go awry. As expected, defensive coordinator Johnny Ray had come through with an aggressive attack. One of Ray's biggest goals was blocking a punt. End Phil Sheridan had come within an eyelash of blocking one late in the second quarter.

As the Irish returned to the field for the second half, Notre Dame students formed a human corridor for them to run through. In the early going of the third quarter, however, it was Wisconsin that felt a new spark. Brandt, with time to pass, began to find his receivers. From the Notre Dame 45, he rolled and kept rolling. He was looking for end Jimmy Jones dragging across the middle, but Irish cornerback Tom Longo knew that Brandt had gone too far. When the quarterback crossed the line of scrimmage, Longo abandoned pass coverage and took off. At that instant, Brandt planted his right foot and lifted an arcing pass over Longo and into the arms of Jones, who caught the pass at the 30 and sprinted uncontested into the end zone.

The officials did not flag Brandt for passing beyond the line of scrimmage. On the sideline, Parseghian's stomach did a backflip. He turned and glared at Ray, who said, "Don't worry, Ara. We are going to be all right."

Notre Dame failed to make a first down on its next possession and chose to punt. Ray kept his defense on the attack. Minutes later, he called for the blocked punt and, under serious pressure, Ron Yates squirted the ball 10 yards out of bounds at the Wisconsin 30. In three plays, Notre Dame moved the ball to the 1-yard line as Joe Kantor slanted off right guard for the touchdown. Notre Dame led 19–7.

Wisconsin failed to make a single first down and punted. On the next possession, Huarte completed 3 straight passes to Snow as the Irish moved the ball to the 2-yard line. Fullback Joe Farrell slammed the ball into the end zone on the next play, and the 25–7 lead brought great relief to the Notre Dame sideline. Pagna had his arm around Parseghian's shoulders as the head coach signaled the next play.

Again, Huarte stepped under center, looked at Snow, looked away, and then set his eyes on the wide receiver for the second time. Wisconsin had no idea what it meant. Before the Badgers could react, Snow was behind the safety and hauling in Huarte's pass for a 42-yard touchdown.

The only offensive glitch in the 31–7 victory was that Huarte failed to complete three 2-point conversion passes. Still, his passing numbers were terrific: 15 of 24 for 270 yards and 2 touchdowns. In one start, Huarte had gained more passing yards than Notre Dame's leading passer from all nine games the previous season. Frank Budka finished with only 239 total yards in 1963.

In one of the most remarkable scenes anyone could remember inside Camp Randall Stadium, the Notre Dame players scooped up Parseghian and carried him off the field—after the first game of the year, no less—and they didn't just carry him off the field: They ran with him down the field and all the way up the tunnel. As Parseghian balanced himself on the right shoulder of Jim Carroll and the left shoulder of Jack Snow, he looked a little nervous at first. He leaned forward, hoping to keep his balance. He grabbed anything he could get his hands on. As they slowed and finally stopped near the locker room, Parseghian raised both fists and shook them. He was whooping as loud as his players. He even winked at Huarte, who was wide awake by then.

No one questioned the joy that Notre Dame felt at that moment. The Irish had been left for dead in late November of 1963. They had endured scholarship reductions and some of the worst coaching in the history of college football. Only once in the last ten games had the Fighting Irish defeated a Big Ten team.

This was more than just one victory over a team with Rose Bowl aspirations. This was total domination. Wisconsin had finished with minus 51 rushing yards. In an era when quarterback sacks counted as minus rushing yards, Brandt had gone down eight times. Almost as impressive, Notre Dame outgained Wisconsin, 419–173.

Huarte to Snow made headlines across the country. Of Huarte's 270 passing yards, 211 went to Snow, who finished with 9 catches. To think that the duo had previously been relegated to the bench for most of their careers at Notre Dame.

Thanks to heavy pressure from the line, Rassas and cornerback Tony Carey continually came up with big plays in the secondary. In the first half, Carey intercepted a pass and returned it 25 yards to the Wisconsin 30. Then, in the third quarter, he hauled in his second interception, diving to catch a tipped pass. Rassas batted down two passes and, if not for a bad guess by Tom Longo, Wisconsin would not have scored a single point.

In a jubilant locker room, Parseghian yelled to the press, "Did I tell you about Huarte and Snow? Did I tell you what great hands Snow had? Did I tell you about his speed?"

The sportswriters just shook their heads and wrote down the quote. They knew that Parseghian had said nothing of the sort. He had spent most of the preseason poor-mouthing his team. It was the oldest trick in the book, dating all the way back to Rockne. No wonder he spent so much time studying Rock.

Still charged up from his ride off the field, Parseghian said quite loudly to the press, "Purdue is next up at Notre Dame Stadium. Better get there early to beat the crowd."

SOME FORTY-FIVE YEARS later, as he relaxed at his home in South Bend, Parseghian was asked if he could ever remember a coach being carried off the field by his players after the first game of the year.

He paused to reflect on his fifty-something years in the game as a player, coach, and broadcaster. He could also count another twenty-five years of being an avid fan.

Parseghian shook his head.

"No, I can't ever recall that *ever* happening," he said with a wink. "Not ever."

Chapter 19

LIVING THE DREAM

The scene was like a dream from long ago. Men in coats and ties. Women in fashionable dresses, some in hats. The smell of roasting peanuts. The manicured green grass, broken up by white lines, stretching on forever.

Nick Rassas knew he would never forget boarding the South Shore Line of the Illinois Central that morning in 1947 with his family—Frances, his mother, along with his father and brother, George Sr. and George Jr. At age five, he was on his way from South Chicago to South Bend to see his first Notre Dame game. He would hold forever the memory of standing outside of Gate 14 as his dad handed him a bag of roasted peanuts and his mother put the Notre Dame pennant in his hand.

Nick could sing the Notre Dame "Victory March" before he could read *Fun with Dick and Jane*. He knew about Frank Leahy and Johnny Lujack before he could ride a bicycle. When he sat down in the family's seats, the young boy made a promise to himself that he would someday play for the Fighting Irish.

When someone waits so long to fulfill a dream, the senses are elevated. Rassas could see and hear everything at once. He was standing at the south end of Notre Dame Stadium before the start of the Purdue game, preparing for pregame warmups. Seventeen years had passed since the first time he set eyes on the place. It was more beautiful than ever. In the distance, he could see the Golden Dome shining. His eyes now were fixed on a scene of Jesus Christ just beyond the north wall of the stadium. Jesus was standing tall with raised arms. He loomed above the disciples.

A few months earlier, a mural entitled the "Word of Life" had been un-veiled on the south side of the new Memorial Library. Constructed of granite, it was 134 feet tall and 68 feet wide. Like many Domers, Rassas thought that Jesus seemed to be signaling a touchdown. Before long, ev-ery student at Notre Dame was calling it "Touchdown Jesus." Ironically, the $200,000 gift for "Touchdown Jesus" was made by Mr. and Mrs. Howard Phalanx of Winnetka, Illinois, Nick's hometown.

Rassas could feel his heart kick into gear as the Notre Dame band marched into the stadium and cranked out the "Victory March." He began to sing, "Cheer, cheer for Old Notre Dame. Wake up the echoes cheering her name."

It was like watching a movie of his life. In the distance, sitting in a box in Section 29, he could see his mother and father standing and wav-ing. He remembered his father's words when it seemed Nick would never make the team. "A bear never leaves the woods with honey in the trees," George Rassas wrote in a letter. He also penned these words: "Remem-ber what Lombardi said. A winner never quits, and a quitter never wins."

An hour until kickoff and already the fans were chanting, "Rassas! Rassas! Knock 'em on their asses!" That is when Rassas saw Purdue as-sistant coach Lenny Jardine walking toward him with an outstretched hand.

Rassas and Jardine never thought they would see this day. Jardine coached Nick in high school and then practically begged the kid to fol-low him to Purdue. Head coach Jack Mollenkopf had offered a scholar-ship and pledged a starting role by his junior year. But Nick was too stubborn—"I am going to Notre Dame. Period. End of story." Jardine lit out for Purdue, his alma mater, sixty miles south of Notre Dame, then waited to read in the newspaper that Rassas was climbing his way to-ward stardom. He waited three years and it still did not happen. He heard that Nick was cut from the team, then received some kind of re-prieve.

After almost three years on the bench, Rassas was finally standing in the sunlight. Jardine strode toward him and grabbed Nick's hand.

"Nick, Nick, you made it," he said.

"Coach, a lot of people told me that I'd never get this far," he said. "They said I'd never walk into Notre Dame Stadium wearing a Notre Dame uniform."

"Nick, I am proud of you. I still wish you'd gone to Purdue with me. You'd gotten to play a lot earlier, but time doesn't matter when you reach your dream."

Rassas's eyes were filling with tears as he shook hands with Jardine.

"Coach, I gotta go warm up. See you after the game."

As he ran up the field, a million images seemed to pass through his mind. He could remember sitting in the stadium for the first time back in 1947 and watching Lujack in a leather helmet slinging the ball to his receivers. He could still see the punter booming the ball high and deep. At that moment, Rassas looked up into a bright blue sky. A spiraling football turned over in midflight and dived straight down into his arms. He was already running, then ducking, then dodging, and cutting up the sideline en route to the end zone. His legs felt strong, his spirit free.

As he trotted back up the field, Rassas saw Ara Parseghian, eyes ablaze, swaggering toward him with the energy of a twenty-year-old.

"Nick, be ready for anything today," the coach said. "I know you didn't get to play much on offense last week, but you'll carry the ball a lot today. You'll be starting at safety again. You'll be returning punts. I need you today, Nick. This is a tough Purdue team."

As Parseghian walked away, Rassas thought about the biggest day of his life. *Be careful*, he told himself. A few weeks earlier, he had suffered what appeared to be an emotional breakdown. Right in the middle of a practice, he pulled off his helmet and started to cry. Then he started shaking. Defensive secondary coach Paul Shoults approached and said, "What's wrong, Nick?"

"Coach, I am like an overtuned race car," he said. "You don't know what this opportunity means to me. I've worked all of my life for this. I think I might have worked too hard."

"Nick, you don't look too good."

"I've been running and lifting weights and working on a ranch and busting my ass. Fact is, Coach, I'm stressed. I feel like my heart is about to pop. I'm ready for the season to start."

Shoults put his hand on Rassas's shoulder. "Stay right there. Don't move. I'll be right back."

The coach sprinted over to Parseghian for a quick conversation. Then he sprinted right back.

"Nick, Coach Parseghian wants you to take the day off. Go take a stroll through the bookstore. Take a walk around the lake. But don't come back till tomorrow."

"Thanks, Coach, I hope you understand—"

"Say no more, Nick. Now get your ass out of here."

Nick walked away in tears. He would return the next day with a new fire.

THE WHOLE WORLD was now watching Notre Dame. Suddenly the matchup with Purdue was the biggest game of the year—in Week 2, no less. It seemed that only yesterday the sporting press was writing off Notre Dame.

But two days following the monster win over Wisconsin, Notre Dame had climbed all the way to No. 9 in both the AP and UPI polls. Teams rarely get that kind of respect after being shut out of the preseason polls. Based on what had been written and said, the Fighting Irish were no better than 50 to 1 to crack the top 10—even by the end of the season.

Most of the players knew why they were sitting at No. 9. It was preparation, preparation, and more preparation. Parseghian and staff were relentless, and they were not letting up. When the players gathered for Sunday dinner following the Wisconsin win, they were handed a twenty-page breakdown on Purdue. It included formations, tendencies, schemes, and special team alignments. It included everything but the color of the Boilermakers' eyes.

That night, Ken Maglicic thumbed through the poop sheet, then turned to Norm Nicola. "I have never seen anything like this in my whole life."

"I bet that no team in the country gets this kind of information," Nicola said. "This means the coaches were up all night after we got back from Wisconsin. Man!"

Some of the pregame facts concerning Notre Dame–Purdue were startling. The Boilermakers had not lost a game at Notre Dame Stadium since 1951, beating the Irish in seven of the last ten games.

Purdue held another advantage that worried Parseghian. Two years earlier, quarterback Bob Griese had been one of the most highly recruited quarterbacks in the Midwest. He grew up in Evansville, Indiana, situated on the gentle horseshoe bend of the Ohio River, right across from the Kentucky border. He spent a good part of his youth listening to the Irish games on the radio and dreamed of being the next Paul Hornung. It was easy for Griese to indentify with Hornung since he grew up sixty miles away in Louisville. All Griese wanted in life was to play for the Fighting Irish, and he was pleased when Hughie Devore started to recruit him. Without warning, though, Devore pulled the scholarship offer a week before the signing date. A broken-hearted Griese settled on Purdue.

As the Purdue players warmed up that day in their white jerseys and gold helmets, Parseghian set his eyes on Griese. This was going to be a difficult assignment, especially with an inexperienced secondary. A week earlier, the Irish had shut down Wisconsin, but most of the heavy lifting was done by a defensive line that sacked Harold Brandt 8 times.

Purdue's offensive line was both talented and experienced, and Parseghian could tell from warm-ups that Griese possessed a quick release. Defensive coordinator John Ray, just as he had done against Wisconsin, had devised an attacking game plan. The Irish would blitz often from the 4-4-3 scheme.

THE DAY BEFORE the Purdue game, Parseghiean could barely believe his eyes and ears as he walked into the Old Fieldhouse and the players filed in behind him.

From the balcony on the north side of the antique building, they all looked down on an organized chaos that no other university in America could match. Students were hanging from the rafters. They were crawling up on each other's shoulders. The real daredevils climbed all the way to the top to create a third level. Toilet paper flew everywhere, and the rafters were now festooned with it. In all, more than 10,000 students and fans were crammed into the Old Fieldhouse, built in 1898 to hold 2,000.

Tom Pagna wrote in *Era of Ara,* "We could have flipped a dime from the balcony where the players sat and it would have never reached the ground; the people were packed that tightly."

But there was more to come. Just then, the Notre Dame Marching Band broke through the side door, belting out the "Victory March."

Tom Pagna leaned into Parseghian's ear. "Ever wonder what might happen if food poisoning broke out around this place?"

"No," Parseghian said with a quizzical expression.

"Look around. All the toilet paper on campus is now hanging from those rafters," Pagna said, smiling.

It was an unwritten rule that every student had to attend the pep rallies. The no-shows would be dragged from the dorm, hauled down to St. Mary's Lake, and thrown in. Notre Dame had no fraternities, so the dorms were left to replace the Greek system's wacky ideas on good, clean fun.

Students spent a good part of the day getting ready for the pep rallies as they painted their faces and chests. They spent hours on banners. One that had been unfurled at the back of the arena read RAY'S RAIDERS LYNCH GRIESE. John Huarte and Jack Snow might have grabbed most of the headlines, but defense was still all the rage with the students. On game days, the defensive unit received a standing ovation every time they trotted onto the field.

As the band continued to play, several students ripped off their shirts to reveal GO IRISH! in green paint across their chests. Then everyone began to chant, "We want Ara! We want Ara!"

It was Frank Gaul's duty to introduce Parseghian. Gaul was the senior chairman of the pep rally committee and had prepared a cute speech, but when the masses began to chant "Ara! Ara! Ara!," Gaul knew to introduce the star and to get out of the way.

Parseghian stepped toward the microphone. The chant grew louder: "We want Ara! We want Ara! *We want Ara!*"

Parseghian cleared his throat and said, "We wanted to bring you a winner."

They shouted back, "You did! You did! You did!"

Parseghian stepped back, paused, and tried to clear his head. One victory over Wisconsin and the starved faithful were going bananas. They practically drowned him out every time he tried to speak that day. Even though he was standing on a second-floor balcony, he found himself eyeball to eyeball with the kids at the top of the pyramids. He could only laugh and try to yell over them.

By the time he finished speaking, Parseghian felt warm all over. He knew inside of his soul that this was where he was supposed to be. And the best was yet to come.

BY DAWN THE next morning, he wasn't so sure.

His excitement leading to the Purdue game had turned to anxiety and stress. Most of the night he had walked the anxious floor. The team had spent Friday night at Moreau Seminary on the opposite side of the lake from campus, away from the excitement that was building for the season's first home game. Energy on campus was almost palpable as the out-of-town fans started to arrive.

Moreau Seminary was the perfect place to rest and relax for the big game. It was built to hold four hundred seminarians, but attendance was now closer to seventy-five. Every player and coach would have his own room. They watched a movie the night before the game and hit the sack early.

All but Parseghian. His mind was still racing at the crack of dawn, and, as the sky turned pink beyond the lake cedars, he took off for a walk. A nip of autumn was in the air. He had some thinking to do.

Parseghian decided to take a long, slow stroll around St. Mary's Lake. On these shores, a young French priest named Father Edward Sorin had built a cabin to house himself and the Six Brothers of St. Joseph's in the hard winter of 1842. Father Sorin had been dispatched by the C.S.C.—Congregatio a Sancta Cruce (Congregation of the Holy Cross). He had come to America to continue the work of the missionaries who had worked to convert the Miami and Potawatomi Indians to Christianity. In 1685, Father Claude-Jean Allouez had established a mission post on the shores of St. Mary's Lake known as the St. Joseph

Mission. Nearly two centuries later, thanks to the work of the missionaries, Father Sorin was shipped to America to build a school called
L'Universite de Notre Dame du Lac.

Father Sorin, like many pioneers in the wilderness, was a visionary
with grand dreams. Believing the place should be independent and self-
sustaining, he first cobbled together a stable and a bakery and, when
winter finally broke, his flock began to farm the land. Sacrifices and
hardships were never-ending. The Civil War brought more issues, and
Father Sorin soon dispatched Father William Corby, C.S.C, to become
a chaplain for the Union's Army Brigade.

Over the years, Notre Dame had survived long, frigid winters and
hot summer droughts. At first, there was no money and few students. Desperate for finances, Father Sorin sent some of the brothers and laymen to
California in 1850 to dig for gold. Most of them never returned.

The majority of Father Sorin's students could not even speak English, but he was determined to make the experiment work through
sheer willpower. He was convinced that the Virgin Mary had summoned him to America to accomplish his work. Some said he was capable of pettiness and ruthlessness, but no one ever doubted his courage.
When the Main Building on campus was destroyed by fire in 1889, he
vowed to rebuild it. This was accomplished in a matter of months. To an
extent, Father Sorin was a precursor to the hard-willed Knute Rockne,
minus all of the bluster.

As Parseghian moved slowly around the lake and watched the sun
break over the horizon, he thought about the wonderful history of Notre
Dame. He thought about Rockne and all that he had accomplished in
the 1920s. It seemed hard to believe that he was now standing in the
midst of such a historical place. He wondered if he belonged there. The
issue of not being Catholic still bothered him. The words of Father Edmund Joyce rang in his head: *Ara, religion is not an issue here. Do not
worry that you are not part of the Catholic faith.* Still, he could not help
but think about it.

As he listened to the birds sing and watched the sun climb higher in
the sky, Parseghian allowed many thoughts to cross his mind. Already, he
had reawakened the echoes. He had lifted their hopes and expectations.

What if he failed them? What if the Fighting Irish lost that afternoon to Purdue? Finally, he said to himself, "It's not going to happen. *Never* going to happen."

He looked into the sky and said, "Father, I hope that I am worthy. Because, by God, I am here for the long haul."

A few minutes later, after circling the lake, he walked back in the Moreau Seminary and into the dining hall where the players were enjoying breakfast. He looked around and smiled. He was home. It was time to play football.

Chapter 20

SHAKE DOWN THE THUNDER

A football sailed high against the hard blue sky and into the arms of Joe Kantor. The big fullback returned it to the 27-yard line.

On the first two plays, a crowd of 59,677 was on its feet as big Joe Farrell gained 6 yards on 2 carries. On third down, John Huarte arced a high spiral toward Nick Eddy down the left sideline. Eddy dropped it. Everyone knew he had a clear shot to the end zone, but he *dropped* it. The fans groaned and wondered if the Irish were returning to their dismal past. The sight of Jack Snow retreating into punt formation seemed quite sobering. Was this 1963 all over again?

Everyone knew that Purdue quarterback Bob Griese might be the second coming of Otto Graham. The previous week against Ohio, he had scored all 17 points—2 rushing touchdowns, 2 extra point kicks, and a field goal. So when Griese sneaked for 10 yards on Purdue's first possession, the crowd grew even more nervous.

Two plays later, Griese was introduced to the dogged Notre Dame pass rush and forced to throw off his back foot. The pass wobbled straight into the arms of cornerback Tom Longo, and he took off down the left sideline with room to run. Griese hit Longo at the 25, knocking the ball loose as the crowd groaned once more. Purdue's Dennis Pabich recovered and the Boilermakers were back in business.

Everyone in the stadium knew that Griese would be looking for his favorite receiver, Bob Hadrick, and the two quickly connected to the Purdue 41. Johnny Ray decided to counter with a blitz, sending outside linebacker Jim Lynch from the left side and Jim Carroll shooting up the middle. End Alan Page bull-rushed the left tackle. Now Lynch, Carroll, and Page were in the Purdue backfield, bearing down on Griese, but the sophomore quarterback coolly retreated two steps and arced another wobbler down the middle. Teter caught it at the Irish 17 and was tackled by Tom Kostelnik. Notre Dame Stadium fell silent once more.

Fullback Bill Harmon took the pitch around right end all the way to the Notre Dame 7. He carried three more times to the 1. On fourth down, Griese shuffled two steps to his right and dived between center and guard into the end zone. He also added the extra point kick for a 7–0 lead.

Neither team could move the ball on the next two possessions, and Nick Rassas set up at the Notre Dame 30 to return a punt. He felt his heart shift gears as the ball sailed toward him. Catching it on the run, he broke two tacklers and carried all the way to midfield. That is when he felt his breathing accelerate. The anxiety attacks in recent weeks were coming more frequently, and Rassas knew why. Waiting three years for this one chance to prove himself had turned him into a ball of nerves. Running toward the sideline, he began to hyperventilate again. He felt his chest rise and fall as his breathing ran away with him. He was dizzy and light-headed, and the entire stadium was turning white. One of the trainers instantly diagnosed the problem.

"Get the oxygen bottle fast," he yelled. "Nick needs it bad."

The trainers normally kept one oxygen bottle on the sideline. They had recently added a second just for Rassas.

Parseghian hustled over to the bench to check on his player.

"Are you okay, Nick?" he said. "You don't look too good."

Rassas pulled the oxygen mask from his mouth. "Same old crap, Coach," he said. "I'll be okay when I get my breath."

In a matter of minutes, he was ready to play again.

On the first play after Rassas's punt return, Huarte found Jack Snow open over the middle to the 25. Huarte wasted not a play hitting Snow again, and this time luck was on his side. The ball bounced off the hands of linebacker Randy Minniear at the 7 and straight into the arms of Snow at the 3. On the next play, taking the pitch around right end, Bill Wolksi rumbled untouched into the end zone. The score was tied 7–7.

Griese, again under pressure, was intercepted at the Notre Dame 47 by Longo. A screen pass to Joe Farrell down the sideline worked beautifully as he followed two crushing blocks by left tackle Bob Meeker and center Norm Nicola. A third-down pass to Rassas kept the drive going at the 9-yard line. Purdue should have figured what was coming next— Huarte to Snow for 5 yards, followed by the same hookup for the touchdown.

Still, the 14–7 halftime lead still did not set well with Parseghian. The strong-armed Griese was enough to worry anyone, and Purdue had more offensive yards than Notre Dame at half. Before starting the chalk talk at halftime, Parseghian approached Johnny Ray.

"Look, I think we should try to block a punt early in the third quarter," he said. "See if you can pull it off."

Ray knew he could. End Phil Sheridan had come within inches of blocking a punt against Wisconsin the previous week, and during the practices leading to the Purdue game, Ray had worked on countless schemes. Ken Maglicic had come within a heartbeat of blocking a punt against the Boilermakers in the second quarter. Now Ray had the right one in mind. Again, Maglicic would be the key to making it happen. Lining up at right guard, Maglicic got a jump on the snap and was almost flagged for being offsides. He slammed into Purdue center Larry Kaminsky, pushing him to the left, as 6'5" tackle Kevin Hardy followed him through the hole—almost like a running back. Hardy had a clear path into the backfield and smothered the punt attempt by Russ Pfahler as the ball shot straight up.

Sitting in the south end-zone stands, watching it all unfold, Charlie Kenny jumped to his feet. Kenny had the perfect view of the play, and from the moment the ball was snapped, he knew that Hardy had a chance.

Kenny was back at Notre Dame Stadium for the first time since the fall of 1962, his senior year. He was wearing a worn cap from his student days, with N.D. sewn onto the front. He was sitting next to his favorite uncle, Bill Kenny, who had taken Charlie countless times to the Brooklyn Dodgers games at Ebbets Field. Uncle Bill had once pitched against the great Satchel Paige in an exhibition game and knew more about sports than anyone Charlie knew.

The previous day, Charlie had traveled to South Bend from Worcester, Massachusetts, where he was working on his Ph.D. in psychology at Clark College. Nothing felt better than being back at Notre Dame and sitting in his favorite stadium. The 1963 season had caused him great pain. This was his first live game since watching the depressing loss to Syracuse ten months earlier at Yankee Stadium.

Kenny, along with nearly 60,000 others, was on his feet as the blocked punt sailed high and tumbled end over end into the long arms of Alan Page. The defensive end gathered the ball at the Purdue 49 and took off in a gallop. After three strides, no one could believe how fast the big man was running.

Kenny grabbed his uncle by the shoulder and yelled, "Look at Ara!"

Sprinting down the sideline, matching Page stride for stride, was Parseghian, his arms pumping wildly like a drum major. The coach leaped high and threw a left-right combination that might have felled anyone in his wake.

"Ara Parseghian is the happiest man in America right now," Kenny yelled. "Who could blame him!"

Watching the large and athletic Alan Page bounding for the end zone would have made any coach happy. The only flaw was that Page carried the ball loosely in his right arm. Running behind him, Maglicic yelled, "Tuck the ball, you big sonofabitch! Tuck the ball!" But there was little doubt he was going to make it. Page, swallowing the ground with every step, covered the 49 yards in only twenty strides.

"That's the fastest I've ever seen anyone run in this stadium in my life!" Kenny howled.

Moments after the play, Maglicic and Hardy knelt down next to each other on the Notre Dame sideline. Both felt relieved.

Maglicic smiled. "I was beginning to wonder if we were going to hold Purdue off. I'm damned glad you blocked that punt."

The sensational play by Hardy tilted all of the momentum to Notre Dame. Early in the fourth quarter, Pete Andreotti took a wide pitch around right end, swiveled to the inside, and broke through a corridor of seven Purdue players 22 yards to the end zone.

Midway in the fourth quarter, Jack Snow's quick kick bounded along benignly inside the 10-yard line when Purdue defensive back Charlie King mistakenly concluded it was necessary to pounce on the ball. King exacerbated his error by knocking the ball into the arms of Phil Sheridan at the three.

On the next play, Rassas lined up in the left slot. This was the play he had been waiting for all of his life. He knew the ball was coming his way. Snow was lined up farther to the outside and drew coverage from two defensive backs. Rassas made a quick cut to the middle of the end zone and Huarte's pass was on the mark. The back judge signaled touchdown and Rassas flipped him the ball, then looked up into the stadium to the seats where he had watched his first Notre Dame game seventeen years ago. His mother and father were cheering and waving, along with several friends and relatives. He knew that his brother George Jr., listening to the game at the seminary, would be proud. A few years earlier, George Jr. had decided he wanted to be a priest.

Instead of angling for the sideline, Rassas took off straight up the field. He wanted to finish crying before coaches and teammates could see him. Tears were streaming down his face so rapidly that his jersey was getting wet. As he turned toward the Notre Dame bench, Rassas could see Parseghian waiting with a wide grin on his face. The coach extended his right hand.

"Coach, all I've ever wanted to do in my whole life is to play for Notre Dame and score a touchdown," Rassas said. "You will never know how much this means to me."

Parseghian clasped him on the shoulder. "Nick, son, you are a fine football player. There are going to be plenty more touchdowns for you."

Purdue scored a meaningless touchdown in the final minutes, and the score of 34–15 was as impressive as it looked. Six more receptions for Snow brought his season total to 15 and his 2 touchdown receptions upped that total to four. Tony Carey grabbed his third interception of the season and Tom Longo added 2 more.

After the game, Charlie Kenny ran to the pay phone to call one of his former classmates, Bob Krug from Long Island, now living in South Bend.

"Bob, can you believe the turnaround?" Kenny yelled into the phone. "Can you believe that we've now got one of the best teams in the country?"

Later that night, Bill Gleason sat down to type his lead for Sunday's edition in the *Chicago's American*:

"They were singing the old songs last night in the hotels and motels where Notre Dame alumni and ladies gathered to lift a glass to Ara Parseghian and his football men."

They had waited a long time to celebrate.

Chapter 21

LETTER FROM HOME

George and Frances Rassas experienced the most joyous ride of all back to Chicago after the game. They talked about all of the things that Nick had overcome to become a starter on the Notre Dame team. They recalled how their son at age five proudly announced that he would someday play football for Notre Dame. The process had been long and difficult with many sacrifices. Most people would have given up, but not this Rassas kid. He would have endured the pain until he finally walked across the stage at the Convocation Center and picked up his Notre Dame diploma. Then he would have strolled off as a proud fifth-stringer, saying that he had given it his best. He would have harbored no bitterness.

As the South Shore Line of the Illinois Central rumbled on toward Chicago that night, Frances said to George, "Did you ever think that Doc was ever going to make it?" She called her son "Doc" because she dreamed he might someday become a successful medical doctor, like her father, Dr. Walter McGuire, an Irish immigrant who rose up to become one of the most successful in Chicago.

"I knew that Doc would never quit," George said. "When you've got that kind of fortitude, anything can happen. I think we can thank God and I think we can thank Ara Parseghian for Doc reaching his dream. I think that if Ara had never come along, this would never have happened."

Frances Rassas spent the next two days thinking about the obstacles her son had overcome. He had been a tough little rascal as a kid. She knew that nothing would ever stop him. When she tried to cut him off at the pass, he would say, "Oh, come on, Grandma, let me have some fun."

Frances could accept being called Grandma as long as she could call him Doc.

On Monday morning, October 6th, two days after the Purdue game, Frances Rassas sat down and wrote this letter to her son:

My Dearest Nick,

Since you started at Notre Dame, I've written you a few letters. Most were sent to try and encourage you when everything turned so hopeless. Today I take my pen in hand and hope I can express the pride and gratitude I feel in my heart for you.

You have always been a son to be proud of. I admit that when you and George were small you gave me a run for my money in painting the car pink—wetting a week's wash so it had to be done over again—finding, after searching your room because of a strange odor, a dead bird under your shirts—discovering a dead snake in your suitcase of treasures (nails, stones, sticks, string). Teaching you to read—"could and would." So many happy memories and I can honestly say you have never done anything to cause me a moment's anxiety.

You have worked against every odd to achieve your goal. Nick, you are a real Notre Dame man. You never would have gone anywhere else.

When I saw you run on that field to take part in your first home game, I thought my heart would burst with pride. When you scored, the tears came out but good. You looked so much like Dad out there that I couldn't get over it. The two of us waited until the crowd left and stood hand in hand listening to the band. I looked up at Dad and he had that proud look on his face and of course the tears were streaming down my face.

I am grateful to you, Doc (excuse the expression) for having the guts to stick it out. You are not a quitter. You have learned your lesson: "Nothing worthwhile ever comes easy."

Never forget to thank God and Our Lady for what they have done for you. Promise me, Doc, you will never change.

I love you, Grandma

P.S. Thanks for not leading the band.

Chapter 22

CRASH LANDING

Physical condition + desire + team loyalty + spirit = victories.

—PARSEGHIAN'S PRESEASON LETTER

All of the formulas were clicking. The hard work was paying off. Late hours inside the coaching offices at the Rockne Memorial were reaping terrific game plans. After pulverizing Purdue, the Fighting Irish rose to No. 6 in the Associated Press poll released on October 5.

The new top 10:

1. Texas
2. Illinois
3. Alabama
4. Ohio State
5. Kentucky
6. Notre Dame
7. Michigan
8. Nebraska
9. Michigan State
10. Arkansas

Everything was sailing along beautifully until the phone rang at the football fieldhouse and Parseghian was summoned.

He picked up the phone and could not believe what he was hearing: "Coach, this is the airport calling. Your chartered plane isn't here, and I have no idea when it will be. We'll have to reschedule you."

Parseghian wanted to slam the phone back into the wall mounting. Instead, he began to shout so loudly that the players wondered if he really needed the telephone anymore. "You've got to be kidding me," he yelled. "What is this? Some kind of a *joke*?"

"No sir," he said. "I just wanted to give you a little heads-up, that's all."

"Heads-up, my ass," Parseghian shouted.

In exactly one hour, the Fighting Irish were scheduled to take off from St. Joseph's County Airport en route to Colorado Springs for a game the next day against the Air Force Academy. The plan was to have a walk-through at the stadium late that afternoon, because Parseghian wanted his team to become accustomed to the playing surface and to adjust to the altitude—which was not a realistic expectation in one day.

No one loved a plan better than Parseghian. He was constantly thinking, working, trying to find a better way. Now a week's worth of work had been blown to smithereens.

To keep the players calm, they were bussed to a local theater. The only movie playing was *The Ten Commandments*, and this excited them almost as much as the Sunday Benediction. They were so bored with Charlton Heston as Moses that most were asleep when the lights went up an hour later and Parseghian announced that the jet was now ready for takeoff.

They were bussed out to the airport and upon arrival found the airline pilot wearing a long face.

"Coach, the darn thing is broken down," he said. "It will take at least an hour or so. I don't know what to do."

Joe Farrell spoke up. "We could always go back to the theater and watch the *The Ten Commandments*." Everyone laughed but Parseghian.

A couple of hours later, the Lockheed Electric with four engines was ready to go. The plane lifted off at five o'clock that afternoon and the trip was going smoothly until they crossed over the Rocky Mountains and turbulence caused the plane to dip two hundred feet in a matter of seconds. The sound of forty football players screaming at the top of their lungs was a bit strange, but no one would ever forget the sight of ticket manager Bob Cahill exiting the rear restroom. He threw up all over himself. Cahill actually laughed. Then he said, "Well, it's a good thing this suit is a two-panter."

Colorado Springs, situated on the eastern edge of the southern Rocky Mountains, is one of the most picturesque cities in America. The elevation at the center of town is 6,050 feet, but the peaks are normally 3,000 feet higher. As the Lockheed glided over the mountains, Parseghian leaned against the window for a look at the runway. He wondered what possibly could go wrong next. What he saw, though, made him smile. Two buses were parked on the tarmac. At least Notre Dame would have a ride to the hotel.

Parseghian knew that the Broadmoor Hotel was one of the leading resorts in the country. Too bad he couldn't have brought his golf clubs along. Waltzing his two handicap onto one of the resort's challenging golf courses would have been invigorating.

As the bus moved closer to the Broadmoor, Parseghian was finally beginning to relax, until the bus driver completely bypassed the resort and started to circle around Cheyenne Lake.

"Where are you going, busie," said Parseghian, sitting on the front row.

"Oh, you guys are staying around back," the bus driver said. "They didn't tell you?"

"What do you mean we're around back? We've got reservations at the Broadmoor Hotel."

"Sorry, Coach. They don't have any rooms in the Broadmoor."

"Around back" meant that the team was headed for the rodeo grounds. The smell as they stepped off the bus could have choked a mule. It was like driving straight into the Chicago stockyards. Parseghian instantly knew this was never going to work. He grabbed Charlie Callahan by the arm and the public relations man grimaced.

"Look, you've got to fix this, Charlie," he said. "My guys aren't smelling cow manure all night. This is one of the biggest games of the year."

"I don't know," Callahan said. "They didn't tell me anything about this."

As they checked into their little cabins out back, the players seemed happy. Some of the Chicago kids had never been around horses. This was almost like going to a dude ranch.

"Hey, Goose," Tony Carey said to Rassas. "You've got to feel right at home. We'll saddle you up a bronc and let you ride. This has got to look just like Wyoming."

"Right you are, Topcat," Rassas said.

Before the buses pulled away Parseghian decided to take matters into his own hands. This was no job for a public relations man and, besides, he was in charge here. He reboarded the lead bus and rode back around the lake to the hotel lobby. What the coach heard from the hotel manager was the same excuse delivered by the bus driver. There were no regular rooms available.

"Okay, then put my players in the suites," he said.

"We don't have enough available," the manager said.

"I'm not talking about one per room. We can put as many as five players in a suite. Just get the suites ready."

"Will do, Mr. Parseghian."

With darkness settling over the city, it was too late to bus over to the stadium for a walk-through. This mystified Parseghian, who dreaded the thought of walking cold into a strange stadium an hour before kick-off the next day. Falcon Stadium was located at the base of Rampart Range with an elevation of 6,621 feet. He had heard that the Air Force crowds could be wild and raucous, and that the mile-high altitude would suck the oxygen straight out of his players' lungs in the fourth quarter.

Parseghian had worried about this matchup from the minute he had set eyes on the 1964 schedule. The previous season, Air Force finished 7-3 while defeating two top teams, Washington and UCLA, scoring 48 points on the Bruins. The Falcons boasted a fast, versatile offense. Parseghian had written this evaluation of Air Force in his preseason letter: "This is a dangerous football team. I just returned from the Academy and saw with my own eyes their tremendous conditioning program. We will need to prepare for the altitude."

The Falcons had made huge strides since starting their football program in 1956. The team was initially coached by Buck Shaw, who had played on Knute Rockne's first undefeated team in 1919. He would leave Air Force to coach the Philadelphia Eagles all the way to the NFL championship in 1960, thus becoming the only coach to ever defeat Vince Lombardi in a championship game.

Shaw's departure opened the door for Ben Martin, a flamboyant coach with a passion for wide-open football. The academy was forced to recruit smaller players due to size restrictions for pilots. So Martin took his little players and designed an offense with receivers darting all over the field. Remarkably, Air Force finished 9-0-1 in his first season and tied No. 10–ranked TCU 0–0 in the Cotton Bowl. Over the next six years, Martin's teams would defeat five more top 10 teams. Up next was No. 6 Notre Dame, and the entire town, the entire state, could not wait to unleash their hate on the mighty Fighting Irish.

The night before the game, Parseghian was more nervous than an expectant father. The airplane breakdown and then the hotel disaster had done nothing for his mood, and he wondered what could go wrong next.

He said to Tom Pagna, "We've got to do something to get this team calmed down. They need to relax."

"Ara, I don't know if you've checked lately, but I don't think our players could be any more relaxed. I have never seen a more confident bunch of kids in my life."

Pagna wanted to tell his boss to calm down, but the timing was not right.

PARSEGHIAN TURNED THE corner the next morning and strode into the banquet room, where the players were eating breakfast. His coffee count was already at five cups. He thought he was going to blow a gasket when he saw what the players were eating. Instead of piles of steak and bacon— protein builders—they were chowing down on pancakes and fruit.

"What the hell is going on here?" he demanded for everyone to hear. "Can someone please find the hotel manager for me?"

A stooped man with a pale complexion walked slowly through the door. He was the same sad figure who had incurred the coach's wrath the previous night.

"Mr. Parseghian, what's wrong now?" he asked.

"Nothing, besides you poisoning my boys' bodies. Can you please get some steak and baked potatoes over here so my players can have some energy today?"

"Right away, sir," he said, pivoting on his heel and speeding away.

Thirty minutes later, all the players and coaches—including the non-Catholics—walked into Mass together. Standing at the front of the room was a dark-robed priest whom Parseghian did not recognize. He had specifically requested a priest from Notre Dame, but not this man.

"Our priest somehow missed his flight," Charlie Callahan said. "We will have to go with this guy."

Parseghian just shook his head, knowing it would be rude to raise hell at Mass.

A kneeler had been set up in the front for the players to pray and take sacrament. The first to kneel were Paul Costa and Tom Regner, a combined 500 pounds of muscle and bulk. Under that weight the kneeler collapsed, throwing bodies and dust in all directions. The players laughed. Parseghian did not.

Fifteen minutes later, as Mass ended, the players were walking toward the lobby when Parseghian said, "Let's get out of this hotel. I think it's a jinx. Let's jump on the buses and ride over to the stadium and get ready to play some football."

They strolled outside into the bright Colorado sunshine with the mountains all around them. They breathed the refreshing morning air. They would be fine, Parseghian said to himself. Then he looked around and realized the buses were nowhere in sight.

Parseghian walked back into the hotel but could not find the manager. Callahan was quickly on the phone to the bus company, but another thirty minutes would pass before they were rolling toward the stadium—with no police escort.

A few miles down the highway, the buses were soon idling at a dead stop. They were already stuck in stadium traffic with Air Force fans all around them. Football mania had gripped the city six years earlier when Air Force completed an undefeated season, but nothing could compare to the day that Notre Dame came to town. The biggest crowd in the history of Falcon Stadium was expected. Parseghian checked his watch. Teams normally arrived at least ninety minutes before kickoff, but the Fighting Irish would be lucky to make it a half hour ahead of the game.

As they inched toward the stadium, Parseghian instructed the bus driver to let the players walk the final half mile. They were hurrying over a hill toward the stadium when they encountered a mob. Actually, it was 750 Notre Dame students who had flown in from South Bend for the game. At the moment, the Domers were standing about fifty yards from an Air Force pep rally, taunting the crowd and hurling insults.

As the players moved toward them, one of the Notre Dame students yelled, "Look, there's our football team."

"Can't be," one of them said. "They should've been here over an hour ago."

"Looks like we beat 'em here," another one said.

Tony Carey surveyed the long line of Domers atop the hill and said, "It looks like the Irish army ready to attack."

By the time the team reached the dressing room, they had twenty minutes to dress and get onto the field. The referee would provide no extra time.

"It's not my fault you're late," he told the coaches. "If you wanted to warm up, you should've gotten here an hour ago."

The team squeezed in about ten minutes of warm-ups before Ken Ivan placed the ball on the tee and booted it through the end zone. On their first possession, Air Force moved the ball to the Notre Dame 44, where they were forced to punt. The ball bounced out of bounds at the 6.

John Huarte, shaky on his first play, fired a bullet far over the head of Jack Snow, who was so wide open at the Notre Dame 45 that he might have scored. Nick Eddy gained 2 yards off right tackle. On third down, Air Force defensive end Miles Clay was not blocked and he roared into the backfield. Clay clamped an arm around Huarte's waist as he uncorked a high wobbler that sailed over Snow's head and into the arms of cornerback Jeff Jarvis, who beat a straight path to the end zone. For the second straight week, the Irish were down 7–0 early.

As Huarte ran past Parseghian on the sideline, the coach said, "Don't worry about it, John. It's way, way, way too early to worry about it."

For the past nine months, Parseghian had religiously studied a talented but somewhat troubled Nick Eddy. Like Carey, he had been suspended from Notre Dame a year earlier for what amounted to be a dorm prank. Eddy went home to California during his suspension and, like

Carey, turned down offers from other schools. Instead, he went to work for a few months and returned to South Bend.

Eddy was a long-striding slasher with a quick burst. He could not be stopped in the open field by one man. That said, Parseghian often found Eddy to be laconic and unfocused.

Late in the first quarter, with Notre Dame trailing 7–0 and the crowd growing louder, Air Force was beginning to believe they could play with the sixth-ranked team in the country. The Falcons' undersized lines were holding their ground against the likes of Dick Arrington, Alan Page, and Tom Regner.

The time had come to find out what Eddy could do. At the Air Force 46, the Irish lined up in the power I formation with Farrell at fullback, Eddy as the I back, and Bill Wolski at right halfback. The play was called 41 trap, and center Norm Nicola knocked down the right tackle. Farrell eighteen-wheeled the inside linebacker, and Eddy shot through a hole up the middle. Then he broke to the left sideline, sprinting the 46 yards to the end zone without a hand being placed on him. The game was now tied at 7–7, and the momentum was already turning.

In the second quarter, the Irish started to pound the line with Wolski and Joe Kantor. The offense, now in sync, moved the ball to the Air Force 1-yard line. Huarte stepped into the huddle and said, "Boys just give me a little crease. That's all I need. Quarterback sweep right on two."

Again from the power I formation, Huarte slipped the ball into the belly of Joe Kantor. Half of the Air Force defense jumped on top of him, so Huarte pulled the ball away, rolled around right end behind blocks by Eddy and Wolski, and slid into the end zone. Notre Dame led 14–7 at halftime.

In the third quarter, Eddy killed a drive at the Air Force 21 by fumbling, but the Irish offense from that point forward could count on good field position, thanks to the attacking defense. Linebacker Tom Kostelnik dropped into deep middle for coverage and intercepted Air Force quarterback Tim Murphy's pass and returned it 8 yards to the 37. Huarte completed 2 straight to Snow and then hit a wide-open Wolksi in the left flat as he rumbled down the left sideline 20 yards for the touchdown. The Irish led 21–7 at the end of the third quarter.

One of the best stories in college football became even better on Air Force's next possession. Tony Carey, leading the nation with 3 interceptions, stepped in front of Murphy's pass at the Falcons' 48 and returned it all the way to the 9. Swerving and dodging four tacklers, Carey was reminded of his days at Mount Carmel High when he quarterbacked the Carmelites to the 1960 Chicago City Championship.

Farrell carried the next 3 times, winding up at the 1-foot line. Huarte, on fourth down, sneaked the ball into the end zone behind Nicola and Arrington. The Irish led 28–7.

Murphy, now on a roll, threw his third straight interception on the next play to Rassas, who grabbed the deflected pass at the Air Force 27 and sliced his way down to the 8. On the next play, Huarte flicked his wrist and found Snow wide open in the middle of the end zone. It almost looked too easy.

Leading 34–7, Parseghian took his foot off the accelerator and brought in the second team. Sandy Bonvechio replaced Huarte midway in the fourth quarter as the Irish ran out the clock on the ground. Ten different players carried the ball for Notre Dame, with Wolski again the leading rusher with 14 carries for 86 yards.

Huarte did not need flashy numbers to produce the victory as he completed 7 of 15 passes for 96 yards. Five of those completions were to Jack Snow for 59 yards and a touchdown. It was hard to fathom that one of the worst teams of 1963 had outscored its first three opponents by the aggregate score of 99–29.

To the surprise of everyone, the buses were on time and a police escort was in place. They reached the Colorado Springs airport in about ten minutes. They arrived in South Bend without incident and, remarkably, were on time. As the plane pulled up to the terminal, however, they heard the bad news. A Lockheed Electric filled with Notre Dame students was in trouble. The landing gear was stuck and the airplane was running out of gas. All looked up and could see it circling the airport once more.

"This is really bad," said one of the terminal workers. "A local radio station is actually carrying this live. They might have to crash-land."

Everyone prayed and then held their breath. They could hear the four engines whining as the plane banked once more and this time descended toward the runway. They could hear the screeching of the tires as the plane braked.

"I bet everybody on that plane is scared to death," Bill Wolski said.

Moments later, the plane taxied to the terminal. As the steel stairwell was set into place, the door flew open. In seconds, students were running—almost flying—down the stairs. Their voices could be heard well into the Indiana cornfields.

"We're No. 1! We're No. 1! We're No. 1!"

It seemed that nothing could faze them.

Chapter 23

STEVIE WONDER

Fourteen-year-old Steveland Morris stepped onto the stage at "American Bandstand" in the fall of 1964 wearing a beige suit and a black tie. Since the release of his first album two years earlier, Morris had come a long way. No longer did Motown CEO Berry Gordy need to introduce him as the "Eighth Wonder of the World." He had already changed his name to Stevie Wonder.

That day, Stevie Wonder danced and sang "Fingertips Pt. 1" (*Now I want ya to clap yo' hand, come on!*) as the kids in the audience screamed in ecstasy. He also played the harmonica like he owned it. News was spreading fast, and, before long, a bunch of big, hulking guys at Notre Dame knew all about Stevie Wonder. They saw potential in the name.

Nicknames at Notre Dame in 1964 were not just popular—they were part of the turf. Ken Maglicic became "Binks" when his teammates got word of his childhood obsession with his binkie. Nick Rassas was "Goose" thanks to his long neck. Tony Carey became "Topcat" because it fit his initials and he played like one. Tackle Bob Meeker was "Meeks." His teammates liked to chant it in high squeaky voices: "Meeks! Meeks! "Meeks!" He hated it. Even worse, some called him "Dr. Beeker" and "Jelly Ass."

Guard Dick Arrington was a smiling and cheerful man off the field. But when the team was running gassers one afternoon after practice, Arrington began to grumble loudly on the twelfth trip from goal line to goal line. He stumbled and fell, and when his ample body hit the ground, he laid on his back and yelled, "Oh, Lord, please let me die! Just let me die!" As a result, Arrington got a nickname, "RIP"—standing for "Rest in Peace."

"Bossy the Cow" was still Parseghian's tag, but it was fading fast, thanks to a 3-0 record and a No. 4 ranking in the country. After three games, these were the top five teams in the country:

1. Texas
2. Ohio State
3. Alabama
4. Notre Dame
5. Michigan

No one figured that John Huarte would ever need a nickname. He was smart, studious, and often withdrawn. Not many descriptions fit him. He could be boring. Over the previous three seasons, Huarte hadn't just stood around on the sideline. He had languished in the deepening shadows. His confidence was so completely routed by the end of the 1963 season that he rarely spoke. He was the Marcel Marceau of college football. His teammates knew little about him—just that he hailed from Southern California, which explained his laid-back persona.

Then it happened. Huarte opened the 1964 season passing for 270 yards and 2 touchdowns against Wisconsin—in a driving rainstorm. Then, against Purdue, he passed for 2 more touchdowns and 127 yards. He played only three quarters against Air Force, but completed 2 more TD passes. His 483 yards led the country through three games and was already approaching Notre Dame's passing total for the entire 1963 season. His favorite receiver Jack Snow also led college football with 18 catches.

After much discussion, one day at practice his teammates came up with a nickname for Huarte, but he still could not believe what he was hearing.

"How the hell are you doing there, Stevie Wonder?" asked Nick Rassas.

"What do you mean?" Huarte responded.

"You know, Stevie Wonder. Everybody's heard his songs on the radio. If anybody deserves to be called Stevie Wonder, it's you, buddy!"

Before the next play, Jack Snow stepped into the huddle and said, "So, Stevie, how do you like your new name?"

Huarte shook his head and smiled. "It's a helluva lot better than some I've heard."

In many regards, Huarte was already the Stevie Wonder of college football. He was cool on the field. He dropped into the pocket with rat-a-tat feet and fired the ball on a line. Each game seemed like just another day at the office. His savvy was so evident by the third week that even Parseghian and Tom Pagna were surprised. Overnight he was on the cover of every sports page in the country. His name was being spoken in the same sentence with Paul Hornung and Johnny Lujack. Until the start of the 1964 season, few people could pronounce Huarte (*Hugh*-ert). Now they were pronouncing his name just fine—Stevie Wonder.

One day, while closely observing Huarte in practice, Parseghian turned to Pagna and said, "I never thought he would develop this fast, but don't get me wrong. I'm doggone glad he did."

"Let's just hope that it never ends," Pagna said.

The best way to describe Huarte's throwing motion was to compare him to two latter-day quarterbacks: Joe Montana and Dan Marino. Huarte was lean with quick, intelligent feet, just like Montana. His release was lightning fast and across the body, just like Marino. This combination made him almost lethal against defensive units that were still stacking for the run. In 1964, there was no such thing as the nickel package in the secondary. On most plays, Huarte was throwing against three defensive backs and cutting them to pieces. Few people knew he'd been considered a top major league pitching prospect in high school. Even fewer knew that he'd strengthened his arm on the farm by throwing oranges.

Parseghian knew that Huarte and Snow might rewrite the record book if opposing teams did not adjust quickly. Snow was killing defensive backs on the deep route. Huarte clicked along at 60 percent accuracy with only 1 interception. With only three games under their belts together, Huarte and Snow looked like they had been playing pitch and catch all of their lives.

"Huarte's success is not a great surprise to us," Parseghian told the *Chicago Sun-Times*. "What worried us was when he hurt his shoulder during spring drills. We knew that if he could get past that injury, we might have something. This guy can throw the ball. Man, can the guy throw the football."

Not everyone believed in the Fighting Irish, however. There was great anticipation leading to the UCLA game in the fourth week of the season, but from the opening kickoff at Notre Dame Stadium, it was clear this offensive machine was not about to slow down. Rassas returned the ball to the 37 and Huarte stuck to the ground on 11 straight plays en route to the opening touchdown. It was Joe Farrell right, Nick Eddy left, and Bill Wolski up the middle. Wolski was nicknamed "Muscle Face" because of the hard muscles in his body that seemed to extend through his jaws. He bore a slight resemblance to legendary Chicago Bears fullback Bronko Nagurski. His running style was comparable to the Bronk, who carried the ball as if he were boiling over with rage.

With Notre Dame at the UCLA 15-yard line, Muscle Face carried 6 tough yards for a first down. A couple of plays later, he bowled into the end zone from the 1. After a botched extra point, Notre Dame led 6–0.

In the second quarter, with the ball at the UCLA 37-yard line, Huarte sensed the blitz coming. He made eye contact with end Phil Sheridan and gave him a quick nod. The signal was for Sheridan to run a quick post pattern. Huarte retreated three steps on catlike feet and arced the ball off his back foot to Sheridan, almost 10 yards behind the secondary. A 12–0 lead suited Parseghian just fine, even though both extra points had failed. All week leading up to the game, Parseghian had warned his players about UCLA quarterback Larry Zeno, an All-American candidate who would finish the 1964 season with 1,363 yards and 13 touchdown passes.

Still, against one of the leading defenses in the country, Zeno looked out of place wearing the number 73. His jersey had been left in Los Angeles, so he was forced to wear one of the Notre Dame whites. His wobbly passes seemed the work of a big, clumsy tackle. He did have a handy excuse. Irish linebackers Tom Kostelnik, Ken Maglicic, Jim Carroll, and Jim Lynch spent most of the day in the UCLA backfield, along with defensive end Alan Page. Sacks by Page and Maglicic caused fumbles recovered by Notre Dame. Once again, Johnny Ray's attacking defensive game plan was right on the money.

In the third quarter, Huarte tossed a 16-yard pass to Jack Snow, wide open in the middle of the end zone, but Wolski's dive for the 2-point conversion came up inches short. Then Page's sack of Zeno caused a fumble recovered by Paul Costa. That set up the Notre Dame offense at the UCLA 15. Eddy carried for 5, Farrell for 9, and then Farrell bulled his way into the end zone from the one. With a 24–0 lead, Parseghian could now relax.

Early in the fourth quarter, halfback Denny Conway came trotting onto the field, giving Rassas the thumb.

"You're out," Conway said.

"What do you mean I'm out?" Rassas said.

"Coach can explain it to you."

Rassas felt his heart sinking as he ran to the sideline. He believed that he was playing as well as anyone on the team. He was the only player listed in each of these statistical categories: rushing (3 carries for 37 yards), scoring (6 points), pass receptions (2 for 24 yards), kickoff returns (2 for 54 yards), punt returns (5 for 64 yards), pass interceptions (1), passes broken up (2), and tackles (19).

Bill Jauss of the *Chicago Sun-Times* had recently quoted him as saying, "Oh, I like carrying the ball the most, of course, but an offensive back takes a lot of punishment. That's why I like to play defense and on the suicide squads. There I get to dish it out. That's where I get even."

After Rassas's long jog to the sideline, Parseghian approached his downcast safety. "I've got to take you out on offense, Nick," he said. "I know this disappoints you. But you've lost 9 pounds since the start of the season. I'm wearing you out. I need you to focus on defense and kick returns."

Rassas unbuckled his chin strap and removed his helmet. He smiled. "Okay, Coach," he said. "After all, you are the boss."

He walked to the bench, sat down, and began to focus on his new role. To think that a year earlier he had logged a grand total of twenty-four minutes of playing time. Sure, he could be happy playing defense and returning kicks.

The 24–0 rout of UCLA was impressive. It could have been a lot worse if Parseghian had not cleared the bench in the fourth quarter.

Still, it was easy to question the overall strength of the Bruins. They had won only six games the previous two seasons, and would finish 1964 with four victories. Coach Tommy Prothro was still a year away from resigning at Oregon State to lead the Bruins back into national prominence and Rose Bowl days once again.

The AP and UPI polls could have cared less about the inadequacies of UCLA. Both polls voted Notre Dame up the ladder to No. 2. No one could believe how far the Fighting Irish had come.

Chapter 24

WOOOO PIG SOOOOIE

I was eleven years old in 1964, and my blood flowed Razorback red. My life's focus was on football. I was already playing tackle football in full pads for the local YMCA on Saturday mornings, but the center of my universe was the Arkansas Razorbacks. When I slept, little piggies leaped over my bed. My all-time hero was Lance Alworth, and I was still mad he didn't win the 1960 Heisman Trophy. Someday, I knew I would wear the cardinal and white with jersey number 23—just like Lance.

There is a confession I have to make, though. In those days, I did have a mistress—if that is possible at age eleven. The team I was seeing on the side wore blue and gold and they played in a faraway place called South Bend.

I grew up just outside of Little Rock, and my parents took me to my first Razorback game at War Memorial Stadium in 1960 when I was seven. You cannot imagine what 50,000 fans howling "Woooo Pig Sooie" sounded like for the first time through the ears of a seven-year-old. We didn't miss a game in Little Rock for ten years and sometimes made the four-hour trek across thin, twisting roads to Fayetteville for some others.

Arkansas versus Texas on October 17, 1964, was the biggest game in the history of Razorback football. We were ready. My mom, Leanna, my dad, Jimmy, and I were at our lake cabin in northern Arkansas. We were nervous all day that we wouldn't be able to pick up the radio broadcast. Texas was the No. 1–ranked team in the country and Arkansas stood at No. 8. The game against the hated Longhorns was to be played under the lights down in Austin. Man, I really hated the Longhorns. The previous season, I had watched Texas beat my team 17–13 in Little Rock. I still wasn't over it.

(Ironically, the 1964 Arkansas roster had two players whom I would cross paths with twenty-five years later—Jerry Jones and Jimmy Johnson. We all met up in Dallas in 1989, during an era when I covered the Cowboys as a newspaperman. Jones would become the subject of my first book, *King of the Cowboys*.)

On the night of the big game against Texas, I was so nervous that I was running to the bathroom every five minutes. Right before kickoff, we realized that our Motorola radio would not get the signal, so our next-door neighbor, Dwight Beard, ran back to his cabin. As an eleven-year-old I was amazed beyond belief when Mr. Beard placed his radio on top of ours and—sha-zam!—we had a signal. Plenty of static, but I could still make out the call of Mr. Bud Campbell, the voice of Razorback football.

As the game progressed, I decided to apply my own brand of science to the little box invented by Marconi. I put our cat on top of both radios, and you could hear Bud Campbell's voice as clear as Wooo Pig Sooie.

It was a night that no one would ever forget—and I'm not just talking about the Hog-wild crazies from the mountains of Arkansas. The Arkansas–Texas game in 1964 rocked the college football world. The Razorbacks' Kenny Hatfield returned a punt 81 yards for a touchdown, and Freddie Marshall passed 34 yards to Bobby Crockett for another. The line-pounding of Ernie Koy and Phil Harris produced 1 Texas touchdown, and with 1:27 to play, Koy bolted 1 yard off right guard for another. It was now 14–13 in favor of Arkansas.

We soon found out just how gutsy Darrell Royal was. He could have kicked the extra point, settled for a tie, and felt sufficiently certain that he would wake up Monday morning still number one, but he chose to try the 2-point conversion.

Some thirty years later, Arkansas coach Frank Broyles related to me this conversation between Royal and him the next off-season during a golf outing.

Broyles: "Darrell, were you stealing my signals that night?"

Royal: "Were you stealing mine?"

Broyles: "Yeah."

Royal: "Yeah."

Oddly enough, they were still best friends.

As it turned out, Broyles did not steal Royal's signal just before the 2-point conversion attempt. He waited to see which halfbacks he would send into the game. When Royal dispatched Hix Green, his smallest back and best receiver, Broyles started yelling to his defense, "Watch the pass! Watch the pass!"

Outland Trophy winner Lloyd Phillips bowled over the blocker in front of him as end James Finch joined him in the backfield. Under heavy pressure, quarterback Marv Kristynik threw the ball into the ground. The No. 1 team in the country was no more.

The reverberations could be felt all the way to South Bend.

The next morning, I closed my bedroom door and turned on my twelve-inch, black-and-white TV. As I did every Sunday, in the dark and quiet sanctity of my own little room, I watched my secret team—the Notre Dame Fighting Irish. Many kids from those days will tell you about watching the hour-long highlights every Sunday morning and the fabulous voice of Lindsey Nelson—"Now moving along to further action." I had discovered Notre Dame football that fall of 1964, and it was like getting an extra scoop of ice cream on your birthday cake. I could not wait to hear Nelson each Sunday—his smooth and high-pitched delivery. Paul Hornung once said, "When you heard Lindsey Nelson's voice, you knew it was football season."

Verne Lundquist, the longtime CBS sports broadcaster, once told me, "Lindsey Nelson was the greatest announcer of his time, and there will never be another one who sounds just like him." Nelson was elected into the College Football Hall of Fame in 1986.

It seemed that every five seconds, Nelson was saying, "That was John Huarte to Jack Snow!" Nelson had this way of crisply breaking off the "k" in Jack. It provided a sense of excitement that I cannot describe. I thought the name "Huarte" was cool, and I even knew how to spell it.

As I watched the Fighting Irish every Sunday morning, I tried to compare them to the Razorbacks. I thought Notre Dame looked more like a pro team. The Fighting Irish seemed more polished than Arkansas.

Their gold helmets were shiny even in black and white. I would have given my entire marble collection—including the clearies—to see Arkansas and Notre Dame square off that year.

One Sunday morning, my mother knocked gently on my door and walked in. I'm sure she thought that I was watching an NFL game.

"Whatcha watching, Jimbo?" she said.

I was busted. I could not lie. Besides, her eyes were now on the screen.

"Mom, I'm watching Notre Dame football highlights."

She gave me the look that reminded me of the time I stayed out past midnight playing football in the street. She turned on her heel and walked away. When she reached the door, she turned and glared at me again.

"I should have made you go to church," she said.

My mother was not anti-Catholic. She was not even anti-Notre Dame. Still, I was a traitor in her eyes. We were Razorback people, and after beating Texas, we were in the hunt for No. 1.

Here is how the Associated Press poll stacked up on Monday following Arkansas–Texas:

1. Ohio State
2. Notre Dame
3. Alabama
4. Arkansas
5. Nebraska

With six weeks remaining in the regular schedule, college football was the most exciting thing in my life. I could not wait for Saturday's games. After all, I had two horses in the race.

Chapter 25

WAKE UP THE ECHOES

The national media arrived on the Notre Dame campus the next week like army platoons storming onto the shores of France.

One of the first to arrive was thirty-five-year-old Dan Jenkins of *Sports Illustrated,* the best football writer ever. He came to do a cover story on the turnaround of the team. Notre Dame was officially back. You could read it in Jenkins's lead:

Once every ten years or so Notre Dame recoats the golden dome rising above its campus so that it glows brightly, especially during football season when the orange-and-red fire of autumn sweeps through the trees below. Last Saturday, as Notre Dame defeated Stanford 28–6 to remain unbeaten in five games, the dome on the main building seemed to be giving off beams of inspiration as it did in the days of Frank Leahy and Knute Rockne. Notre Dame is winning again.

On the cover of *Sports Illustrated* was a photo of John Huarte trotting onto the field before the opening kickoff with the rest of the team in the background. Against Stanford, Huarte completed 21 of 37 passes for 300 yards, a school record. Already he had surpassed last season's total passing yards in just five games. His totals were now 1,009 passing yards and 8 touchdowns.

Eight of those passes against Stanford were completed to Snow for 113 yards. Snow's total catches were now up to 34, and the season was only halfway over.

Bill Wolski scored three touchdowns, the first on a 54-yard reception when the big halfback somehow got behind the entire secondary. He scored 2 others on runs of 1 and 9 yards. Little wonder that Notre Dame was off to its best start since 1953 when the Frank Leahy lads were 5-0. Stanford coach John Ralston could not have been more impressed, and why not? Notre Dame finished with 29 first downs to four for Stanford.

"This is the most physical team that I've ever come up against in thirteen years of coaching," Ralston told Joe Doyle. "It's not only the defense. It's that offense, too. That Jack Snow creates certain problems. We tried to give him room and then hit him as he caught the ball. That didn't work. No doubt, that Notre Dame is the toughest team we've faced. Ara is going to win a lot of games."

Parseghian was asked after the game to put his finger on the reasons for the turnaround.

"Platoons," he said. "That's the story behind our five wins. We've got an offensive team and a defensive team, strictly using platoons under the new rules, but believe me, there is no depth on this team. If two or three of our boys had to go both ways, I'm not so sure that people around here would be so excited."

Indeed, they all had something to cheer about. Frank Gaul, the senior chairman of the pep rally committee said, "We can finally cheer, not because Notre Dame was great in the '20s or '40s, but because we're great now."

After the game, Parseghian awarded one of the game balls to Hughie Devore for his contributions in recruiting the players now on the team. Devore, still knocking around as an assistant athletic director, broke down and cried in the middle of the locker room.

Notre Dame might have been undefeated, but there were still questions. How good had the first five opponents been? Stanford was hardly top 20 material. Not since 1957 had the Indians finished with a winning record, and they would go .500 in 1964. Still, Notre Dame was dominating week after week and they would pick up four more first-place votes in the Associated Press poll. They were starting to close ground on Ohio State for No. 1. Little wonder. Notre Dame had defeated its first five opponents by the aggregate score of 151–35.

Next up would be their biggest test of the season against the Heisman Trophy winner from 1963.

Chapter 26

TOUGH IRISH THIEF

The Notre Dame uniform for 1964 was basic and sleek and lacking in gimmicks, until Ara Parseghian decided to make one addition to the helmet. For every interception that season, a Notre Dame defender would receive a blue star on his gold helmet.

No wonder that after the second game of the season, Parseghian was already calling Tony Carey the "Three-Star General." After the fourth game, Carey was a "Five-Star General." After a 28–6 defeat of Stanford in the sixth week of the season, Carey was now was an astonishing "Six-Star General."

Not only was Carey leading the nation in interceptions, he was running away with the race. Two others were tied for second place with 3 apiece. Just a year earlier, the tough Irish kid had been all but forgotten. This year he was the second biggest story behind Huarte-to-Snow.

The *Chicago Sun-Times* was quick to pick up on the story of the blue stars. The newspaper ran pictures of Carey's gold helmet after every game. Carey had so many stars that his helmet was now more blue than gold.

John Huarte was earning most of the headlines with his nation leading 1,009 passing yards, but going into the Navy game versus Heisman Trophy–winner Roger Staubach, Carey was the man of the hour. The previous year, Staubach had led the Midshipmen to a 35–14 embarrassment of the Irish at Notre Dame Stadium. By the end of the season, he had scrambled and passed Navy to what amounted to be a national championship game showdown against Texas in the Cotton Bowl.

Five games deep into the 1964 season, in spite of an ankle injury,

Staubach was still one of the most dangerous players in college football. It would be Carey versus Staubach in the main event at John F. Kennedy Stadium in Philadelphia.

A year earlier, no one could have imagined such a matchup. While Staubach was taking home the Heisman, Carey was watching the Notre Dame games from the stands. He had to buy his own ticket. He was not offered a single scrap of chicken from the pregame dinner. He was not invited to pregame Mass.

Halfway through the 1963 season, Carey asked for a meeting with head coach Hughie Devore to discuss his disappointment. Not once had he been allowed to suit up for a Notre Dame game—home or away. Sitting in front of Devore's desk, Carey broke down and cried.

"Hughie, I don't understand why you won't give me a chance," he cried. "Why won't you at least give me a chance to play? You know I can play."

Devore never relented. He recalled how Carey had been kicked out of school. He couldn't care less that Carey was one of the top recruits in the country in 1961. Forget the fact that he had quarterbacked his team to the Chicago City Title. Besides, Devore never could quite figure out where to play him—quarterback or cornerback.

A year after being fired as the Notre Dame coach, Devore was still haunted by the presence of Tony Carey. He could barely believe his eyes as he watched the lanky right corner suffocating opposing receivers week after week. Carey, with his attacking style and ability to close on receivers, was the perfect bandit in Johnny Ray's blitzing defense. He was one of the strongest forces on the nation's No. 1–ranked defense. In a way, Devore did not like what he was seeing.

"You never played that hard for me," he told Carey one day in the locker room. "I don't understand why you'd play so damn hard this season and not for me. If you had played like this, you'd have been a starter for me."

Carey smiled. "Hold on, Hughie. The only reason that I never played this hard for you is that you never gave me a chance to. I would have played this hard for you—maybe even harder—but you never let me on the field."

Devore shook his head. "That's not how I remember it. None of you guys played for me, but you're all busting your asses for Ara."

Because Carey had labored the last three years on the fourth string, no one could foresee just how effective he would be in Ray's 4-4-3 scheme. What most of the experts had underestimated was just how tough this South Sider could be. From about the third grade on, Carey had fought his way through the playground at St. Phillip Neri grammar school. Fighting was just another part of recess. Kids fought because they felt like it.

"I was a good street fighter," Carey remembered. "In those days, fighting was acceptable on the playgrounds. Nobody got hurt, really, just a bunch of bloody noses, but I kept fighting and fighting. I found out I was pretty good, but later I realized I needed to tone it down a little."

Boxing around South Chicago was organized by the Catholic Youth Organization. The next step for Carey was to seek higher learning at the boxing clubs around town. Carey was not messing around when he walked into Johnny Coulon's gym on Sixty-third Street, close to Stoney Island and three blocks from Mount Carmel High. Coulon had held the bantamweight world belt from 1910, when he defeated England's Jim Kendrick, until 1914 when he lost to Kid Williams. Among the notable names that had trained in his gym since 1921 were Jack Dempsey, Gene Tunney, Jim Braddock, Joe Louis, Sugar Ray Robinson, and Muhammad Ali. The latter kept himself toned at Coulon's Gym during his exile from boxing.

Coulon, in the years that Carey trained in his gym, was a bona fide Chicago celebrity. He had befriended every heavyweight champ since John L. Sullivan. He celebrated his seventy-sixth birthday by walking the length of the gym on his hands. He always departed the ring by springing over the top rope and lighting like a butterfly on the other side. Little wonder that a kid named Carey would become mesmerized by the fight game at an early age. His intensive training at Coulon's Gym meant that he was headed straight to the boxing team when he reached Notre Dame.

The Bengal Bouts on campus had been started on campus back in

1920 by Knute Rockne, who was looking for yet another way to condition his players for the long grind of the football season. Under the guidance of Dominic "Nappy" Napolitano, the event flourished. The Bengal Bouts followed the mantra of the Men's Boxing Club—"Strong bodies fight that weak bodies may be nourished." All of the proceeds benefitted the Holy Cross Missions in Bangladesh.

In 1963, when Carey began to train for the Bengal Bouts, the event was held in the rickety Old Fieldhouse. Training was done in a small gym with a wooden floor just behind the balcony seats. Every afternoon, the pounding of the heavy bags and the slamming of the speed bags echoed through the gym.

The Bengal Bouts always began in mid-February, and the excitement around campus was somewhat comparable to football season. Crowds often swelled to 4,000, and it seemed they all sat right on top of the ring. The Old Fieldhouse was known for its ear-splitting noise during the pep rallies and basketball games. During the Bengal Bouts, each dormitory was like a fraternity house, and they backed their own fighters to the hilt. Carey knew that he could count on a few hundred supporters from Fisher Hall, along with his football teammates. He cherished every moment of every bout.

"I knew that if I could climb into the ring in front of three or four thousand people, I could handle anything on the football field," he remembered. "I think that fighting in the Bengal Bouts got me ready physically and mentally to play football."

He made it to all the finals of the 185–pound division in both 1963 and 1964. To qualify for the finals, he won five three-round bouts. He lost both times in the final but still left with a smile on his face, knowing that he had gone further than anyone expected.

"I would do it all again in a heartbeat," he said. "I wish I could have won, but, man, did it make me tougher."

Boxing improved his confidence, but Carey had yet another weapon that not many inside the football program knew about. He was an accomplished handball player, thanks to the long days he spent at Rainbow Beach in the summer leading up to the season. He took a summer job in high school at Rainbow Beach on the shore of Lake Michigan, just a few blocks from his house in South Chicago. He began his morning at 5:30 by hosing down the buildings and the courts, then worked until dusk. The handball courts were 20×40 feet with wooden floors. The 40-foot walls on the side tapered down from the front wall all the way to the end of the court.

Nothing builds hand-eye coordination more than handball, a better sport than racquetball because it forces you to use your nondominant hand, and there was little question that Carey possessed a terrific hand-eye reflex. He plucked interceptions from the air with lightning-quick hands. His eyes were so well trained that he knew precisely when the quarterback would release the ball, and where it was going. Carey was the type of cornerback that coaches call a "cluer," one who checks the quarterback's eyes to see if he is telegraphing his passes. A cornerback who can gauge the moment of release, along with the direction, is far ahead of the game. Carey possessed all of these tools.

Yet another factor that made Carey the perfect cornerback for Johnny Ray's system was that he knew angles. In covering a wide receiver, or tackling a running back, he instinctively knew the angle to take. Some of this he picked up on the sandlots as a kid playing tackle football.

"We never once played touch football when I was a kid," he remembered. "We always played tackle. I think that's the biggest reason I knew the angles to take to the ball carrier."

Halfway through his dream season, Carey took the time to think about all of the obstacles he had overcome. Few knew that his mother, Ann, had almost died in a car accident in the fall of 1962, when Tony was ineligible to play because of his suspension. This was yet another crushing blow that the kid had to deal with privately.

Ann Carey had been riding in a car with her sister to the Notre Dame–Purdue game in West Lafayette. They were driving through the cornfields of Indiana when the driver lost control of the car and it swerved onto a soft shoulder, broke through a fence, and then plunged into a culvert. Ann Carey crashed through the windshield and landed in the ditch. She was unconscious and near death.

A doctor riding in the car behind them jumped out and grabbed his medical bag. He discovered that Ann Carey's heart had stopped beating. He injected adrenaline into her heart and restarted it. She was then rushed to a local hospital. Hours later, she was care-flighted to a Chicago hospital. Tony borrowed a fellow student's car and rushed back to Chicago where he learned that his mother was going to be okay.

She would live to see him play during the 1964 season.

BECAUSE NOTRE DAME possessed three top-flight defensive backs in Tom Longo, Rassas, and Carey, the Fighting Irish were able to gamble more on defense than were most teams—and no one loved to roll the dice more than Johnny Ray. This philosophy was totally supported by Parseghian, who often said, "We don't make mental mistakes. We force the other team to make mental mistakes."

One reason that Notre Dame could afford to play defense like a riverboat gambler was the long days of preparation. This attention to detail cut down on mental mistakes by his players.

"Johnny Ray could tell you what a team was going to do on first down from their own 21 in the first quarter," Carey said. "Or he could tell you what they were going to do on third down from the 33 in the third quarter. I've never in my life seen anyone who knew more about trends."

Ray was also a driver and a taskmaster. Thanks to the Camels he chain-smoked, he spoke in a deep, raspy, and often angry voice. He sounded like Bear Bryant without the southern drawl. His voice could be dripping with sarcasm when his defense did not play up to standard. One day on the practice field leading to the Navy game, Ray started yelling, "Where is my All-Star linebacker? Jimmy Carroll. Why didn't you make that tackle? Page! Page! You let them get around you *again*. If you let Staubach do that to us Saturday, Navy will beat the crap out of us. You hear me, Page?"

On the next play, Page drove his shoulder into a ball carrier and jarred the ball loose. Suddenly, they were on a first-name basis again.

"Alan, that was a great job," Ray said in a much calmer voice. "You make that play every time, big fella, and we'll win the national championship. A national championship, big fella!"

At 6'6" and 230 pounds, Page was the most impressive specimen on the entire Fighting Irish team. He was also the strongest and the fastest. Students in the stands at the Purdue game in 1962 would never forget the sight of Page walking onto the field before the game. He was there on a recruiting trip and would stand on the Notre Dame sideline that day. As he strolled along the sideline, some of the students actually pointed and gawked. Soon, the word got around that it was Alan Page, a senior at Central Catholic High School in Canton.

Page had grown up poor and one of six children. As a youngster, he had promised his mother that he would attend parochial school. It was not easy being one of the few black faces, but he excelled in the classroom. He also gained statewide notoriety as a football and basketball player.

One hardship was getting a ride home after practice. He approached high school teammate Norm Nicola one day and asked if he knew of a solution. Canton was a working-class town with a large white population, but Nicola had been hitchhiking for years and knew the ropes.

"Put on your letter jacket and stand next to the entrance to the turnpike," he said. "I can assure you that somebody will pick you up." It worked, just as Nicola had suggested. When Page made his recruiting visit to Notre Dame, it was his friend Norm who showed him around campus.

A black dentist from Canton had convinced Page that he should consider Notre Dame. The dentist telephoned Hughie Devore and told him all about Page. Before long, he was on his way to Notre Dame. As a freshman, he soon learned that Notre Dame had 1 percent black students. He spent most of his time on football and academics. The priests called him by his full name of Alan Cedric.

"I know that he was lonely at first," Nicola said, "but I can tell you the guy was never unhappy. He handled everything very well."

Handling Johnny Ray was another matter. Of all the Notre Dame defensive players, Ray was the hardest on Page, constantly driving him.

"Alan Page," he would say, "I am going to make you a great player, dead or alive." At times, Page retreated into a shell. He did not speak for days. He talked with a slight lisp that seemed bothersome. At the end of practice one day, he was approached by Ken Maglicic.

"I need to tell you something, Alan," Maglicic said. "It might seem that Coach Ray is picking on you. The reason he's spending so much time with you is that he likes you, believe it or not. He really does want to make you a better player."

Ray was not exactly friendly to any of the players. This does not mean he was disliked or disrespected. Ray was the kind of coach that expressed his love with a balled fist. Not that he would ever strike one of the players, or that Parseghian would allow it. Ray loved to raise the roof with that deep, gravelly voice. He craved a national title as much as anyone in South Bend. Most of his football life, he had scratched and clawed his way to gain whatever ground he could. It was never easy. He played center at Notre Dame in 1944 and was drawing praise from the fans and the press when he was drafted into the Army and shipped off to Europe to fight in War World II. He returned to South Bend in 1947 as a married man and was informed that he could give up his wife or his roster spot. He gave up the latter. He chose to transfer to Olivet College, an obscure little school in Michigan. The offer made by Frank Ham, his former high school coach, was too good to turn down. Ham also offered him a position on the coaching staff. As a player/coach, Ray would be able to augment his GI Bill income as a paid member of the staff.

Upon graduating from Olivet, the big, lucrative coaching offers did not come rolling in. So Ray chose the high school route, first at Sturgis High, then at Three Rivers High, both in Michigan. He latched on to an assistant's position at the University of Detroit. In 1959, he moved into the head coaching ranks, but it was on the NAIA level at John Carroll University. The Blue Streaks were hardly the talk of college football. Yet, in five seasons, he put together a 29-6 record, the best in school history, along with three undefeated seasons in 1959, '62, and '63.

No one in college football knew more about Ohio football than Ara Parseghian. He grew up in Akron and then played and coached at Miami of Ohio. He instantly knew he wanted to hire Ray as the defensive coordinator. That Ray had also applied for the Notre Dame head coaching job did not worry Parseghian in the least. His self-confidence would never allow him to worry that Ray might take his job. He even bowed to Ray's desire to be totally in charge of the defense.

So far it was working out just fine. Notre Dame led the nation in rushing defense, allowing just 22.1 yards per game. Only 2 touchdowns had been scored on the first-team defense. In turn, that No. 1 Notre Dame unit had scored 10 touchdowns in punt, interception, and fumbles returned.

At that time John Ray was one of the biggest names in college football. All he had to do was stop the 1963 Heisman Trophy winner—Roger Staubach himself.

NICK RASSAS WAS standing inside the horseshoe at John F. Kennedy Stadium an hour before kickoff, preparing to field a punt in pregame warm-ups. Notre Dame special teams were always the first on the field, and that meant Rassas was right in the thick of it, returning punts and kickoffs.

Rassas heard the roll of the cannon behind him and then felt the concussion. It was a Howitzer 105, and he instantly knew it was no more than ten yards away. The cannon was fired because the Navy team was coming down the tunnel for warm-ups. Rassas was blown forward a few feet and hit the ground face-first. He was slowly getting up when he turned to see the Midshipmen in their blue and gold uniforms running onto the field.

"Those guys look like a bunch of midgets," he said, laughing to himself. "We are going to beat the crap out of these guys."

Funny that Rassas would say that. He was one of the smallest players on the Notre Dame team.

Service academies, especially in the early sixties, were known for their undersized players. Moreover, the Navy roster of 1964 had been thinned by graduation, then shredded by injuries. The same team that went 9-2 in 1963 was now 2-3-1. A much larger concern was that Staubach had injured his right ankle in the second game against William and Mary and reinjured it the following week against Michigan. He had missed some playing time. The Navy trainers were reporting that Staubach would be ready to go against Notre Dame, but no one knew how effective he would be as a scrambler. That, however, did not stop coach Wayne Hardin from singing his praises from the tallest buildings at Annapolis.

"He's the finest football player that I've ever seen in my life," Hardin said. "He reminds me of Wyatt Earp. He's already become a legend in his own time. I've seen Tittle. I've seen Unitas. I've seen some of the top players in this day and age, and Staubach is as good or better than any of them."

On that first play of the game, as Staubach gazed into the secondary, he saw Tony Carey's heavily decorated gold helmet. Someone suggested the Midshipmen might actually salute Carey because of all the blue stars.

The previous season, Staubach had passed for two touchdowns in the 35–14 defeat of the Irish. Now he was facing a new secondary. These strangers, however, were no stranger to success. They were already being called the "Thieving Trio" by the Chicago sporting press. Between them, Longo, Rassas, and Carey had stolen 10 passes in five games, and no one was sure if it would ever stop.

The Johnny Ray scheme for Staubach was far more conservative than the previous five quarterbacks. Blitzing linebackers were now assigned to contain "Roger the Dodger" so he could not scramble around the ends. In the first half, Staubach and the Navy offense did make 10 first downs, but they could not get the ball into the end zone.

The Notre Dame offense was a different story. The same unit that had fallen on its face against Navy in 1963 was rolling again. Huarte-to-Snow, plus the power running of Bill Wolski, helped the Irish average 30 points a game. Even so, nothing all season could compare to what happened two minutes deep into the second quarter.

Huarte dropped to pass. He kept dropping and dropping. He was more than 15 yards behind the line of scrimmage and retreating fast with three Midshipmen in his face. Then he whipped a pass over the heads of seven onrushing players and into the arms of Nick Eddy. Ahead of Eddy was a forward wall of five blockers—John Meyer, Dick Arrington, Norm Nicola, John Atamian, and Bob Meeker. A middle screen had never been more perfectly executed.

Eddy followed his blockers to the Navy 40, then swerved to the right sideline and outran the secondary to the end zone. The touchdown covered 74 yards. It was one of three touchdowns in the second quarter. Five minutes later, Huarte's 50-yard touchdown pass to Jack Snow, accomplished with astonishing ease, made it 14–0. Snow was five yards behind the secondary. On the next possession, Huarte mixed his plays well, throwing to Snow and Phil Sheridan, then handing off to Wolski around right end to the 1. On the next play, fullback Joe Kantor kicked the defensive end to the outside and Wolksi bowled into the end zone for his sixth touchdown of the season. Notre Dame led 21–0 at halftime.

A 3-touchdown lead would have felt comfortable if not for the strong arm of Staubach, whose accuracy approached 70 percent over three seasons. He had completed 10 passes in the first half and moved the Navy offense to the Notre Dame 8-yard line before a fumble killed the drive. The shotgun formation, used on every play, was giving Staubach more time to pass.

At halftime, Ray went to the chalkboard and changed the defense to a blitzing scheme. They would go after Staubach. Early in the third quarter, from the Notre Dame 43, Staubach took the snap from the shotgun and instantly knew he was in trouble. Linebacker John Horney blitzed up the middle as Jim Carroll swooped down from the left side. Alan Page threw his blocker to the ground and began his pursuit. Staubach retreated to the right, then spun and reversed field. He looked like a calf being herded by cutting horses. All the while Tony Carey was lurking in the shadows, reading Staubach's eyes. He knew that the Navy quarterback was desperately seeking tight end Bill Studt.

Staubach never saw Carey, who stepped in front of Studt just as the pass was released. Carey was two steps ahead of the tight end when he made his most coveted interception of the season against the best quarterback in the country. He returned the ball 5 yards to midfield. It seemed inconceivable that a former outcast would now have 7 interceptions in six games.

Backup quarterback Sandy Bonvechio greeted every defensive player with a handshake on the sideline.

"Man, I was getting worried," he said. "Until you guys started blitzing, I thought Staubach might get us."

Three plays later, Joe Farrell scored on a 3-yard run. Try as he may,

Staubach could not kick the Navy offense into gear, and the blitz was getting to him more than ever. After yet another punt, Huarte rolled left and fired into the left corner of the end zone to Jack Snow for a 34–0 lead. Once again, the backups flooded the field in the fourth quarter as Denny Conway added the final touchdown on a 15-yard run.

The 40–zip victory over Navy was a 61-point swing from the previous season. Remarkably, Notre Dame held Navy and Staubach scoreless in spite of a school-record 19 completions.

After the game, Navy coach Wayne Hardin said, "Notre Dame has the best football team I've ever seen. They are truly the No. 1 team in the country."

As the team filed onto the bus after the game, Parseghian noticed that sophomore linebacker Jim Lynch was limping.

"I'll be just fine," he said. "I hurt my knee. The trainer says it's just a nick. I'll be ready to play next week."

"If it's just a nick, then why are you limping?" the coach asked. "Looks to me like you're in pain."

"I don't know," Lynch said. "I've never had one of these things."

Lynch was one of five sophomores on defense and, in spite of his lack of experience, he was practically indispensable. Parseghian was worried as he walked away.

Lynch's knee had buckled when he was hit from the side. He felt it pop but figured the swelling would subside the following week, and that he would be ready for the Pitt game. Knee injuries were one of the trickiest to diagnose in the mid-1960s because orthopedic doctors did not fully understand the intricate structure of the four ligaments and countless tendons. Instead of shaving off a torn section of the cartilage, they were harvesting the whole thing back in the '60s. An X-ray was not effective in revealing a tear, so no one was really sure how badly Lynch's knee was damaged.

Upon returning to St. Joseph's County Airport late that night, the team was greeted by 1,500 howling students. Airport officials estimated the crowd would have been 5,000 if they had not been thirty minutes early. As the plane stopped on the tarmac and the stairway was pushed into place, the students began to chant, "We're No. 1! We're No. 1!"

As the buses rolled along the three-and-a-half mile two-laner to campus, horns blared and students stood along the shoulder and waved. It seemed that everyone in South Bend (population 135,000) wanted a glimpse of the Fighting Irish. Some said it was the greatest celebration since Knute Rockne and George Gipp returned to the train station after the 1920 victory over Army.

And to think there were still four games to be played.

Chapter 27

NO. 1

Hitchhiking was still the number-one mode of transportation for students who had yet to reach their senior year, thus qualifying for the use of a personal car. Upon catching a ride around town, they were accustomed to hearing the grumbling about Notre Dame football, but all the complaining officially stopped on November 2 when the Associated Press and United Press International polls were released.

Notre Dame was No. 1. There was bedlam in South Bend once more.

Ohio State, after a 21–19 victory over 16th-ranked Iowa, fell from the top ranking to No. 2. The Buckeyes had barely averted a tie with two seconds remaining when Iowa failed to execute a 2-point conversion.

The previous week, Notre Dame had received six first-place votes, but that number jumped to 29 after the 40–0 shellacking of Navy. This was the order of the top 5:

1. Notre Dame
2. Ohio State
3. Alabama
4. Arkansas
5. Nebraska

Parseghian was beaming when he heard about the No. 1 ranking.

"We're delighted," he said. "That is what we've been striving for—to be the No. 1 team in the country again—but I'm sure that every team that we face is really going to be shooting for us now."

The miracle season rolled on the next Saturday as Notre Dame broke six offensive school records in the first half and rolled to a 14–0 lead at Pitt Stadium against the Panthers. This was not surprising when you consider that Pitt had tied Navy 14–14, and everyone knew that Notre Dame was 40 points better than Navy. In the first half, Jack Snow surpassed the school record for receptions (43) in a season and yards (776). John Huarte broke Bob Williams's season passing record with 1,493 yards. Also in that first half, Huarte and Nick Eddy eclipsed the school mark with a 91-yard touchdown completion. Huarte found Eddy wide open in the middle of the field at the Irish 35. The fleet halfback, as he did against Navy, pulled away from the secondary with a fluid ease.

By this time, it seemed the only team that might beat Notre Dame Irish was the Green Bay Packers—the NFL's best of the 1960s—but just as the nation's sporting press was about to coronate the Irish, the season fell apart.

By the end of the second quarter, the Pitt Panthers were starting to abuse the vaunted Notre Dame defense. The Panthers were gashing the right side of the line with big gains. This seemed impossible. The first six games, Notre Dame had led the nation in rushing defense, allowing just 22.1 yards per game, but Pitt right tackle Ron Linaburg was tearing huge holes in the left side of the Notre Dame line as halfbacks Barry McKnight and Fred Mazurek rolled into the secondary. Tackle Kevin Hardy, another sophomore, was having a superb season until he ran into Linaburg.

Defensive coordinator Johnny Ray was faced with a hard reality. Jim Lynch's knee injury was a bigger blow than he thought. (Two years later, Lynch would captain the national championship team and win the Maxwell Award as college football's best player.) At first, Lynch's knee injury was regarded as a mild sprain. In truth, he had partially torn two ligaments. Against Navy, Ray had replaced Lynch with John Horney, who at 180 pounds was big enough to handle the undersized service academy players. But Pitt was built with muscle and bulk, like most eastern teams, so Ray inserted Arunas Vasys into Lynch's spot with hopes he could slow Pitt down.

Pitt began to dominate the game by the third quarter. The Panthers moved 60 yards on 5 rushing plays. On third down from the 10, Mc-Knight carried for 9 yards off right tackle, then slanted into the same hole for the touchdown. For the 2-point conversion, McKnight cracked the same spot in the line. It was now 14–8.

On the sideline, Parseghian's stomach was doing backflips. He knew that Pitt had found Notre Dame's Achilles' heal. Thanks to recent injuries, there were soft spots in the Notre Dame defense. The most valuable missing players were Pete Duranko (broken wrist), Paul Costa (knee), Harry Long (knee), Mike Wadsworth (knee), and Lynch. The Irish were now starting four sophomores in the line—Alan Page, Don Gmitter, Tom Regner, and Hardy. All four were grading high in Ray's book, with Regner at the head of the class. Nevertheless, so many inexperienced players in one place, combined with a recent string of injuries, was making Parseghian nervous. Now Hardy was being manhandled.

In the huddle, Hardy began to tear up when one of his teammates said, "Why don't you get your ass to the sideline." To the surprise of everyone, Hardy started trotting, head down, to the Notre Dame bench. He was replaced by Mike Wadsworth, coming off an injury.

Parseghian's worries were mounting. Twice in his career at North-western—in 1959 and 1962—his Wildcats had begun the season 6-0, only to fall apart down the stretch. He wondered if it was about to happen again.

Parseghian breathed a little easier when Joe Azzaro kicked a 30-yard field goal with forty-nine seconds left in the third quarter. But Pitt was rolling again within a matter of minutes, driving 80-yards with only 1 pass. McKnight made the final three inches into the end zone and Jim Jones's kick made it 17–15.

Now the sellout crowd of 56,628, the largest to see a Pitt game in seven years, was on the brink of hysteria. The Notre Dame players could barely hear themselves think. The Pitt backs looked like sledgehammers swinging into the line. Notre Dame knew precisely where they were going—off right tackle for 5, 10, 15 yards a pop—but the Irish still could not stop them. The crowd was on its feet in the final minutes and yelling itself hoarse. On fourth down and inches from the Notre Dame 17, coach John Michelson faced the decision of a lifetime. Like most coaches of his era, Michelson adhered to the Bear Bryant school of coaching. "If you can't make a foot on fourth down, you might as well put on a dress."

Michelson disdained the short field and sent Mazurek into the line, this time off left tackle. He never made it back to the line of scrimmage. Linebacker Jim Carroll and Regner body-slammed him to the turf in the same manner that "The Great Bolo" pounded championship wrestlers into the mat.

The day had been saved. The No. 1 ranking was still intact. Notre Dame remained the glamour team of 1964.

But only by inches.

Chapter 28

HAYWIRE

Four days before the biggest game that anyone could ever remember at Notre Dame, 3,000 students descended upon the football practice facility at Cartier Field.

"Beat State," they chanted again and again. Thanks to the green tarpaulin that completely covered the ten-foot fence all the way around the field, the students could not see what was taking place. Otherwise, they would have caught a glimpse of Ara Parseghian smiling. They were so loud that the offensive players could not hear John Huarte barking signals. Parseghian finally shrugged his shoulders, turned up his palms, and yelled to the team manager guarding the gate, "Let 'em in! We can't practice until we get some quiet anyway."

Parseghian was wary about allowing anyone into practice. He knew there might be spies in the crowd that began to flood through the front gate and form lines on the sideline. All of them looked like Notre Dame crazies, but Parseghian had learned long ago that you could trust no one, not with the biggest game of the season coming up.

"Everybody take a knee," he yelled to his players. "I'm going to talk to these kids for awhile."

Parseghian walked over to the sideline, where the army was now standing. You could have heard a pin drop. These kids would have paid all of the money in their pockets just to hear a few words from the Notre Dame messiah. Most of them could not remember a bigger moment in their lives. They had been in grammar school the last time Notre Dame played a game of this significance.

Parseghian crossed his arms and momentarily surveyed his audience. Then he began. "I know what you are thinking. You think that we aren't taking this Saturday's game seriously enough."

The laughter could be heard all the way to the Old Fieldhouse, but in the blink of an eye, the quiet returned.

"You can be sure that I realize how big this game is," he continued. "I can assure you that our players know how big this game is. Yes, I know from looking at your faces that this is the biggest game Notre Dame will ever play. It's not, but I can tell you from a personal standpoint, it sure feels like it to me!"

A cheer went up. This was like the old days with Knute Rockne. No one could work a crowd into a frenzy like Rock, but they said that Parseghian was the second coming of the most famous coach in the history of college football. The two hardly looked alike. Yet Parseghian certainly knew how to deal the Rockne magic.

Over the next fifteen minutes, Parseghian introduced his starting lineup to the students. As each player stood, the coach provided an evaluation: "John Huarte is the best quarterback in America . . . Jack Snow leads the country in receptions and he's going to be a first team All American . . . Tony Carey is the No. 1 interception man in college football and nobody's going to catch him . . . Nick Rassas. Man, Nick Rassas. What can you say about him? He finally gets his butt on the playing field and then he shows everybody that he might just be our most valuable all-round player. . . . Jim Carroll is our captain and our leading tackler . . . Ken Maglicic is our second leading tackler and our number-one comedian."

By the time Parseghian finished, the students were floating on air. Their feet barely touched the ground as they filed out the gate and back onto campus. Most would not attend another class all week. Homecoming was coming up, and Michigan State was coming to town. It was the biggest football week at Notre Dame that anyone could remember.

TERRY BRENNAN BECAME the Notre Dame coach in 1954 just as Duffy Daughtery succeeded Biggie Munn at Michigan State. That year, Notre Dame defeated Michigan State 20–19. It was Notre Dame's last victory over the hated Spartans. After eight straight losses there was only one reason to smile—Notre Dame did not lose to Michigan State in 1958 because the teams did not play.

November 14 had been circled all the way back in December of 1963, about the time Parseghian arrived. The new coach knew his fans wanted to beat Michigan State in the worst way. The previous summer he had traveled from town to town, making speeches on the rubber-chicken banquet circuit. This was the one phrase he repeated to every audience: "The team that we want to beat the most is Michigan State." Duffy Daughtery got word of the speeches and said, "That Armenian rugmaker better be careful about what he's saying."

The rivalry between Notre Dame and Michigan ran as deep as Lake Superior. Reasons abounded for all the hate. For one, the two schools were less than 120 miles apart. While Michigan State rarely played on the national stage like Notre Dame, the Spartans were always a tough opponent. Notre Dame's most important win during the last national championship season of 1949 was 34–21 over Michigan State.

Notre Dame versus Michigan State was a case of the blue bloods against the urban rowdies. Many Michigan State students had applied to Notre Dame, only to learn they could not qualify. So they came to resent the small, high-toned private Catholic university situated on the south bend of the St. Joseph's River.

The biggest reason that Notre Dame was so fired up for Michigan State was the prospect of having a great season ruined. A loss to the Spartans, and No. 1 would be flushed. No question that Michigan State was the benchmark game of 1964. That is why students staged pep rallies every night at the different dormitories and worked around the clock on homecoming floats.

Returning from the dining hall two nights before the big game, Maglicic was soaking up the atmosphere when he turned to Tony Carey.

"This campus is on fire," he said. "This place is electrifying."

"I've never seen anything like it in my life, Binks."

"I think we can beat Michigan State," Maglicic said.

"You better think that," Carey said, "or our asses are history."

Carey was having trouble sleeping that night at Fisher Hall. At 3:00

A.M., he rolled off the bed and his feet hit the floor. He needed a book to read or something to occupy his mind. He peered through the window that faced the Rockne Memorial Center. His eyes widened.

"Wake up Bonvechio," Carey said. "You've got to see this."

Sandy Bonvechio rolled over, his eyes bleary from sleep.

"What the hell do you want, Carey?" he grumped. "Most people are sleeping, you know."

"I know one man who isn't," Carey said, pointing at the Rock. "Look."

Bonvechio rose to a sitting position and looked out the window. He could see a light burning in the corner office.

"Good God," Bonvechio said. "That's Ara's office. He's still up there working."

"Yep. It's three o'clock in the morning. The man hasn't gone home yet. He's still working on the game plan. What does that tell you?"

"It tells me this game's bigger than we ever imagined."

The rest of the coaching staff had worked until midnight before Parseghian sent them home. He decided to stay a couple more hours to study some film and to rediagram a couple of plays. The coach was planning a big surprise for Daughtery and Michigan State. They would never see it coming, and Parseghian wanted to make sure he had it right.

THEY WERE WALL-TO-WALL on the dirt floor of the Old Fieldhouse on Friday night, an hour after the sun had set over Indiana. Crowd estimates were around 9,000. Not bad for a university of 6,500 students. The rest of the crowd were local fans and alumni that had arrived early for the game.

As the football players climbed the steel stairway to the north balcony, the Notre Dame band, 175 strong, roared through the side door of the Old Fieldhouse, belting out the "Victory March." No one could ever remember that level of noise. Rolls of toilet paper flew through the air and students held up signs that read HATE STATE and SPARTANS DIE!

In his book *Era of Ara*, Tom Pagna wrote of the Old Fieldhouse crowds, "The unsophistication, the absolute abandon, the spontaneity of these people was incredible."

As Parseghian moved close to the railing and became visible to the crowd, 9,000 voices began to chant, "Ara! Ara! Ara!" They wanted to hear from the Notre Dame coach, and they wanted to hear from him right away. His popularity knew no bounds. Less than two weeks earlier, on November 3, a couple of Indiana priests had walked into the polling both and written in the name of Ara Parseghian for president.

Before he hit the stage, there was one piece of business to take care of. Because of the enormity of the game, Notre Dame president Father Theodore Hesburgh had been invited to speak. The invitation was extended by Frank Gaul.

Father Hesburgh's presence in the sea of delirium hardly made sense. The Notre Dame president stood for intellectualism, spirituality, and somberness. He lived in a quiet world of dark robes, antique books, and academia. Standing before the chaotic masses—not all of them sober—Father Hesburgh looked a bit uncomfortable, but some of the shouting did subside and the students seemed ready to pay attention.

"This is a great day for Notre Dame," he began. "Not just for football, but for academia as well. We have made great strides in all areas of the university. I am proud to say that Notre Dame is now regarded as one of the leading centers of academia in all of the world. . . ."

Father Hesburgh continued down this path for about a minute before the revolt began. A "Boo!" popped up from the back of the arena, then another and another. These were not sustained boos. They were more like comic-book dialogue balloons. Now they were popping up everywhere as the priest tried to speak. Near the stage, a student shouted, "Bowl Game!" Several others followed his lead. Father Hesburgh was not a popular figure among the football enthusiasts because he had forbidden postseason bowls. This was decried by students, alumni, and the subway alums everywhere. Seeing as how the Irish were No. 1, the issue was boiling up once more.

More than ten years earlier, Father Hesburgh had set out to decelerate the fabled football program. Why? Because he hated the term "football factory." He believed a win-at-all-costs image was sacrilegious to a university seeking a kind of Ivy League reputation for academics. At this time, standing in the midst of the football lion-hearted, he looked worried. His face was turning red. He knew that addressing the student body in such a whipped-up frenzy was a bad idea. Again they were starting to chant, "Ara! Ara! Ara!'

Father Hesburgh leaned into the microphone and said, "I want to congratulate Coach Parseghian for having a great season thus far." Then he wheeled away and walked toward the stairwell. He caught Gaul's eye along the way.

"You can be sure, Frank, that this will be the last time I will ever speak in this place," he said.

A loud cheer went up. Was it a response to Father Hesburgh's departure, or Parseghian's arrival? Probably a combination of both. Parseghian beamed as he looked out at the crowd. These moments reminded him just how much he loved his work. Here was the reason for his burning passion.

"We wanted to bring you the No. 1 team in the country," he said.

"You did! You did!" they shouted back.

SMOKE WAS THE only thing missing from the fire raging across campus the next morning. Students rushed from the dormitory to Mass to the dining hall to St. Mary's to pick up their dates and finally to the stadium. Toilet paper streamers festooned the trees. Firecrackers clattered like machine guns. It seemed that every student was wearing a HATE STATE button.

This was no place for the faint of heart—or for a Michigan State fan, either. The students spoke in a militant tone as they approached total strangers. "You wouldn't be a State man, now would you?" Some wore buttons that read SONS OF ERIN, UNITE and RUB THEIR NOSES IN THE IRISH SOD. They shouted, "Hate State" with a hardness in their voices.

An hour before kickoff, standing in the press box, Moose Krause peered down at the sellout crowd of 59,265 filing in. "We could have sold 250,000 tickets to this game," he said. That figure might have gone much higher if Notre Dame were still playing an annual game in New York. The Army game in 1924 had drawn a request of 750,000 tickets from both schools.

For the last couple of weeks, the sporting press had called Notre Dame–Michigan State the "Game of the year." More than 35 million were expected to watch the nationally televised game on ABC. Broadcast executives prayed that Notre Dame was back to stay.

In the locker room, Parseghian paced back and forth like an angry tiger. He approached Nick Eddy's locker.

"Nick, I have a question for you," he said. "What were you doing at this time in 1951?"

Eddy shrugged his shoulders. His mind searched for an answer that was not there.

"I'll tell you what you were doing," Parseghian said. "You were only seven years old in 1951, and that's the last time Notre Dame beat Purdue in this stadium."

Eddy smiled and said, "Wow!"

As he walked away, Parseghian bowed his head, closed his eyes, and focused on the speech he was about to give. Losing was not an option. He reached into his mind for his best Rockne.

"Everybody, stay where you are!" he yelled to the players. Then he began to bang his fist into the palm of his hand.

"Boys *(bang)* you read the newspapers *(bang)*. The predictors *(bang, bang)* say that Michigan State is going to beat us. But we *(bang)* are a better team than they are. We're going out there *(bang)* and prove it *(BANG)*!"

Parseghian then sank to his knees and bowed his head. "Hail Mary, full of grace . . ."

As the team headed for the field, captain Jim Carroll yelled, "Hey, everybody *stop*! I've got something to say. I want you to listen to me. I've played with nothing but losing teams all of my life. I am sick and tired of losing. Michigan State is not about to take No. 1 away from us now!" The players were now buckling their chinstraps and scraping their cleats more rapidly across the concrete floor.

Out on the field, the Notre Dame mascot, a.k.a "The Lep," had a surprise cooked up for the crowd. Dressed in his green suit and bowler hat, the bearded Lep (Robert Guenard) brandished a sword and was chasing someone dressed up in a Michigan State uniform. The Michigan State fans in the audience hoped this was a prank, because the Lep seemed intent on ramming his sword into someone. He chased the Spartan all over the field and finally stabbed his prey. Actually, the Spartan was Bill Harrigan from Morrissey Hall and he did a pretty good job of acting. Running away from the Lep, he headed into the stands, where the students grabbed him. They began to pass him up from row to row. Harrigan was missing a chinstrap on his helmet, so he held it with both hands. He prayed they didn't drop him. They passed him all the way to the fiftieth row and pretended to dump him over the side. Symbolically, they were throwing the Spartan out of the stadium. When they set him free, Harrigan ran back down the aisle to the stadium tunnel, ripped off his uniform, put on his slacks and shirt, and was sitting in the student section as Nick Eddy ripped off one of the most memorable Notre Dame runs of the last twenty years.

All that Harrigan missed was Michigan State punting after three plays. On Notre Dame's second offensive play, the Irish lined up in the double wing formation that had not been used all season. Eddy bolted around right end, picked up a crushing block from guard John Atamian, threaded his way back against the grain, split the secondary, and was into the end zone in the blink of an eye. Sixty-one yards to the end zone and the crowd went haywire. Even the fake Spartan, still smarting from Lep abuse, was on his feet and yelling his lungs out.

As the Notre Dame defense took the field again, Ken Maglicic noticed the glaze that had come over Tony Carey's eyes. The players were accustomed to seeing the happy-go-lucky Carey turn into a madman on game day. On Michigan State's next play, wide receiver Gene Washington ran a sideline pattern and the ball slipped through his fingers, but Carey clobbered him anyway. Ken Maglicic was quickly on the scene, yelling at his friend.

"Topcat, you've got to be careful. They'll flag you for that crap. Let him catch the ball and *then* knock the shit out of him!" He made sure Washington heard him.

The Irish defense was on its toes once more. Johnny Ray had used some caution in the early going of the last two games that did not work. This time he was going after Michigan State quarterback Steve Juday with everything but the Lep's sword. The Spartans would go nowhere in the first half, making one first down on their first six possessions.

Halfback Bill Wolksi had reinjured his hamstring in warm-ups, so Joe Farrell did most of the inside power running. Farrell and reserve fullback Bob Merkle pounded the ball down the field before Farrell caught a 13-yard touchdown pass from Huarte. Kicking woes continued as Joe Azzaro had also suffered a pregame leg injury. The Irish missed yet another 2-point conversion try and led 12–0.

The Nick Eddy show continued early in the second quarter with a 78-yard touchdown run, but this one was called back because of illegal procedure. Beginning with the Navy game two weeks earlier, Eddy had produced touchdowns of 74, 91, and 61 yards. If the 78-yarder had stood up, the sporting press would have been marking his name on every All-American ballot. The Notre Dame press box that day was jammed with enough typewriters to fill a Smith-Corona factory. The writers had come from all parts of the country.

In the view of the Notre Dame coaches, Eddy was actually two people. He was a terrific talent and a player who might wind up with the Heisman Trophy one day. Upon seeing Eddy for the first time, Pagna compared him to Gale Sayers, the "Kansas Comet," and one of the most elusive running backs in the history of college football. Like Sayers, Eddy could jiggle, hop, pivot, skip, and side-step just about anyone. When he turned his shoulders up the field, few could catch him.

After watching Eddy during the first week of practice, Pagna provided this analysis to Parseghian: "This kid is going to be great. The sky is the limit. I had no idea how good he was going to be."

Parseghian gave Pagna the look—the black eyes burning straight through him.

"Are you willing to make a black-box statement that he'll be a superstar?" Parseghian asked.

A black-box statement was written and circled on the blackboard in the coaches' meeting room. It was never erased. If a prediction fell through, Parseghian would never let you forget it.

"I will make the black-box statement," Pagna said. It was quickly chalked up on the blackboard.

What the coaches saw of Eddy on the field, they loved, but away from the field, he strayed. He and some other students were caught stealing cigarettes during their freshman year. Eddy told the dorm priest that he did not smoke, but, yes, he had participated. Like Tony Carey, he was sent home for a semester.

Eddy had grown up poor in northern California and his parents, Joseph and Angelina, divorced when he was young. Going home in the middle of a semester was not the easiest thing to do. It was his mother's dream that he play football and graduate from Notre Dame. She had been wined and dined by many coaches, but she liked Notre Dame the best.

When the young boy was growing up, Nick and Angelina listened to the Notre Dame games on the radio. They fell in love with the Fighting Irish.

"I was so naïve that I didn't even know where Notre Dame was," Eddy remembered. "I thought it might be in California. When I got on the plane to South Bend, I never thought it was going to land."

It was not long before he was on a plane back to California. Coaches started calling the day he got home. UCLA and USC wanted him badly. Marv Goux, an assistant coach at USC, called at least once a day. Goux coached for twenty-six years at USC, and most of his time was spent on John McKay's staff. He was considered the spiritual leader of the team. Mike Garrett credited Goux for giving him the inspiration to win the Heisman Trophy in 1965.

Goux told Eddy, "You come to USC and *you* will win the Heisman Trophy. Go back to Notre Dame, and they'll forget about you. Remember, Nick, you've already got one strike against you back in South Bend. Those Catholic priests are not forgiving."

Eddy refused to disappoint his mother. He went to work for a gasoline pipeline company outside of Tracy, California. He reconditioned 36-inch pipe by getting down on his knees and sandblasting it. He wore a hood and heavy protection and almost suffocated during the 100-degree days in desertlike conditions. The heavy clothing started to wear his skin off. Eddy was motivated by the hard labor. By the end of the summer, he was more determined than ever to revive his football career at Notre Dame. He was going back.

At preseason practice, Parseghian and Pagna were overwhelmed by what they witnessed of Eddy. He turned short gains into long touchdown runs. Yet, a few weeks later, they were left scratching their heads when they learned he was getting married. Vows were spoken at a small ceremony in a chapel behind the Sacred Heart Church. In 1964, unlike the old days of Knute Rockne and Frank Leahy, players were not forbidden from getting married. Eddy was homesick for his girlfriend, Audrey Jean. They would have two daughters, Carol and Nicole, before Nick graduated.

The coaches might have been unhappy to see Nick get married, but he seemed to improve each week in every phase of the game. He was not only a terrific runner but a polished receiver, averaging almost 30 yards per catch. The 74-yard screen pass against Navy looked like the work of a pro.

Late in the second quarter against Michigan State, Eddy scored his sixth touchdown of the season on a 5-yard sweep around right end. Jack Snow made the 2-point conversion on a quick slant from Huarte, and Notre Dame led 20–0 at halftime.

It was evident from the early minutes of the third quarter that Notre Dame was not about to slow down. Carey leaped high and seemed to hang in the air over Gene Washington as he registered his eighth interception of the season.

Washington did catch a 51-yard touchdown pass, but Notre Dame countered with a 21-yard dash to the end zone by Huarte, and Pete Andreotti's 2-yard sweep for 6 more points. For the seventh time in the 1964 season, Notre Dame had throttled another opponent, this time 34–7.

One of the heroes of the day was Joe Farrell, who rushed for 86 yards and took up the slack for Wolski. Standing outside the locker room, Farrell told the press, "We wanted to win it for our fans. I have never in my life seen so much spirit on the Notre Dame campus."

Farrell then walked into the locker room, lay down on the training table, and cried his eyes out. All his life he had wanted to play on a winning team at Notre Dame, and as a fifth-year senior, this was his last chance. He wanted nothing more as a kid than to wear the blue and gold. He was not so sure he would reach that dream. Tuition and room and board was $2,500. His dad, William Farrell Sr., was a Chicago firefighter and made that amount annually. Fortunately, Farrell won a football scholarship, and no one was prouder than his dad. Every time the Notre Dame tuition bill arrived in the mail, he showed it off around the firehouse.

"Look at this, boys," he would say. "Twenty-five hundred bucks and zero balance."

For the fourth game that season, Snow finished with more than 100 yards receiving, and Huarte was 11 of 17 for 197.

The players carried Parseghian off the field and then handed him the game ball. He held on to it like he would never let it go.

Duffy Daugherty smiled, shook Parseghian's hand, and said, "You might not have the best team in the world, but I would never want to play you again."

TWO DAYS BEFORE the Iowa game, *Time* magazine hit the newsstands with a picture of Ara Parseghian on the cover. To think that only a year ago, Notre Dame football was not worth a single line in America's most circulated periodical.

On the morning of the game, the sky cleared, and the blizzard that had passed through South Bend the previous day had moved to the east. Still, the temperature at game time was a bone-chilling 13 degrees, with winds gusting to twenty-eight miles per hour.

Nothing, however, was going to stop the Irish en route to their ninth straight win. Huarte threw only 10 passes against Iowa, but completed a 66-yard touchdown pass to Jack Snow, an appropriate name for all of the white stuff piled along the sideline. Nick Eddy continued his amazing surge with 17 carries for 92 yards and a touchdown run of 17 yards. Bill Wolski returned from his hamstring injury for touchdown plunges of 3 and 1 yard.

Notre Dame 28, Iowa 0 was not surprising when you consider the Hawkeyes had registered one win in Big Ten play.

Then it was time to focus on USC at the Coliseum in one week. Two days after beating the Hawkeyes, Notre Dame grabbed thirty-six votes in the Associated Press poll, compared to six for second-place Alabama. So it was clear that the slightest victory over USC would ensure a national title.

Out in Las Vegas, a renowned sports linesmaker named Bob Martin sat down with a pencil and a legal pad and wrote down the strengths and weaknesses of Notre Dame and USC. The Notre Dame side of the page was filled with "strengths" while "weaknesses" dominated the USC side. A few minutes later, he looked up just as a local bookmaker walked into his office. "You're going to laugh," Martin said. "But I'm making Notre Dame a fourteen-point favorite. I know the game's in L.A., but Notre Dame is one of the best teams I've ever seen."

Chapter 29

MISTER HEISMAN

S having in his dorm room on Tuesday before the USC game, John Huarte heard his name echoing down the hallway.

"John Huuuuugh-ert," came the voice. "You have a telephone call."

Huarte wiped the shaving cream from his face and wondered who might be calling before eight in the morning. His parents knew he was headed for class at this time of day, and he did not have a regular girlfriend.

Huarte picked up the receiver dangling from the hall phone. The voice on the other end of the line said, "Good morning, John, hope you are doing well."

Huarte recognized the dulcet tones belonging to Charlie Callahan, the sports information director at Notre Dame. He had called several times during the last few months to summon Huarte to his office for publicity pictures. Callahan, with his bow tie and horn-rimmed glasses, was one of the nicest men ever to grace the university.

Huarte had no idea why he was calling, but the words pouring from Callahan's mouth sent a rush up his spine. "Johnny, I am proud to announce that you have won the John Heisman Memorial Trophy as the best college football player in America for 1964."

The silence on the other end of the line did not surprise Callahan. He knew Huarte. He knew that the young man could be as excitable as warm milk.

"Gee, Charlie, how in the world did this happen?" Huarte said. "I never imagined—"

"Simply, Johnny, you are the best player in the country. You have been all season. This team would not be where it is right now if not for you. I congratulate you on a great season."

"But I had no idea—"

"Johnny, you will fly to New York at the end of the season for the awards banquet that will be held December the third at the Downtown Athletic Club. Ara will go with you. Your parents will be flown in from California."

"Sounds great."

"One other thing," Callahan continued. "The Heisman people want you to bring along your letter jacket for publicity pictures."

"Charlie," Huarte said. "I still don't have a letter jacket."

"Oh my God," he said. "I didn't think about that. We won't issue letter jackets till the end of the season, and you've never won one till now."

"Maybe I can borrow one," Huarte said.

"That would be a great idea, Johnny. By the way, I need you to come over to my office at two o'clock for some pictures with Ara."

As Huarte hung up and turned around, he found several Notre Dame students huddled around him. They had been listening to the conversation.

"Guys, I guess I just won the Heisman Trophy."

They all cheered. One of the students ran down the hallway like his hair was on fire.

"Stevie Wonder has won the Heisman Trophy!" he bellowed.

Later in the day, Parseghian extended his hand and said, "Johnny, you are not only the greatest player in college football, you are the comeback story of the year."

"All I can say is this, Coach. Thank God you came along at the right time in my life."

In one fourteen-year stretch, Notre Dame had won five Heismans— Angelo Bertelli, 1943; Johnny Lujack, 1947; Leon Hart, 1949; Johnny Lattner, 1953; and Paul Hornung in 1956. The next eight years without one seemed like a drought.

During Notre Dame's dark ages in the 1950s, the national sporting press began to turn up its collective nose on the program. The alumni had tried to pressure Callahan to beat the drums more loudly, but what did he have to work with? Hornung might have won the award on a 2-8 team. Still, no one ever expected that to happen again.

Callahan had never campaigned for Huarte, but he did say to his key contacts around the country, "We would be nowhere without this kid, and to think he never played until this season."

The top vote-getters in 1964 might have comprised the best Heisman Trophy class of all time:

1. John Huarte, Notre Dame, 1,026 votes
2. Jerry Rhome, Tulsa, 952
3. Dick Butkus, Illinois, 505
4. Bob Timberlake, Michigan, 361
5. Jack Snow, Notre Dame, 183

Perhaps the biggest surprise was that Kansas's Gale Sayers, who led the nation in rushing in 1964, did not finish in the top 10. Sayers was considered the greatest open-field runner in the history of the game.

Nevertheless, in 1964 the Heisman Trophy did not carry the prestige that it would in years to come. Not until 1977, when the presentations were first televised, did the award become a national treasure.

Not in the sixty-five-year history of the award has anyone other than Johnny Huarte won it without ever having first earned a letter jacket.

Chapter 30

THE TRAP

Few people completely understood USC coach John McKay. The man with the white flattop and the ever-present cigar always had that twinkle in his eye that said, the punch line was coming.

After losing a crucial game in the final seconds back in 1961, he said, "I told our players that there were 700 million Chinese in the world who didn't even know the game was played. The next week, I got five letters from China saying, 'What happened?'"

Make no mistake, McKay might laugh and joke with the best of them. He was known to hang out with Frank Sinatra and the Rat Pack. Be that as it may, there was not a more serious-minded man in college football—unless his name was Ara Parseghian or Bear Bryant. It took McKay only two years to turn a sodden program into national champions in 1962. He was one of the best game planners in the country. Of a larger concern, his halftime adjustments bordered on genius.

McKay wanted to keep the enemy off guard. He had the best poker face in the business. Never smiling, McKay had said this to the West Coast sportswriters two days before the big game against Notre Dame, "I've decided that if we play our very best and make no mistakes whatsoever, we will definitely make a first down."

He definitely wanted this quote to make the Notre Dame billboard: "I studied the Notre Dame–Stanford tape for six hours last night. I have reached one conclusion: Notre Dame can't be beaten."

That Thursday night before the game, he sat down for a steak dinner with a group of friends that included John Underwood from *Sports*

Illustrated. McKay lifted his knife and fork, shrugged, and said, "The condemned man ate a hearty meal."

McKay loved to bemoan the fact that USC was 6-3 and barely hanging on to a top 20 spot. This was especially disappointing because the Trojans had defeated the University of Oklahoma 40–14 early in the season when they jumped from twelfth in the national polls all the way to No 2. That week, USC received three more first-place votes than the No. 1 Texas Longhorns, but the season came unraveled the following Saturday when the Trojans lost 17–7 to Michigan State. If you believed in the accuracy of comparative scores, Notre Dame, thanks to destroying Michigan State, was 37 points better than USC.

It would be easy to assume that USC might pack it in against Notre Dame, but a strange rule in the Athletic Association of Western Universities, also known as the Western Conference, kept slim hopes alive. The Trojans could still reach the Rose Bowl if they beat Notre Dame. USC and Oregon State were tied with 3-1 records at the end of the conference schedule. To break the tie, a vote by the Western Conference faculty athletics representatives would be held that Saturday night in San Francisco. Word had been sent from the conference office to McKay that the Trojans would be Rose Bowl–bound if they upset America's top-ranked team. It just made sense.

Notre Dame–USC was the biggest game of the year in college football. An upset by USC would open the door for undefeated Alabama or Arkansas to inherit the top ranking.

McKay knew deep in his heart that the Trojans could hang tough with the Fighting Irish. The film of the Pitt game told him so. It revealed that USC could run inside against Notre Dame's No. 1 rush defense. All season, opposing teams had double-teamed the Notre Dame tackles. McKay's plan was to block down on the tackles with one man, then pull the guard to block the outside linebacker. He knew how badly the Irish missed sophomore linebacker Jim Lynch. Arunas Vasys was a big step-down from Lynch. Other Notre Dame defenders to miss the game with injuries would be Paul Costa, Pete Duranko, and Mike Webster. The forward wall had virtually no depth to fall back on.

McKay knew the Irish were hurting, but in public, he was still giving the impression that he had no hope of winning. He wanted the Irish to think that USC was already calling it a season.

Privately, though, he was building a fire under his team. He didn't mind calling upon old bulletin board tricks. Photos of every Notre Dame player had been taped to the bulletin board in USC's locker room. In the midst of this artwork was the *Time* magazine cover of Parseghian. Friday afternoon, after the final practice of the week, the players tore down the Notre Dame photos, then danced and stomped on them as fellow teammates clapped, chanted, and hollered.

Meeting the press that afternoon, McKay was still packing punch lines. "You know that if we knock these guys off, I could become the governor of Arkansas or Alabama." He paused and said, "Naw. Just tell them to send money."

Alabama had come from behind to win three games in 1964, alternating quarterbacks between Steve Sloan and Joe Namath, bothered by a trick knee. When Namath was well, he was hell on opposing teams. Against Vanderbilt, Namath absorbed a hard lick from a defender who said, "Hey, number 12, what's your name?" Namath smiled and said, "You'll see it in the headlines tomorrow."

Down the stretch, the Crimson Tide had defeated archrivals Georgia Tech 24-7 and Auburn 21-14. Folks in Alabama were happy that their team had decided never to play Georgia Tech again. The acrimony between the schools had turned ugly. Georgia Tech fans were so fond of Bryant that they decided to throw empty whiskey bottles at him. That is why Bryant chose to wear an Alabama football helmet onto the field in Atlanta.

"I don't mean to insinuate that these people in Atlanta are not good people," Bryant said. "They probably have good mamas and papas, too, but I think that some of them have forgot their training."

Bryant was angry with the Georgia Tech fans, but he was incensed that the Fighting Irish were running away with the national title. Three weeks earlier, Alabama had gained three first-place votes on Notre Dame following a near loss to Pitt, but the Irish proceeded to maul Michigan State and Iowa, and now held a 30-point lead over Alabama.

Bryant's frustration had recently boiled over at a press conference in Tuscaloosa.

"I don't know why y'all people who call yourselves sportswriters are voting Notre Dame No. 1 every week," he said. "Notre Dame doesn't play anybody. If they had to come down here and play our schedule, there's no damn way they'd be undefeated."

Bryant was not finished.

"Everybody in Alabama believes we're No. 1," he said. "Except for the Auburn people, who probably think we're No. 20."

Asked about Bryant's comments, Parseghian looked like he was ready to fight. "I guess he doesn't know anything about Midwestern football," he said. "Maybe he should think before he speaks."

Arkansas had also made a strong case for No. 1. After defeating top-ranked Texas 14-13 in mid-October, the Razorbacks' defense did not allow another point the rest of the way, shutting out Wichita State, Texas A&M, Rice, SMU, and Texas Tech. The Hogs would meet Nebraska in the Cotton Bowl while Alabama was headed to the Orange Bowl to play Texas. Thanks to the outdated thinking of the Notre Dame administration, the Fighting Irish would stay home once more during the bowl season.

In spite of Bryant's cynical view, Notre Dame still held the admiration and support of America's sporting press. The staff of college football writers at *Sports Illustrated* had unanimously voted Notre Dame No. 1. How could you not be impressed with a team averaging more than 30 points a game on offense while allowing 1 touchdown each Saturday? The critics pointed out that only one of Notre Dame's nine opponents currently resided in the top 20; Purdue was No. 16. The overall record of those nine teams, when you excluded the losses to Notre Dame, was 36-36, but the average margin of victory was almost 4 touchdowns.

Notre Dame–USC always stirred the blood because the teams had played thirty-six times since 1926. The rivalry was dreamed up by the greatest motivator in the history of college football, Knute Rockne himself. Rock agreed to travel west by train in 1926 to get the party started. No one admired Rockne more than Parseghian. Perhaps no one since Rockne knew how to inspire, cajole, and arouse like Parseghian. The first nine games of the season, the Irish were bubbling over with energy. Nevertheless, some experts wondered how much was left in the tank.

Before leaving South Bend, Parseghian had scattered notes around the locker room that were aimed at keeping the team focused. The coaches in recent weeks had watched a "laconic" Alan Page develop into one of the best players on defense. All the same, they still worried that he might retreat into his old form. The note on his locker read, "Go in with reckless abandon."

Left tackle Bob Meeker received a similar message: "Aggressiveness is a virtue."

Given all the hype and high expectations, Jim Murray of the *Los Angeles Times* could not wait for the game to begin. He wrote, "There is something reassuring about a Notre Dame team being No. 1 in the country, a reaffirmation of old verities. It's fitting—like ham and eggs, a good five-cent cigar and apple pie and ice cream. It takes us back to a time when Maine went Republican, heavyweight champions didn't quit on their stools, singers got haircuts and barbershop quartets wore straw hats."

Saturday's game would be Parseghian's first at the Coliseum. After a week of studying the USC films, he knew his hands were full. "USC is the most balanced team that we will play all year," he said. "They've got two speedbacks and a quarterback who can flat-throw the ball."

Before the game, McKay was handed a scouting report on Notre Dame that was two inches thick. He could never remember USC scout Mel Hein delivering a larger one, and; after poring over it, McKay realized that the Irish would be difficult to beat. The toughest chore would be slowing down the No. 1 offense in the country. So McKay set his priorities thusly: one, slow down the strong-side running game; two, keep Nick Eddy in check on the screen pass; and three, play a deep zone against Jack Snow. For the first time all season, a defense was going to respect Snow's speed. Little wonder. The big receiver had scored 6 touchdowns of more than 50 yards.

How would USC match up against the Irish? The Trojans possessed only one marquee player; Mike Garrett with his 869 rushing yards that ranked ninth nationally was still a year away from becoming the talk of college football.

Notre Dame would be leaving behind the snowy weather in South Bend for warmer climes in Southern California. Hoping to adjust to the heat, Parseghian scheduled a flight Thursday morning to Phoenix, where the team enjoyed Thanksgiving lunch and then worked out in temperatures that ranged into the high eighties. They flew to Los Angeles Friday morning. Notre Dame players were not accustomed to the adulation they received on the West Coast. They were mobbed at Los Angeles International Airport. A half hour later, as the buses pulled up to the Beverly Wilshire Hotel, they found the building ringed with fans. A year ago, hotels and airports were far more subdued when the Fighting Irish rolled into town. Now it was like traveling with The Beatles.

The change in the travel schedule bothered Tony Carey. Like most players, he was comforted by the same routine week after week.

"I think it was a dumb idea to stop in Phoenix," he told Ken Maglicic.

When Jack Snow walked into his hotel room, the phone was already ringing. He was about to become a target of the NFL-AFL bidding war, and with the draft two days away, club executives were desperately trying to gain a contract commitment from the prized wide receiver.

"Look," Snow said to his roommate Dan McGinn. "I don't want to talk to these pro people. When the phone rings, tell them I'm not here."

McGinn smiled. "But, Jack, they know you're here."

"I know, but lie to them anyway."

Saturday morning broke beautifully in Los Angeles. The sky was cerulean blue with temperatures in the eighties. The Coliseum would have its largest crowd since the national championship season of 1962—83,840, half of them wearing green and pulling for the Irish. A story in the *Times* under the headline of SCALPERS' BONANZA decried the work of ticket brokers who were getting $25 a pop for sideline seats. The regular price was six bucks.

Sitting among the movie stars, the raconteurs, the Big Cigars, and the beautiful people were Joseph and Dorothy Huarte, parents of the Heisman Trophy winner. Not far away were Jack Snow Sr. and his wife, Mabel. Also in the stands, wearing I LIKE ARA buttons, were Monsignor Thomas Foley and Father Charles Cranham, a stogie stuck between his teeth. Both were subway alums.

As Nick Rassas trotted toward the Notre Dame bench minutes before kickoff, he remembered the words of his father, George: *The Coliseum is the loudest place you will ever play. Sometimes the noise is so loud that you almost feel like you can't think. And that band. That band never stops playing that same song.*

Rassas turned to watch the Trojan Band marching up the tunnel. Indeed, they were playing "Hail Troy." The crowd was going bananas. Tony Carey, standing next to Rassas, tried to speak but was not sure his buddy could hear him. "I think I just felt the earth move," Carey said.

Rassas nodded, but Carey was not sure he'd heard every word.

Carey and Rassas and several members of the Notre Dame defense were worried about the defense they would put on the field. Arunas Vasys and Vince Mattera were hardly Jim Lynch and Pete Duranko. McKay was known to isolate on one part of a defense and hammer it down. Like Pitt, the Trojans were going to pound the line at right tackle. He was going to test the inexperienced Notre Dame line.

Rassas returned the opening kickoff from the 3-yard line to the 30. Three straight running plays failed to net a first down, and Bill Wolski was stopped cold at the 38. Jack Snow's first punt was a beauty, traveling 50 yards and rolling out of bounds at the USC 10.

McKay made no secret of his game plan. The first 9 snaps were running plays at right tackle—straight at Vasys, Mattera, and Kevin Hardy. The Trojans rolled up three straight first downs and seemed on the verge of wearing down the defense when Rod Sherman fumbled at the 48 and Tom Longo recovered.

Huarte quickly completed a 15-yard pass to Phil Sheridan over the middle. On second down, he rolled right and fired a bullet into the seam of the USC defense that Eddy caught at the 15 and carried down to the eight. Two running plays netted zero yards and, on third down, Huarte dropped straight back to pass. Jack Snow was covered on the right side so Huarte chose Eddy just outside of the right goalpost, but the pass was high, leading to a 25-yard field goal by Ken Ivan.

McKay began the first quarter by picking on Vasys and Matera, but as the game wore on, it became evident that he could not run at the left side even if he wanted to. Alan Page was completely dominating the blocker in front of him, Bob Svihus, throwing him around like a rag doll. After every snap, Page was in the USC backfield in the blink of an eye. That is why USC ran three plays, gained 2 yards, and punted.

Wolski quickly gained 22 yards and crossed midfield, but the play was called back due to holding. Eddy picked up 30 yards on a perfectly executed screen pass, which was reversed because of an illegal man downfield.

By the start of the second quarter, officials' flags were flying everywhere. A nervous Parseghian already knew he might be fighting an uphill battle. This entire five-man crew was from the Western Conference. The agreement to have an entire Western Conference crew had been approved the previous year by Parseghian's predecessor, Hughie Devore. Parseghian would have demanded a split crew with at least two officials from the Midwest. At that very moment, he had never felt more like an outsider. Here was an entire crew from a conference that worshiped USC, a team fighting to reach the Rose Bowl.

Remarkably, the penalties did not slow Notre Dame. Huarte completed two straight passes to Sheridan, another to Snow, and the ground game took over as Wolski, Kantor, and Eddy accounted for 30 more yards. Notre Dame faced a second down at the USC 22 and lined up in the power I formation with Snow flexed 3 yards to the right. USC smelled a run, but Huarte dialed up the pass. Jack Snow was 2 yards behind cornerback Bob Moss when he hauled in the pass at the goal. Notre Dame had marched 70 yards for the touchdown. Fifty yards in gains had been wiped out by flags, so the drive actually covered 102 yards. Ivan's PAT kick gave the Irish a 10–0 lead.

After the first play of USC's next possession, Page left the game with a hand injury. Mattera moved to right end. No surprise, the Trojans were now running at Mattera on every play. Garrett carried on 5 straight carries as USC moved all the way to the Notre Dame 9. But on fourth down, quarterback Craig Fertig overthrew a wide open Sherman in the right corner of the end zone.

After a Huarte interception, USC again moved inside the 20 with most of the carries around left end, but Fertig again overthrew an open receiver on fourth down.

The next time Notre Dame got the ball, Huarte made everything work—quick strikes to Sheridan and Snow, a screen pass of 20 yards to Eddy. At the USC 5-yard line, Huarte ran the option to perfection. He carried around right end and waited for the defensive end to move toward him. As he did, Huarte pitched quickly to Wolski, now in the clear, and he carried five easy yards for the touchdown. The drive of 74 yards made it 17–0.

As the teams left the field at halftime, the consensus was that Notre Dame could not be beaten. John McKay was right. Not once all season had the Notre Dame offense clicked this well in the first half. Huarte had been typically modest five days earlier when he won the Heisman Trophy, but the award was yet another boost to his confidence. He completed 11 of 15 for 176 yards in the first half. Mr. Heisman was well on his way to posting his best statistical day of the season—and he was doing it with ease.

During the intermission, former Notre Dame coach Frank Leahy did an interview with the USC radio broadcast team. If overconfidence could be contagious, Leahy already had the bug.

"USC is fighting to make it to the Rose Bowl, but they are not going to make it against this great Notre Dame team," he said. "Ara is running an imaginative offense that just cannot be beaten."

In the locker room, Parseghian drew up three more plays on the chalkboard that he thought would work. Then near the top, he wrote JUST 30 MORE MINUTES.

Wearing a white shirt, dark slacks, and a blue tie, Parseghian walked to the front of the room and made a fist. This was to remind the players of the first speech he had made back in December—*When I make a fist it's strong and you can't tear it apart. As long as there's unity, there's strength.*

Parseghian knew this halftime speech would be the most important one of his life. A national championship was on the line. Notre Dame had USC on the ropes.

"Let's have your attention up here," he began. "Thirty minutes stands between us and the greatest sports comeback in history. Thirty minutes! You gotta go out and play this second half, boys, like a 60-minute team. This is the way we started this season and this is the way we're going to finish, you understand. I want that defense down there knocking them on their butts. You go after it, understand. You did a damn good job in there and I'm real proud of you. I want to be prouder of you when you come back here after the second half, boys. Let's really go out there and give them thirty more minutes of Notre Dame football!"

The Irish players stormed down the tunnel toward the field like a team en route to a 50–zip victory. Nevertheless, in the other locker room, another coach was working his magic.

"Our game plan is working," McKay hollered at the Trojans. "Keep doing your stuff and we'll get some points. They've won nine games and never really been under duress. If we can get on the scoreboard quick, we can get some pressure on them."

On the way out of the locker room door, McKay grabbed Garrett by the arm. "Mike, we are going to do some different things in the second half. I don't want you to think about it. I just want you to run the damn football. Believe me, this is going to work."

In the first half, the USC offense had worked between the tackles like a boxer delivering body shots. This time they were going to attack the outside. Moreover, McKay planned to turn quarterback Craig Fertig loose. He once called Fertig "the best pure passer in college football."

McKay's confidence was no illusion. With Garrett sweeping the ends, and Fertig completing quick hits to Sherman and Garrett, USC rolled down the field. Garrett carried to the Notre Dame 17 when yet another flag flew from the back pocket of referee Jack Sprenger. A personal foul on Gmitter moved the ball to the Irish 6. It took USC three plays to score as Garrett bowled over from the 1. The lead had been cut to 17–7.

As if to say "never fear," Huarte moved the offense goalward once more. Wolski and Eddy tore holes in the center of the USC line. Not a single time all season had the Notre Dame offense looked this dominant. On second down, Huarte fired a 17-yard completion to Sheridan all the way to the USC eight.

Just minutes earlier, USC cornerback Ed Blecksmith had approached McKay on the sideline with a plan to stop the Irish. "Coach, on that option pitch Notre Dame is running, I noticed that I can break it up," Blecksmith said. "If you'll let me blitz, I can get the ball."

"Go for it," the coach said. McKay was running out of guesses on how to stop Huarte.

On first down at the 8, Blecksmith sensed that Huarte was going to run the same option that had produced the 5-yard touchdown run by Wolski. As Huarte took the snap from Norm Nicola, Blecksmith looped around the left defensive end and quickly was on a collision course with Huarte. Blecksmith actually hid behind the end and Huarte did not see him coming until the last second. Blecksmith wrapped his hands around Huarte's waist and caused the quarterback to hurry the pitch. It bounced off Wolski's shoulder pad and linebacker John Lockwood recovered.

The Trojans offense was going nowhere. They ran three plays and punted. From the Notre Dame 40, Huarte and the offense started powering up once more. It seemed too easy. Wolski right, Eddy left, Kantor up the middle; Huarte to Snow on the quick post. Huarte to Sheridan at the sideline. It took Notre Dame only three minutes to reach the 1-inch line after a 2-yard dive by Kantor. Now it was first down and the Irish were ready to stick the dagger into the Trojans' hearts.

A hand-off at left tackle and Kantor was in the end zone before USC could blink. Touchdown! Forty thousand Irish fans were now having the time of their lives. As 23–7 flashed on the scoreboard, the game was all but over. But as the players unpiled, a flag came sailing in from the far right side. Snow had been elbowed in the helmet by a USC player. The Notre Dame players expected a flag for unnecessary roughness, but umpire David Queen had something else in mind. He nailed left tackle Bob Meeker for holding.

In the era of the five-man crew, the umpire was permitted to line up just about anywhere he wanted to go. (In today's game of seven officials, the umpire always lines up in front of the center.) With Notre Dame at the 1-inch line, Queen chose to line up outside of Jack Snow, who was at right end. This placed Queen more than a dozen yards from Meeker. Two officials—back judge Everett Bannister and referee Jack Sprenger— had a better view of the play.

Holding on Meeker would be remembered as one of the most controversial calls in the history of Notre Dame football. For many reasons. The first and most obvious is that Meeker did not hold. To be called for holding, a player must first block someone. Meeker barely brushed tackle Denis Moore and then fell forward on his face. A study of the film by the most unbiased viewer will confirm that Meeker could not have held Moore. His hands never released from his jersey until he tried to brace for his fall. As Carey joked years later, "Meeks, you *deserved* a flag because that was the lousiest block I've ever seen in my life."

If Meeker had never come out of his stance, Kantor still would have scored with ease. Kantor was such a powerful runner that the entire offensive line could have stood still and he would have hammered his way across the goal. Frustrating to the Notre Dame coaches was that Queen was completely out of position to make the call. His view of Meeker was blocked by several Notre Dame and USC linemen. Little wonder that USC play-by-play man Tom Kelly yelled into the microphone, "Ara Parseghian is jumping up and down! Up and down!"

"I have never seen holding called from the one-inch line in my life," Parseghian yelled at Sprenger, "It's just not possible. That is a bad, bad call."

"I guess it's possible, Coach," Sprenger said. "Because my guy called it."

Now the Notre Dame offense was all the way back at the sixteen. Kantor carried twice for a total of 4 yards, and Huarte overthrew Sheridan in the end zone on third down, the ball banging off the crossbar. Parseghian could have opted for a 29 field goal attempt. Ivan already had connected from 25, but Huarte was too hot and the offense too powerful to pull back now. The Heisman quarterback dropped five steps into the pocket and had all day to throw. He looked left. He looked right. He waited and waited. Snow broke clear in the middle of the end zone and, to the surprise of everyone, Huarte whizzed the ball far over his head. A low groan emanated from the Notre Dame faithful.

On the first play, Garrett lost 4 yards, but on second down, Fertig found Fred Hill down the middle for a gain of 28. USC's red-headed quarterback possessed a strong arm, and like Huarte, had waited three long, frustrating years for his chance to start. After a terrible first half, he was finally making the most of it. Fertig would complete five straight passes on the drive, and the touchdown would come from the 23. His

TD pass to Hill in the right corner of the end zone could not have been more on the mark. Hill had beaten Longo by 3 yards. Dick Brownell's extra-point kick was wide, and with 5:09 to play in the game, Notre Dame's lead had shrunk to 17–13.

McKay paced the USC sideline like a wild man. "We've got 'em!" he yelled to his players. "They've already reached the breaking point. I knew they would."

On the Notre Dame sideline, Maglicic bowed his head and said a Hail Mary. Then he thought to himself, *This is starting to feel like last season.*

How remarkable that Fertig's five straight completions had come against a Notre Dame secondary that had allowed only three touchdown passes all season. Tony Carey, Nick Rassas, and Tom Longo had combined for a nation-leading 18 interceptions. No secondary in the country was more respected, or more talented.

The Notre Dame offense was now dead-legged. They ran three plays and Jack Snow punted. Because USC had rushed only two men, most of the Notre Dame linemen were free to fly down the field in coverage, and, as Mike Garrett caught the ball at the USC 28-yard line, he was eighteen-wheeled by Dick Arrington and Norm Nicola and driven all the way back to the 22. With slightly more than three minutes to play, USC was now stuck 78 yards from the winning touchdown. But wait! There was another flag far upfield.

Head linesman William Settle had dropped a flag on Notre Dame left guard John Atamian for holding just before the ball was punted. Again, the call was a phantom. Atamian had barely brushed linebacker Frank Lopez as he made a halfhearted attempt to rush Snow. It was clear that USC was not coming after the punter because they rushed only two men. After Lopez bounced off Atamian, he took two more steps into the backfield and peeled back to block for Garrett.

Sprenger was asked by Notre Dame captain Jim Carroll the number of the player guilty of holding and the referee said, "Number 68."

Notre Dame did not have a number 68. Atamian's number was 66.

Snow's second punt was fielded by Garrett at the USC 48 and returned to the Notre Dame 42, where he fumbled. The ball rolled to the

39 and was loose for three seconds before it was recovered by USC's Lopez just before Alan Page grabbed it. The penalty had cost Notre Dame 39 yards of priceless field position. On first down, Fertig rifled a pass of 23 yards over to Hill, all the way to the 17. The USC fans were now hollering their lungs out. The Trojan Band played "Hail Troy" over and over. A backward pass to Garrett netted 2 yards.

The USC band was now blasting "Hail Troy" and the Trojan players could barely hear Fertig calling plays in the huddle. On second down, he arced a pass into the end zone that was caught by Fred Hill in front of Carey. A silence fell over the stadium as the fans waited for the official's signal. Hill had landed on his helmet just inches out of bounds and the pass was ruled incomplete.

After injuring his hand earlier in the game, Page had returned in the third quarter and was again tearing through the USC blocking. What defensive coordinator Johnny Ray saw on the next play made him smile. All season, he had worked his backside off to make Alan Page a great player. As Ray shouted encouragement from the sideline, Page knocked down his blocker and swooped down on Fertig, chasing him backward all the way to the 30. Page wrapped his left arm around Fertig's shoulder and was dragging him backward as the quarterback pitched the ball toward fullback Homer Williams. Practically everyone in the stadium believed it was a fumble. Even Kelly in the pressbox yelled into the microphone, "There is a fumble on the play!"

To his credit, Fertig managed to push the ball forward, but Sprenger was so out of position that he almost missed the call. He was standing behind Fertig and Page. With a better view, he likely would have called a sack. Instead he waved his arms across his body just once. Then he waited and hoped that another official would confirm his call. When nothing happened, Sprenger, now a confused man, furiously waved his arms, calling it incomplete.

Even if the call had been a fumble, it was recovered by Williams at the 26. But Parseghian and the Norte Dame coaches wanted a sack that would have set USC back to the 30.

"How can you make that call?" Parseghian yelled at Sprenger. "You missed the damn call—again!" If instant replay had been available for officials in 1964, the most likely call would have been a sack.

Instead, USC still had the ball at the Notre Dame 15 and the biggest play of the game was coming. It was fourth and eight with 1:37 to play. On the sideline, Ray was working through his mind the most important defensive call of a coaching lifetime. Ray's signal to Jimmy Carroll was a bit radical. He was calling for the inside blitz. Notre Dame would be going for broke in the biggest play of the year. Parseghian swallowed hard. He prayed his man was right.

Ray's instructions were for Carroll to line up over the center with Maglicic right behind him. It was the defense's version of the I formation. Left cornerback Tom Longo assumed coverage on Fred Hill on the left side of the defense. Rassas would take tight end Dave Moton. Carey's responsibility was Rod Sherman.

As Fertig prepared to call his play in the huddle, Garrett said to himself, *Please, God, I don't want to carry the ball anymore. This is the toughest defense I've ever been up against in my whole life.* He was relieved when Fertig called 84Z, a quick post to Rod Sherman.

"Good luck, you guys," Garrett said. "I really hope this play works."

As USC lined up, Rassas started yelling, "No! No! No! This won't work!" Maglicic turned to see Rassas madly tapping the top of his helmet. He was signaling "Call off the blitz!" Rassas instantly knew that Fertig was going to throw the ball to Sherman on a quick post pattern. He knew that Carey would need some inside help. Otherwise, Sherman would be wide open.

Maglicic looked at Ray on the sideline and tapped the top of his helmet, trying to call off the blitz. Ray looked back at Maglicic and raised both fists over his head. It meant the blitz was still on.

As Carey lined up on the right side of the defense, he was 8 yards off Sherman and squarely in front of him. The words of coach Paul Shoults from the past nine games rang in his head: *Never let the receiver get inside of you.* Carey checked the Notre Dame defensive alignment and said to himself, *I'm going to have inside help.* Otherwise, he would have taken two steps to his left in order to get a better angle on the inside route.

As Fertig called the signals, Mike Garrett went in motion to the left. Now Carey was certain he would have inside help. According to the Notre Dame defensive formula, a man in motion meant double coverage on the outside. The ball was snapped and Fertig dropped straight back, then took two steps to his left. Carroll blew open a hole in middle of the USC line and Maglicic shot through like a cannonball. He was already bearing down on Fertig as Sherman took five steps upfield and cut hard to his right. Fertig had about half a second to throw. He was leaning so far to the left to avoid Maglicic that he actually released the ball back to his right. As Fertig went down, he prayed that Sherman would catch it.

Tony Carey can still see it in slow motion, like a bad dream. The pass is perfectly placed to the inside of Sherman at the 4-yard line. Carey can't reach the ball. He lunges for Sherman's shoulder pads but loses his grip. He goes down—down on his knees. He hears the crowd roar and the band strike up "Hail Troy." He is facing the opposite way from the end zone and refuses to look back because he knows Sherman is already there. The kid who had once danced on the hood of his 1953 Chevy to celebrate the hiring of Parseghian had just lost the national championship for Notre Dame. Eight stars on his helmet no longer meant a thing.

Carey felt numb all over as he stood up. He started to walk straight up the field and never looked back. He did not want to see the wild celebration taking place in the end zone. Carey kept saying to himself over and over, "I cannot believe it."

In truth, he had been hung out to dry by a defensive scheme that should have never been called. The play would have never worked if Rassas had been assigned double coverage on Sherman; 84Z would have become 84 Zip. The tight end stayed in to block so Rassas had no one to cover. He became a spectator on the play. If he had taken three steps to his right, he would have easily picked off Fertig's pass.

Remembering the thunderous noise that day, Garrett said, "It was so loud that you actually felt paralyzed, if you can imagine that. The sound seemed like it was going straight through me."

On the sideline, Parseghian covered his head with both arms and seemed to be crying. USC now led 20–17. The entire Notre Dame bench was in shock, but after taking a few seconds to recover, they realized there was still 1:33 left on the clock—plenty of time for a Heisman Trophy quarterback to mount a comeback.

Huarte quickly moved Notre Dame to the USC 46, but threw an interception to Nate Shaw. Hope was still alive, though, with three time-outs remaining. The defense stopped USC cold and, after a punt, Notre Dame was back in business at its own 20 with thirty seconds to play. No one could blame Huarte for going straight to Snow for completions of 21 and 12 yards. The Irish were at the USC 47 with five seconds to go. Last play of the game.

Snow would be the only Notre Dame receiver running a route. He sprinted straight up the right sideline as Huarte threw the Hail Mary all the way down to the 10, where five USC defenders were waiting for Snow. It was hopeless, and the ball was knocked down.

Nick Eddy, after blocking on the right side, was starting to drift open over the middle before Huarte released the ball. By then, though the quarterback was already locked into Snow. The game was over. Depression was setting in.

For the first time all season, the Irish would not carry their coach off the field. Instead, Parseghian had to endure the sight of the USC players carrying McKay straight toward him. McKay dismounted and shook hands with Parseghian. The Notre Dame coach stood around for a couple of minutes, shaking the hands of the USC players, acting the part of the good soldier.

The Fighting Irish lumbered off the field like an exhausted battle troop. Upon reaching the tunnel, they slowed to a funeral walk. They barely felt like putting one foot in front of the other. Inside the locker room, three players bounced their gold helmets off the concrete floor. A few others kicked the metal lockers. But for the most part, the fight was out of them. Bob Meeker sat down on one side of the locker room and bawled into his hands. Carey sat down on the other side and did the same. Huarte stood in the corner and stared straight ahead, while Rassas leaned his chair against a wall and studied the ceiling.

Moments later, Parseghian marched into the locker room with the energy of a heavyweight contender about to go fifteen rounds. He pointed to each of the four doors around the locker room.

"Close those doors," he yelled to the managers. "And I want all the players to get to the middle of the locker room. Now!" They slowly trudged to the center of the room and turned to face their coach. Parseghian fell to his knees.

"Dear God, give us the strength in our moment of despair to understand and accept that which we have undergone."

Parseghian stood up and set his eyes on the players. He wiped away a tear.

"I want you to know how proud I am of all of you. We had a great season. I still believe we are the No. 1 team in the country. What happened out there on the field today cannot be blamed on one person. A lot of crazy things occurred. I can't explain all of it to you right now. Most importantly, I want all of you to understand one thing. What we do in the next half hour will follow us the rest of our lives. The press is about to walk in here and they're about to ask a lot of questions. They know we feel cheated by the officials, and maybe we should. But we are Notre Dame men and we don't cry, alibi, or blame a loss on someone else. We won this season with humility. I want us to accept this loss in the same way. I am not going to blame the officials. I don't want you to blame the officials.

"For the next ten minutes, no one else will be allowed in this locker room. If you want to cry, swear, throw your helmets against the wall—I will understand all of those feelings. But when we open up the doors, I want all of you to hold your tongues and to lift your heads high in defeat and to act like Notre Dame men. I have never in my life been associated with a better bunch of people than the guys in this room right now. I want you to know that from the bottom of my heart. No one will ever forget what you achieved this year. No one."

Parseghian walked away and sat down on a black trunk in the corner of the room. He stared at the floor for ten minutes. Then he began the process of healing. The players decided to follow his lead.

Chapter 31

COMING HOME

Two nights later, the Notre Dame chartered flight touched down in the darkness of St. Joseph's County Airport. As the players peered out the windows, they saw nothing stirring. Nothing at all.

They had spent two days on the West Coast at Disneyland and Universal Studios. It did nothing to lift their spirits. Ara Parseghian never would have scheduled the trips if he had anticipated such a crushing loss.

After the plane taxied to the terminal, the players quietly descended the steps to the tarmac and filed on to two buses. They were soon on their way back to campus. The utter stillness of the night was heartbreaking. Not a single headlight pierced the darkness along the highway. No one had come to meet them at the airport.

Sitting across the aisle, Tony Carey said to Ken Maglicic, "Looks like they forgot about us, Binks. I thought there'd be a few people at the airport to meet us."

"Over a thousand showed up when we beat Navy," Maglicic said. "I guess everybody's back at campus studying."

The bus rolled on in to the darkness. The players had spent the last couple of days trying to get over a devastating loss. Now they were sinking more deeply into that mind-numbing depression.

Five minutes later, the players heard the airbrakes hiss as the driver prepared to make the left turn onto Notre Dame Avenue. At the time they were really slowing down. As the bus made the wide turn, the headlights caught a few silhouettes standing at the corner. Then several more figures moved out of the shadows. Suddenly all of the players stood up. They could see thousands upon thousands of eyeballs reflecting in the headlights. People were lined up shoulder to shoulder in the street for more than a half mile. They were chanting, "We're No. 1! We're No. 1!"

"Oh my God," Parseghian said to Tom Pagna. "I thought they'd forgotten about us. I really did."

Pagna smiled. "I knew they'd be here."

Carey laughed. "Look, Binks, they still love me after all!"

At that moment Parseghian and Pagna were standing at the front of the lead bus. "You don't know how much this means to me, Tommy," Parseghian said. "They basically kicked us out of Northwestern. I wanted us to win it all at Notre Dame."

"We will someday," Pagna said. "This is only the beginning."

The driver brought the bus to a halt. Notre Dame Avenue was a sea of students yelling like crazy. The Notre Dame band was a block away, striking up the "Victory March." The driver turned to Parseghian and said, "What do you want me to do, Coach?"

"Open the door," he said. "Let's walk. I think the walk will do us a lot of good."

A roar went up as the players filed off the two buses. Students grabbed their luggage and began acting as bellmen. They all marched together toward the Old Fieldhouse. Players were slapped on the shoulders and pounded on their backs.

Parseghian was met at the front door of the Old Fieldhouse by Frank Gaul, who put his arm around the coach and said, "I know you weren't expecting this—"

"No, I wasn't expecting it all," he said. "I'm just glad to see it happened."

Eighty percent of the student body had been away during Thanksgiving break. They began to return on Sunday, and, as word spread, Gaul knew they were going to have a terrific turn-out. More than 7,000 students and fans were inside the arena, jammed shoulder to shoulder from one side of the arena to the other and all the way to the back wall. It was even louder than the Los Angeles Coliseum.

Jim Carroll was scheduled to speak first. Even before approaching the microphone, Carroll knew his emotions would overcome him.

"I can't tell you how much we all appreciate this," he said, tears streaming down his face. "We were hoping you would be here for us when we got back." He stepped away and listened to the roar. He was really crying now. The standing ovation lasted more than ten minutes. Then, slowly, the chant began: "Ara! Ara! Ara!"

Parseghian knew precisely what he was going to say.

"We wanted to bring you a national championship!" he hollered into the microphone.

"You did! You did!" they shouted back.

He backed up and wiped away a tear. Then he chuckled.

"You know," he said as the crowd settled, "I don't give a damn what they're saying down in Alabama. Notre Dame is still No. 1!"

Parseghian paused and said, "You know, we cried together after the USC loss. But that is okay. There is a deep bond between the players and their coach."

That was all it took. The band played and the students sang and you would have thought the USC game had turned out differently. Parseghian had known for years that nothing could topple the Notre Dame spirit. Beginning with Knute Rockne, they had never stopped believing. Yes, there had been some doubt in the fifties and early sixties, but when the Irish started winning again in 1964, the place sprung to life. Watching from the cornfields that ringed the campus, you would have sworn the Old Fieldhouse was on fire that night. Lightning bolts danced inside. Standing in the shadows about a hundred feet from the side door, Father Theodore Hesburgh smiled. He had promised never to come again, but, in truth, he wanted to feel the Notre Dame spirit rising up. Later, he would write, "It's dark and cold outside. There was a strange quiet on campus after the loss. Then the shouting returned when the team got back. Southern California has done it to us before, and we have done it to them, too, but somehow the world went on. The sun rose again the next morning and the people began to dream of next year."

Many more wonderful seasons would lie ahead under Ara Parseghian. The Fighting Irish had been reborn. Parseghian had taught them how to win again. All Notre Dame needed was someone to remind them of just how great they could be. That someone was Ara Parseghian.

The 1964 season was not for today, but for the days to come. Even in defeat, the Irish had showed the world what they were made of. The Old Fieldhouse was rocking. Championships were coming again.

Notre Dame football was back.

EPILOGUE

Forty-four years after the heartbreaking loss to USC, I was sitting across the desk from Ara Parseghian at his home in Mishawaka, just outside of South Bend. I asked him how it felt to lose a national championship that was so firmly in his grasp.

"What do you mean?" he said, those dark eyes burning. "Stand up and look behind you."

Hanging on the wall behind my chair was the MacArthur Trophy, a silver plate with NOTRE DAME NATIONAL CHAMPIONS 1964 engraved on it. The trophy was presented to Parseghian by the National Football Foundation at the end of the season. It represented one of the year's three national championships. The others belonged to Alabama and Arkansas.

Notre Dame's 20–17 loss to USC in late November was just the beginning of a crazy end to the 1964 college football season. On the afternoon of January 1, 1965, Arkansas rallied to defeat Nebraska in the fourth quarter 10–7 in the Cotton Bowl. Then it was up to Alabama to defeat Texas in the first bowl game ever played at night.

We all gathered around a neighbor's television set to watch the first college postseason bowl game broadcast in color. We were not disappointed with NBC's wonderful experiment that drew 40 million viewers and launched the era of prime-time sports broadcasting. In spite of a terrific performance by Joe Namath, the Texas Longhorns came through with a 21–17 upset of Alabama. A frantic last-minute comeback attempt by the Crimson Tide fell just short.

In the final seconds, a white-shoed Namath made a desperation lunge for the goal line on fourth and inches. Texas middle linebacker Tommy Nobis tackled him about 2 inches short of the stripe. Namath argued the call. "I will go to my grave believing that I scored that touchdown," he said.

The Crimson Tide's loss meant that my team, the Arkansas Razorbacks, would climb to No. 1 in the rankings. But wait! Not so fast. The final AP and UPI polls that year were conducted *before* the bowls. So Alabama was crowned the official national champ and Arkansas was left out in the cold. Both of my teams were shut out. At the age of eleven, after experiencing the most exciting college football of my life, I was left with no choice. I started chasing girls.

This was the final top five:

1. Alabama
2. Arkansas
3. Notre Dame
4. Michigan
5. Texas

I still wonder what would have happened if Arkansas and Notre Dame had played in the Cotton Bowl. With Alabama losing to Texas, the Cotton Bowl would have been a de facto national championship game. The Notre Dame administration did not believe in bowl games, however, and five more years would pass before the ban was lifted.

After the '64 season, Arkansas was awarded the Grantland Rice Trophy as the unofficial national champion of 1964. What irony. Grantland Rice brought national fame to Notre Dame in 1924 with the famous newspaper lead—"Famine, Pestilence, Destruction, and Death." I still think that Notre Dame and Arkansas should have traded trophies. In truth, though, the MacArthur Trophy and the Grantland Rice awards were like bowling trophies compared to the hardware Alabama picked up that season.

All of this would be moot if Notre Dame had taken care of business against USC. I have watched the film of that game more than twenty-five times and I firmly believe Notre Dame was defeated by a far inferior team. Three factors worked against the Irish in the second half. One,

USC quarterback Craig Fertig made up for an abysmal first half by hitting almost every open receiver; two, halftime adjustments by John McKay took advantage of Notre Dame injuries in the defensive front eight; and three, the officials made two phantom calls that day that greatly damaged Notre Dame's chances of winning. I have been covering football for thirty-five years, and I know that officials make mistakes—some big, some small. Most of the time, bad calls go both ways, but the calls I am about to describe were without justification.

The first came early in the fourth quarter with Notre Dame facing a first down at the USC 1-inch line. Fullback Joe Kantor powered into the end zone behind some great blocks by center Norm Nicola and left guard John Atamian. The only player in the Notre Dame line not delivering a good block was left tackle Bob Meeker. The man he was supposed to block, John Lopez, veered to the outside. Meeker barely brushed the tackle, Denis Moore, before he fell on his face. Out of the blue, umpire David Queen, some 12 yards away, threw a flag for holding. It was like arresting a man for stealing a car, only to discover it belonged to him.

Meeker said he received a phone call after the game from NFL referee Fritz Graff, who was from Meeker's hometown of Akron. Graff was sitting in the stands in the east zone, not far from Meeker, when the controversial holding call was made.

"Fritz told me that there was no way I should have been called for holding, that I didn't even touch the guy," Meeker said.

The second most debatable call came with three minutes to play. Notre Dame, leading 17–13, set up to punt at the Irish 23. USC rushed only two men. Neither one was held on the play, but this did not stop head linesman William Settle from digging into his pocket and throwing a flag. He nailed guard John Atamian for holding even though the Notre Dame left guard merely brushed USC's Lopez with his right shoulder. This cost Notre Dame 39 yards in field position and set up the winning touchdown for USC.

Parseghian said in 1964 that he would not blame the officials for the loss. Through the years, he held firm to that pledge. Nevertheless, when I met with him in September of 2008, he'd had a change of heart.

"All of those calls were bad calls," he said. "All of them were 15-yarders and they killed us. We should have won that game. That game belonged to Notre Dame. What really bothers me is the significance of those calls in that loss. Without those calls, we would have won that USC game. And it would have been the most dramatic comeback in the history of college football, one that would have been long remembered. The team was 2-7 the previous season and we would have been 10-0 if we had beaten USC.

"They called holding on Bob Meeker and it was stupid. The man he is trying to block veers down to the outside and Meeker completely misses him. He didn't even touch the guy. We are trying to go off tackle and Meeker completely takes himself out of the play by falling down. How in the world that guy [David Queen] ever made that call I will never know. You make no contact with anybody and therefore it cannot be holding. The official made the call all the way from the other side of the field. How in the hell he saw holding from that far away I will never know. Joe Kantor was already in the end zone. That touchdown would have locked up the game. That would have made it 24–7 and we win the game.

"The holding call on the punt with three minutes to go in the game still gives me nightmares. That caused an incredible swing in field position. We looked at the film, up and down, over and out, and we could never find why they made the call they did. Once again, it was a bad call.

"On the play before the winning touchdown pass, we fully believe that call should have at least been a sack. That would have put the ball at the 30 instead of the 15. Craig Fertig kind of flicks his wrist and the ball goes forward. It either has to be a fumble or grounding. Or the referee should have called the sack. No way that USC gets the ball back at the 15."

Shortly before he died in October of 2008, USC quarterback Craig Fertig was asked about the controversial play in which he was chased backward for 15 yards by Alan Page. Fertig was being pulled backward by Page when he shoved the ball forward in the direction of fullback Homer Williams. Referee Jack Sprenger ruled the pass incomplete.

"You see, I belonged to the Screen Actors Guild back then," Fertig said. "That was one of the best acting jobs that I've ever done." He smiled and continued, "All I can say is that Jack Sprenger showed a lot of guts by making that call."

Sprenger became the Pac-10 supervisor of officials in 1971 and was only the third official inducted into the National Football Foundation Hall of Fame. Notre Dame–USC was not his crowning achievement.

After the 1964 season, Parseghian wrote a letter to Meeker that absolved him of holding at the goal line. "Incidentally, we both know that the worst officiating call in the history of college football took place in Los Angeles in 1964, and through this letter, I document for you that Bob Meeker was the innocent victim of an incompetent official."

Parseghian's greatest regret beyond the officiating was that Notre Dame was not allowed to play in a bowl game in 1964.

"It was very difficult to fight for a national championship when you couldn't go to bowl games," he said. "That was one of the things that really bothered me back then and still does."

MUCH DEBATE WOULD follow the 1964 season concerning the overall value of the Notre Dame team. No one could argue with the fact that Notre Dame defeated its opponents by an average of almost 4 touchdowns per game. The Irish finished with the No. 1 overall defense. John Huarte was the fourth-ranked passer and Jack Snow led the nation in receiving with 60 catches. Huarte finished with 2,062 passing yards and 16 touchdowns. He set twelve school records, four that still stand. Perhaps the most remarkable statistic is that Huarte averaged more than 10 yards per attempt for the season.

The Notre Dame pass defense finished No. 8 in the country, but if you figure in all of the statistics, including the 18 interceptions, the Irish compiled a defensive passer rating of 48.4 that was tops in the country.

Jack Snow and John Huarte were consensus All Americans, and Tony Carey was selected to the second team. Jim Carroll finished with a school record 140 tackles, 52 more than second-place Ken Maglicic. He was selected first-team All American by the Associated Press.

USC running back Mike Garrett, who would win the Heisman Trophy in 1965, was asked more than forty years later to assess the Notre Dame defense. "That was the best defense by far that I ever played against in college. Those guys could hit, run, and put a stranglehold on you. The only defense that I played against with that much discipline were the Green Bay Packers."

The six sophomore starters on the 1964 team—Jim Lynch, Nick Eddy, Tom Regner, Kevin Hardy, Don Gmitter, and Alan Page—would become the driving force of the 1966 national championship team that shut out six opponents. They were fortunate that they came along in 1964 when things were turning around for Notre Dame.

"Those sophomores always looked up to the older guys because they knew just how badly we wanted to win," Tony Carey said. "They knew that we had been through some pretty bad times and that we were going to do what it took to turn it around."

Eight players were drafted off the 1964 team. The first off the board to the Minnesota Vikings was Jack Snow with the eighth pick. He was quickly traded to the Los Angeles Rams. The next two were Carey to the Chicago Bears and John Huarte to the Philadelphia Eagles.

Jack Snow in eleven seasons became one of the Rams' all-time leading receivers with 6,012 yards. Lynch also played eleven years with the Kansas City Chiefs, making the Pro Bowl once. He led the Chiefs to the Super Bowl IV victory over the Minnesota Vikings.

Lynch was elected to the College Football Hall of Fame in 1992. Huarte signed with the New York Jets in 1965 and played with the Eagles, Chiefs, and Vikings among others. Not until May of 2005 was he finally elected into the College Football Hall of Fame.

Of the players who started on the 1964 team, sixteen played professional football. None was more decorated than Alan Page, who played 10½ seasons with the Minnesota Vikings (1967–1978) and 3½ seasons with the Chicago Bears. He was only the second defensive player in the history of the NFL to win Most Valuable Player in 1971. He was named the Defensive Player of the Year in 1973 and led the Vikings to four Super Bowls. He was All-NFL six times, made the Pro Bowl on nine other occasions. The man who inspired Johnny Ray to say, "I'm going to make you a great player, dead or alive," was elected to the Pro Football Hall of Fame in 1988. He has been an associate justice on the Minnesota Supreme Court since 1993.

It would be difficult to question the validity of the 1964 team that came within ninety-three seconds of winning the national championship. Some experts, however, say that Huarte was one of the most overrated

Heisman Trophy winners of all time, and that 1964 was actually a down year for college football.

Dan Jenkins, who wrote some glowing things about Notre Dame in *Sports Illustrated* that season, is not completely sold on the Notre Dame of 1964.

"First of all, it was great to have Notre Dame back among the living," Jenkins wrote in an e-mail that was somewhat tongue-in-cheek. "On the other hand, that team played a fairly weak schedule. The toughest foe they faced, USC, beat them. Notre Dame was blessed. It was destiny. Wrong, of course, Huarte is a great American and a wonderful human being, but what sane person actually thought John Huarte was a greater football player than Gale Sayers, Joe Namath, Tucker Frederickson, Dick Butkus, Tommy Nobis. Stop me before I kill more."

NOTRE DAME COULD not wait to get its hands on USC in 1965. The Irish started plotting their revenge within minutes after the 20–17 upset. Tony Carey was so angry after the loss that he thought about storming into the USC dressing room and demanding they stop singing the song, "Amen."

"They sang that damn song so many times that I was still mad the next year," he said.

The day after the 1964 loss, Nick Rassas bought a framed portrait titled "Custer's Last Stand" that he hung over his locker for the entire 1965 season. The players could not get the USC upset off their minds, and who could blame them? Two days before the 1965 game, a couple of Notre Dame students managed to sneak into the Administration Building, scale the walls of the Golden Dome, and hang a banner that read, BEAT THE HELL OUT OF USC.

Fifteen minutes before kickoff, Johnny Ray gathered the Irish defense around him. "Boys, I want this to be off the record," he said. "But I will make you this promise. The first one of you guys that knocks a USC player out of the game, I will buy you a sport coat."

Carey could not wait to face Rod Sherman on the first play of the game. Sherman split to the left side, just as he had done on that fateful play the previous season. His assignment was to block Carey, but a perfectly placed knee by Carey into Sherman's left thigh sent him sprawling onto the ground. Sherman was carried off on a stretcher and didn't return.

"I knocked him out of the game, but I never got my sport coat," Carey said. "I graduated after the fall semester and then I let Johnny Ray die on me [in 2007]."

On October 23, 1965, USC was the fourth-ranked team in the country and Notre Dame was No 6. Mike Garrett was already being touted as the Heisman Trophy winner. Even so, USC never stood a chance against an angry band of hornets known as the Notre Dame Fighting Irish. Nick Rassas and Jim Lynch were all over Garrett as he gained only 7 yards in the first half and 36 in the second. Notre Dame almost tripled the Trojans in total yards, and Larry Conjar scored 4 rushing touchdowns as Notre Dame won 28–7.

Los Angeles Times columnist Jim Murray wrote, "Outlined against a blue-gray October sky, Notre Dame kicked the bejabbers out of USC on a leaky Saturday afternoon."

Two years earlier, Nick Rassas had promised Louise Turner Bertschy out in Wyoming that he would score a touchdown for her if she would come to Notre Dame for a game. The week following the USC victory, Louise showed up at the stadium for the Navy game wearing all red. Before kickoff, Rassas reiterated his promise. In the second quarter, fielding the ball at the Notre Dame 25, Rassas caught a punt on the run and shot straight up the field like a bullet. He juked two Navy men and was suddenly into the open field. As he crossed the goal, Rassas looked to his left and spotted the red outfit high in the stands. He heaved the ball with all of his might and Louise caught it. The woman who had told him to "slow down that motor, Nick Rassas" could not believe what she had just witnessed.

The 1965 season did not turn out as happily as everyone had hoped. The Irish definitely missed John Huarte and Jack Snow. They lost in the second week to Purdue and the next-to-last game against Michigan State. Then they tied the Miami Hurricanes 0–0 in the season finale at the Orange Bowl.

Following his final game, Rassas sat down at his locker and could not find the willpower to take off his uniform. He started to cry. Teammates and coaches came by to console him, but Nick just sat there.

Finally, Father Edmund Joyce approached him.

"Is there anything I can do for you, Nick?" he said.

"Father, I am twenty-one years old and I have already accomplished everything I've ever wanted to do in my whole life," he said. "The only thing I ever wanted was to wear this uniform and play football for Notre Dame. This will be the last time you'll ever see me in it. I don't want to take it off."

Rassas would be named first team to every All-American team in 1965. He led the nation in punt returns with 24 for 459, an average of 19.1 yards per attempt and 3 touchdowns. He ranked third with 6 interceptions. He was also named the Outstanding Athlete of the Year at Notre Dame.

One of his most prestigious awards was being named to the Kodak All-American team with his good friend Dick Arrington. Not bad for a walk-on who had the patience to hang on for three long years.

A few days before Christmas, Rassas and Arrington were sitting in the lobby of the Waldorf-Astoria Hotel in New York. They were dressed in blue sport coats with the Notre Dame insignia. That night, they would be introduced on the *Ed Sullivan Show.*

Rassas soon spotted Mike Garrett walking up the stairs beside Michigan State defensive end Bubba Smith. Garrett began to yell at the top of his lungs.

"Please, Bubba, Save me!" he wailed. "Please don't let those mean Notre Dame boys beat me up again. Don't let them hurt me! Save me, Bubba!"

It was a laugh they would all share for many years.

MOST OF THE participants from the 1964 team are retired, but success stories are abundant. Ara Parseghian won national championships at Notre Dame in 1966 and 1973 before retiring from coaching in 1974. He spent eight years in the ABC broadcast booth as a color commentator. Ara and his wife, Katie, have raised $433 million the last fifteen years for medical research to cure Neiman-Pick Type C disease. Three of their grandchildren were diagnosed with the disease in 1994. By 1997, thanks to contributions to the Ara Parseghian Medical Research Foundation, the gene responsible for the disease was identified. The Parseghians, however, lost their three grandchildren, Cowboy Mike in 1997, Christa in 2001, and Marcia in 2005. A recent family portrait on the wall of their home includes cutout pictures of the children.

Ara and Katie now split their time between South Bend and south Florida. In spite of five hip surgeries, and three more on his left knee, Parseghian plays golf almost every day. During his heyday, his golf handicap was a two. He now plays with an eleven handicap.

Nick Rassas was drafted in the second round by the Atlanta Falcons in the 1965 NFL draft and played three seasons, returning punts and playing safety. He spent more than forty years working in financial markets before retiring to his dream home in Moose, Montana, not far from the Circle X Dude Ranch, where he worked two summers during college days. He finally surrendered to the wishes of Louise Turner Bertschy. "I sit in my chair every day," Rassas said. "And I watch the mountains grow."

Tony Carey went to camp with the Chicago Bears in 1966 but did not make the team. He decided to pursue a career in law. After graduating from DePaul Law School, he worked for several years in different phases of law. Forty years later, he still goes to work every day for the firm of Carey, Filter, White and Bowland in downtown Chicago. He can also be found at Hawthorne Race Course, where he is the Chief Executive Officer of the racetrack that his grandfather, Tom Carey, an Irish immigrant, bought in 1909. The Carey family is about to celebrate their one hundredth anniversary at Hawthorne in 2009.

John Huarte's smartest move was starting Arizona Tile in 1965. Arizona Tile for the last four decades has imported and distributed ceramic tile and natural stone. His company supplied marble columns for Bank One Ballpark, Italian porcelain flooring for the Staples Center, and granite pavement slabs for Invesco Field. Total sales for the company in 2008 were over $140 million. "I have been incredibly lucky," he said, "but I do have a way of sticking with things." Everyone at Notre Dame recognized that years ago.

Nick Eddy finished third in the Heisman Trophy balloting in 1966, a national championship season, then played five years with the Detroit Lions. He was in the insurance business for almost thirty years until he discovered his calling. Soon after returning to Modesto, California, in 1997, Nick and his wife, Audrey Jean, attended a speech given by Colin Powell, and even managed to arrange a private meeting. "I was lost at the time," he remembered, "and when Colin Powell spoke about community involvement, I felt like he was talking to me." Not long after that, a friend asked him to do some substitute teaching in a special education class and he fell in love with kids. He went back to school and earned his master's degree and began teaching special education classes nine years ago. "I'm an old football player who barely graduated from Notre Dame and now I have a master's," he said. His first day on the job, one of his students threw a flurry of punches, but he did not punch back or walk away. "All of my friends tell me I'm crazy, but this is one of my great achievements. I wouldn't change it for the world."

As a sophomore in 1964, Tom Regner was considered Notre Dame's best defensive linemen. He played in the 1967 College All-Star game as the starting right guard. Future Hall of Famer Gene Upshaw was the left guard. Regner was drafted by the Houston Oilers and enjoyed six outstanding seasons. He is now retired and lives with his wife in Reno.

Pete Duranko, who walked on his hands up the stadium steps while singing the fight song in Polish, lives back in his hometown of Johnstown, Pennsylvania. He suffers from ALS, also known as Lou Gehrig's disease. He continues to receive both financial and moral support from his former coaches and teammates. "Ara has been just great to me," he said. "I can't tell you how much that guy has helped me."

Ken Maglicic played one season for the Winnipeg Blue Bombers of the CFL under Hall of Fame coach Bud Grant. When he realized that he was too small for the pro game, he went to work in management for U.S. Steel and later was an occupational and health inspector for the U.S. government. He retired in 2004 and lives in suburban Cleveland.

Like many of the Notre Dame players, it took Maglicic several years to get over the USC loss. On the winning touchdown pass, he blitzed up the middle and had his hands on quarterback Craig Fertig when Fertig managed to corkscrew his body into position to release the ball to Rod Sherman.

Maglicic and Joe Kantor were driving to South Bend in 1998 for the Michigan game when Maglicic said, "You know, Joe, if I could have gotten to Fertig a half a second earlier, we could have won that game." Kantor had been hearing these regrets for far too long.

"You know, Kenny," Kantor said. "It just wasn't meant to be."

That is when Maglicic finally started to heal.

"At that moment, I knew it was time to get over it," he said. It only took thirty-four years.

AUTHOR'S NOTE

I was asked to speak at a seminar at Notre Dame in the summer of 2008 by Dr. Charlie Kenny, class of 1963. On my first trip to South Bend, I was surprised to learn that more than five thousand ex-students attended the four-day "Reunion Weekend" each summer. I stayed in the dorm with the Class of 1963, but never slept.

That first day at Notre Dame, Kenny was giving me a campus tour when he pointed out a large outdoor cement patio. "That is where the Old Fieldhouse used to be," he said. "To me, that is where the Notre Dame spirit was born." As it turned out, the Notre Dame spirit almost died in the same place. Until the arrival of Ara Parseghian in 1964, the Old Fieldhouse was just an old, gray building falling down around itself.

In 1959, Kenny attended his first pep rally as a freshman, along with about four thousand other students, to celebrate the hiring of coach Joe Kuharich. Kenny timed the standing ovation that lasted eighteen minutes. A year later, in the midst of an eight-game losing streak, only eighteen students showed up for a Friday night pep rally preceding the Miami game. Football was dying at Notre Dame. Knute Rockne, who practically invented college football, would have whipped off his signature hat and stomped it. Rockne was also responsible for birthing Notre Dame pep rallies at the Old Fieldhouse in the 1920s. Until football was deemphasized in the 1950s, they were some rollicking fun.

In the summer of 2008, no one besides Kenny knew that I was on the prowl for a Notre Dame book. I had researched many angles the past decade only to come up empty. It seemed that every story of the Notre

Dame past was tied to big-time winning—not my style. I write about underdogs. I write coming-of-age stories. My idea of a great sports story is a bunch of 130-pound orphans (*Twelve Mighty Orphans*) who rise up with spirit and grit to win a state championship. Another one of my passions was a college football team (*The Junction Boys*) that was subjected to a hot-as-hell preseason camp in 1954 when seventy-six players quit in ten days. Somehow the Texas A&M Aggies managed to rebound to win a conference title.

As we strolled the emerald Notre Dame campus that day, Kenny told me about the great history of the Old Fieldhouse, along with the sad tales of Notre Dame football in the fifties and early sixties. At that moment, I knew the story had found me. As I later told my editor Pete Wolverton, "Where else can you couch Notre Dame as the underdog?" Indeed, the Fighting Irish, before Parseghian (B.P.), had recorded only two winning seasons the previous eight years.

I'm not so sure that Notre Dame football will ever save itself from this current rut of mediocrity. Those interested in doing so should read every word of this book. Parseghian drew a terrific blueprint to success in 1964 and, believe me, it would work today. Sometimes an old-fashioned underdog story always works.

MORE THAN ANYTHING, this book is the product of interviews that could practically fill the Chicago white pages. My friend David Bradley once told me, "Dent, you couldn't write a book if you didn't have somebody to interview."

I extend my thanks to Ara Parseghian, who invited me into his home and provided insight and stories that could have filled two books. During our time together, I asked him to name his favorite team from his eleven-year career at Notre Dame and, like most coaches, he decided to pass. Nevertheless, I suspect that the 1964 team is closest to his heart— even more than the 1966 and 1974 teams that won national championships.

In no particular order, these 1964 players gave a hundred and ten percent to *Resurrection*: Tony Carey, Nick Rassas, John Huarte, Ken Maglicic, Nick Eddy, Tom Regner, Joe Farrell, Norm Nicola, and Bob

Meeker. (Carey, Rassas, Maglicic, Farrell and Nicola were part of a two-day group interview in Chicago).

For more than a week, Rassas dug through thirteen army trunks that had been sealed up in his basement for more than forty years. The UPS man arrived at my door for six straight days with everything from scrapbooks to the wonderful, heartwarming letters written by his mother, Frances.

I told Maglicic that he could have written this book without breaking a sweat. He remembered the good times and the bad times like they were yesterday. Between Maglicic, Carey, and Rassas I have more than two hundred typewritten pages of notes. This story is an especially important story to Carey because he was kicked out of Notre Dame and then battled his way back to lead the country in interceptions. He was a second team All-American in 1964.

My only regret is that I did not get to interview Jack Snow, Dick Arrington, Mike Wadsworth, and Bill Wolski—all deceased. Snow and I became good friends in the 1990s during my radio talk show days. Rassas once said of Arrington, "He had a smile that could light up a ballroom." As for Wolski, who wouldn't love a guy nicknamed "Muscle Face?"

A bibliography is included within these pages, but the most helpful books were *Talking Irish* by Steve Delsohn and *Era of Ara* by Tom Pagna. Also special thanks to Dan Jenkins and John Underwood for their rich anecdotes and superbly composed stories about Notre Dame in *Sports Illustrated*. No one covered Fighting Irish football better in 1964 than Joe Doyle in the *South Bend Tribune*. Doyle was interviewed extensively for this book.

During this journey, I was privileged to meet and become friends with Jim Connelly, known as the "Mayor of Notre Dame." Connelly has loved Notre Dame all of his life, even though he did not attend the university. You can find him and his wife, Kate, strolling the campus just about every day. They live a mile from Notre Dame and know more about the place than anyone I know.

Sue Shidler, assistant director of the Hammes Notre Dame Bookstore at Notre Dame, provided friendship and great stories. Tom Longeway and David Swire, both members of the Notre Dame class of 1963, listened to my ideas and provided many of their own. My intern in Chicago was Brian McCabe, who graduated from Notre Dame in 2001 and recently received his Masters of Journalism degree from Northwestern. My prediction is that Brian will rise to the top of this business.

Dr. Charlie Kenny, president of The Right Brain People, a strategic research marketing firm in Memphis, walked with me every step of the way. He may know more about the history of Notre Dame football than anyone.

I would also like to thank Rolly "Big Cat" Dent, who recently turned seventeen and loves all of my books.

Resurrection would have never seen the light of day without my agent, Jim Donovan of Dallas, and my editor, Pete Wolverton, associate publisher of Thomas Dunne Books in New York. They are two of the most talented people in publishing. Both did comprehensive editing. Most important, they shape the view of every story I write. They also keep me on track—and sometimes that can prove to be the toughest task of all.

BIBLIOGRAPHY

Anderson, Heartly "Hunk," and Emil Klosinski. *Notre Dame, Chicago Bears and "Hunk"*: Sports Immortals, 1976.

Boyles, Bob, and Paul Guido. *USA Today College Football Encyclopedia*: Skyhorse Publishing, 2008.

Chelland, Patrick. *One for the Gipper*: Henry Regnery, 1973.

Clary, Jack. *PB: The Paul Brown Story*: Atheneum, 1979.

Connor, Jack. *Leahy's Lads*: Diamond Communications, 1979.

Donovan, Jim, Mark Spellen, and Keith Marder. *Notre Dame Football Encyclopedia*: Citadel Press, 1979.

Delsohn, Steve. *Talking Irish*: Avon Books, 1998.

Eden, Scott. *Touchdown Jesus*: Simon & Schuster, 2005.

Hansen, Erik. *Where Have You Gone?*: Sports Publishing, 2005.

Heisler, John. *Echoes of Notre Dame Football*: Triumph Books, 2005.

————*Quotable Rockne*: TowleHouse Books, 2001.

Hesburgh, Theodore M., with Jerry Reedy. *God, Country, Notre Dame*: University of Notre Dame, 1990.

Hornung, Paul. *Golden Boy*: Simon & Schuster, 2004.

Krause, Moose, and Stephen Singular. *Notre Dame's Greatest Coaches*: Pocket Books, 1993.

LaTourette, Larry. *Northwestern Wildcat Football*: Arcadia Publishing, 1975.

Maggio, Frank. *Notre Dame and the Game That Changed Football*: Carroll and Graf, 2007.

Pagna, Tom, and Bob Best. *Era of Ara*: Strode Publishers, 1976.

Pont, Sally. *Fields of Honor:* Harcourt Press, 2001.

Rice, Grantland. *The Tumult and Shouting*: A. S. Barnes, 1954.

Robinson, Ray. *Rockne of Notre Dame*: Oxford University Press, 1999.

Schoor, Gene. *100 Years of Notre Dame Football*: William Morrow, 1987.

Smith, Ron, and Joe Hoppel. *Fighting Irish*: Sporting News Books, 2002.

Sperber, Murray. *Shake Down the Thunder*: Indiana University Press, 2002.

"The Vault." *Sports Illustrated:* 1954–'64.

Ziemba, Joe. *When Football Was Football*: Triumph Books, 1999.

INDEX